# Track Diagrams -England: East

These diagrams cover the lines of former British Rail's Eastern and Anglia Regions, Midland Region, together with a number of private railways and industrial layouts January 1998. They reflect `operational' capabilities.

Mileages often vary slightly between different official records, but, in general, those given in the latest Sectional Appendix have been used. Station mileages are usually taken from the mid-point of the platforms, or, in the case of a terminus, the buffer stops.

These diagrams have been compiled substantially from information supplied from various former British Rail sources up to 31 March 1994 with some subsequent updates, supplemented by other data and amended from observations. In some cases distinctions between Railtrack ownership and other parties are not shown and no inferences concerning ownership should therefore be drawn. The fragmentation of the railway industry has precluded the wider consultation to give a more accurate picture.

The assistance of Railtrack plc & EW & S Railway is gratefully acknowledged. Other acknowledgements are due to the Branch Line Society, the Railway Correspondence & Travel Society, other railway societies, and Michael Oakley; also representatives of the other private and preserved systems featured.

Cartographer: John Yonge

Consultant editor: Gerald Jacobs

## KEY

- Running line } A broken line indicates `in situ' but out of use, proposed or under construction
- Siding }
- Line obstructed
- Line out of use
- Railtrack zone boundary
- Signal box/centre area limits (York (Y) | Doncaster (D))
- Tunnel
- Viaduct
- Selected Motorway/Trunk road bridges over rail
- Level crossing (signalled) } Attributed Number and supervising point may be shown
- Crossing (telephone or unsignalled) }
- Track signalled in both directions (a double arrow indicates normal direction of travel) (On single lies `DN' indicates down direction)
- Limit of Electrification
- Private siding boundary, often marked by a gate
- Turntable
- Wall

- 93 — Whole mileposts, shown on the appropriate side of the line
- 81.3 — End of mileage run
- 3 — Platform with number
- Provisional proposed platform
- Royal mail platform
- Platform out of use
- Loading Bank
- (Y) — Signal box with code (name underlined)
- Gate box
- Ground frame
- Radio Electronic Token Block-Token Exchange Point
- ¶ — Proposed Closure
- ○ — Water Tower
- ^ — Summit
- • — Location Spot
- 86.34 — Distance in miles and chains (80 chains to 1 mile; 22 yards -about 20 metres - equal 1 chain)
- ECM — ELR Engineer's Line Reference (Prefix and suffix numbers indicate sub-divisions and their boundaries)

Guide references are given to pre-nationalisation, pre-grouping and sometimes pioneer railways eg LNE:NE(Stockton & Darlington)

References to adjoining volumes & page nos. refer to previously published books and will not neccessarily be the same in future editions.

PRICE £7.95 ISBN: 1 898319 29 4

Published by the Quail Map Company, 2 Lincoln Road, Exeter EX4 2DZ (Telephone/Fax: 01392 430277) and printed by the Brightsea Press Ltd, Exeter

## ABBREVIATIONS

| | |
|---|---|
| AA | Acid Application |
| ABCL | Automatic Barrier Crossing-(Locally monitored) |
| ABP | Associated British Ports |
| AHB | Automatic Half Barriers |
| AOCL | Automatic Open Crossing-(Locally monitored) |
| AOCR | Automatic Open Crossing-(Remotely monitored) |
| ARR | Arrival |
| ARTS | Anglia Railway Train Services Ltd |
| bdy | boundary |
| BCH | Branch |
| BS | British Steel |
| Cal | former Caledonian Railway |
| CCTV | Closed circuit television |
| CET | Controlled Emission Toilet Discharge |
| COM | Change of mileage |
| CR | Cripple siding |
| CT | Central Trains Ltd |
| CW | Carriage washer |
| C & W | Carriage & Wagon |
| DEP | Departure |
| DGL | Down Goods Loop |
| DN | Down |
| DPL | Down Passenger Loop |
| DRS | Down Refuge Siding |
| E | East |
| e | electrified |
| EB | Eastbound |
| EC | former Eastern Counties Railway |
| EGF | Emergency Ground Frame |
| EMU | Electric multiple-unit |
| Engrs | Engineers' sidings |
| ESP | Emergency Signalling Panel |
| EW & S | English Welsh & Scottish Railway Ltd |
| FA | Flushing Apron |
| FP | Fuelling point or footpath |
| ft | feet |
| GC | former Great Central Railway (Manchester, Sheffield & Lincolnshire prior to 1897) |
| GDS | Goods |
| GE | former Great Eastern Railway |
| GER | Great Eastern Railway Ltd |
| GF | Ground Frame |
| GL | Goods loop |
| GN | former Great Northern Railway |
| GNER | Great North Eastern Railway Ltd |
| GS | Goods Shed |
| GSP | Ground Switch Panel |
| GW | former Great Western Railway |
| H | Headshunt |
| H & B | former Hull & Barnsley Railway |
| HH | Hopper House |
| HST | High Speed Train |
| IECC | Integrated Electronic Control Centre |
| Jn | Junction |
| Jt | Joint |
| L | Wheel Lathe |
| LC | Level Crossing(manned, automatic or open) |
| L & CR | London & Continental Railways Ltd |
| LD & EC | former Lancashire, Derbyshire & East Coast Railway |
| L & Y | former Lancashire & Yorkshire Railway |
| LHS | Loco. Holding Siding |
| LMS | former London, Midland & Scottish Railway (1923-47) |
| LNE | former London & North Eastern Railway (1923-47) |
| LNW | former London & North Western Railway |
| LPG | Liquified petroleum gas |
| LS | Locomotive shed |
| LSW | former London & South Western Railway |
| LT & S | former London, Tilbury & Southend Railway |
| LT & SR | London, Tilbury & Southend Railway Ltd |
| LW | Locomotive washer |
| M & C | former Maryport & Carlisle Railway |
| MCB | Manually Controlled Barriers |
| MGR | Merry-go-round |
| Mid | former Midland Railway |
| MOD | Ministry of Defence |
| N | North |
| n | Not electrified |
| N & SWJn | former North & South Western Jn Railway |
| NB | former North British Railway |
| NE | former North Eastern Railway |
| NIRU | Not in regular use |
| NL | former North London Railway |
| NLR | North London Railways Ltd (Silver Link) |
| NWRR | North West Regional Railways Ltd |
| OHC | Overhead crane |
| OHLE | Overhead Line Equipment |
| OOU | Out of use |
| Open | Open crossing - no lights |
| OTM | On-track Maintenance |
| P | Points padlocked |
| PAD | Prefabricated Assembly depot |
| PL | Passenger Loop |
| PSB | Power signal box |
| PW | Permanent Way |
| Qy | Query concerning distances etc, unresolved |
| RAF | Royal Air force |
| RC | Remotely controlled |
| REC | Reception |
| RETB | Radio Electronic Token Block |
| REV | Reversing Line |
| R/G | Miniature red/green warning lights |
| RNAD | Royal Naval Armaments Depot |
| RR | Run-round |
| RRNE | Regional Railways North East Ltd |
| RT | Railtrack |
| S | South |
| SB | Signal box |
| SC | Signalling Centre |
| S & C | Switches and crossings |
| S & D | former Stockton & Darlington Railway |
| Sdg(s) | Siding(s) |
| SD | Sand Drag |
| SF | Shunting Frame |
| SN | Shunt Neck |
| SP | Switch Panel |
| SR | former Southern Railway |
| SS | Shunt spur |
| T | Tamper siding |
| TL | Traffic lights |
| TMD | Traction Maintenance depot |
| TMO | Traincrew operated |
| TR | Thameslink Rail Ltd |
| TR & SMD | Traction & Rolling Stock Maintenance Depot |
| UF | Up Fast |
| UFN | Until Further Notice |
| UGL | Up Goods Loop |
| UPL | Up Passenger Loop |
| URS | Up Refuge Siding |
| UT | Up Through |
| Vdct | Viaduct |
| W | West |
| WAGN | West Anglia Great Northern Railway Ltd |
| WB | Weighbridge or Westbound |
| X | (After level crossing type abbreviations) - the crossing works automatically for movements in the wrong direction |
| yds | yards |

**FORMER BR NON-PASSENGER BUSINESSES**
**(January 1998)**

| CURRENT TRADING NAME | FORMER NAME | PURCHASED BY |
|---|---|---|
| AMEC Rail Ltd | BRIS - South West Infrastructure Maintenance Co | AMEC plc |
| Amey Railways Ltd | BRIS - Western InfrastructureMaintenance Co | Amey plc Group |
| Balfour Beatty Rail Maintenance | BRIS - South East Infrastructure Maintenance Co | Balfour Beatty Rail Ltd |
| Balfour Beatty Rail Maintenance | BRIS - Eastern Infrastructure Maintenance Co | Balfour Beatty Rail Ltd |
| Balfour Beatty Rail Infrastructure Renewals | BRIS - Southern Track Renewals Co | Balfour Beatty Rail Ltd |
| Centrac Ltd | BRIS - Central Track Renewals Co | Tarmac Construction Ltd |
| Fastline | BRIS - Eastern Track Renewals Co | Jarvis plc |
| Fastline | BRIS - Northern Track Renewals Co | Jarvis plc |
| First Engineering Ltd | BRIS - Scotland Infrastructure Maintenance Co | Track Action Ltd |
| GT Railway Maintenance Ltd | BRIS - Central Infrastructure Maintenance Co | GT Railway Maintenance Ltd (GEC Alsthom/Tarmac) |
| Jarvis Facilities Ltd | BRIS - Northern Infrastructure Maintenance Co | Jarvis plc |
| Red Star Parcels Ltd | Red Star | Rald Ltd |
| Scotland Track Renewals Co Ltd | BRIS - Scotland Track Renewals Co | Jarvis plc |
| Western Track Renewals Co Ltd | BRIS - Western Track Renewals Co | Jarvis plc |
| W S Atkins Rail Electrification | Powertrack | W S Atkins Rail Ltd |

**ENGLISH, WELSH and SCOTTISH RAILWAYS Ltd** - An American consortium led by Wisconsin Central Transportation Corporation. It incorporates the former British Rail Operations of **Mainline, Transrail, Loadhaul and Railfreight Distribution (RfD)** and assets of **Rail Express Systems**

**LONDON & CONTINENTAL RAILWAYS LTD (LCR)** - Owner of **Eurostar (UK) Ltd** also to build in association with Rail Link Engineering (former Union Railways) and operate the high-speed rail link between London and the Channel Tunnel. (Subject to change)

**PASSENGER FRANCHISES**
**(January 1998)**

| TRADING NAME | * FRANCHISE | HOLDER |
|---|---|---|
| Anglia Railways Train Services Ltd | (AR) Anglia Railways | GB Railways Group plc |
| Cardiff Railway Ltd | (CA) Cardiff Railway | Prism Rail plc |
| Central Trains Ltd | (CT) Central Trains | National Express Group plc |
| The Chiltern Railway Company Ltd | (CH) Chiltern Railways | M40 Trains Ltd |
| Connex South Central Ltd | (SC) South Central | Connex Rail Ltd(CGEA (France)) |
| Connex South Eastern Ltd | (SE) South Eastern | Connex Rail Ltd(CGEA (France)) |
| Gatwick Express Ltd | (GX) Gatwick Express | National Express Group plc |
| Great Eastern Railway Ltd | (GE) Great Eastern Railway | FirstGroup plc |
| Great North Eastern Railway Ltd | (GR) InterCity East Coast | GNER Holdings (Sea Containers Ltd) |
| Great Western Trains Ltd | (GW) Great Western | Great Western Holdings Ltd |
| Heathrow Express | | BAA plc |
| Island Line Ltd (Isle of Wight) | (IL) Island Line | Stagecoach Holdings plc |
| LTS Rail Ltd | (LS) London Tilbury & Southend Rail Ltd. | Prism Rail plc |
| Merseyrail Electrics Ltd | (ME) Merseyrail Electrics | MTL Trust Holdings Ltd |
| Midland Mainline Ltd | (ML) Midland Mainline | National Express Group plc |
| North Western Trains Co Ltd | (NW) North West Regional Railways | Great Western Holdings |
| Regional Railways North East Ltd | (RE) Regional Railways North East | MTL Trust Holdings Ltd |
| Silverlink Train Services Ltd | (NL) North London Railways | National Express Group plc |
| South West Trains Ltd | (SW) South West Trains | Stagecoach Holdings plc |
| ScotRail Railways Ltd | (SR) ScotRail | National Express Group plc |
| Thameslink Rail Ltd | (TL) Thameslink Rail | GOVIA (Go-Ahead Bus Group plc(VIA-GTI)) |
| Thames Trains Ltd | (TT) Thames Trains | Victory Railway Holdings Ltd |
| Virgin Trains: CrossCountry Trains Ltd | (VT)InterCity CrossCountry Trains | Virgin Rail Group plc |
| Virgin Trains: West Coast Trains Ltd | (VT)InterCity West Coast Ltd | Virgin Rail Group plc |
| Wales & West Passenger Trains Ltd | (WW)Wales & West | Prism Rail plc |
| West Anglia Great Northern Railway Ltd | (WAGN)West Anglia Great Northern | Prism Rail plc |

* Great Britain Timetable abbreviations

**RAILTRACK ZONES**

| | | | | | |
|---|---|---|---|---|---|
| East Anglia | EA | Great Western | GW | London North East | LNE |
| Midland | MID | North West | NW | Scotland | SC |
| Southern | SO | | | | |

## ENGINEERS LINE REFERENCES

| | |
|---|---|
| ABE | Allington Jn. - Barkston East Jn. |
| ACW | Acton Canal Wharf - Willesden |
| ADH | Alexandra Dock - Hessle Road Jn. (Hull) |
| AGY | Altercliffe Goods Yard (Sheffield) |
| ANL | Acton - Northolt Line (via Greenford East) |
| ATG | Turnham Green (LUL) - Gunnersbury Jn. |
| AWL | Acton East - Acton Wells Jn. |
| AWP | Anlaby Road Jn. - West Parade North Jn. (Hull) |
| | |
| BCB | Black Carr Jn. - Bessacarr Jn. |
| BCE | Bolsover Colliery Empties |
| BCO | Bentley Colliery ( Doncaster) |
| BDH | Brent Curve Jn. - Dudding Hill Jn. |
| BDM | Bow Depot Midland |
| BEC | Bevercotes Colliery |
| BEW | Beighton Jn. - Woodhouse Jn. |
| BGE | Boldon Colliery Jn. - Green Lane Jn. |
| BGK | Bethnal Green - Kings Lynn |
| BHM | Barrow Hill Motive Power Depot |
| BHP | Boultham Jn. - Pyewipe Jn. |
| BIB | Shipley West Jn. - Bradford Jn. |
| BKS | Brancliffe East Jn. - Kirk Sandall Jn. |
| BLF | Bensham Curve Jn. - Low Fell Sidings Jn. |
| BLJ | Shepcote Lane East Jn. - Broughton Lane Jn. |
| BNE | Benton North Jn. - Earsdon Jn. |
| BNJ | Bentley Colliery North Jn. - Bentley Colliery Jn. |
| BNW | Boldon New Curve: Boldon East Jn. - Boldon North Jn. |
| BNY | Green Lane Jn. - Dean Road Sidings |
| BOC | Bolsover Colliery (Seymour Jn. - Bolsover) |
| BOH | Bowesfield Jn. - Hartburn Jn. |
| BOK | Broad Street - Old Kew Jn. (North London line) |
| BOO | Bowers Row Opencast (Castleford) |
| BRA | Braintree Branch (Witham - Braintree) |
| BRI | Brocklesby Jn. - Immingham Dock |
| BTB | Barlow Tip Branch |
| BTE | Barking Tilbury Line Jn. East - Barking East Jn. (Connecting line) |
| BTJ | Brightside - Treeton Jn. (Tinsley Yard) |
| BWC | Bedlington Jn. - Woodhorn Colliery |
| BWO | Ashington Jn. - Butterwell Jn. (Butterwell Disposal Point) |
| BWT | Barking West Jn. - Barking Tilbury Line Jn. \Vest |
| BYE | Bury St. Edmunds Yard |
| | |
| CAW | Cricklewood Curve Jn. - Acton Wells Jn. |
| CBC | Carnforth North Jn. - Carlisle South Jn. via Whitehaven |
| CBE | Cambridge Goods |
| CCB | Rectory Jn. - Cotgrave Colliery |
| CCH | Cambridge - Haughley Jn. |
| CCN | Clipstone Colliery North ( Rufford Jn. - Clipstone Colliery) |
| CDY | Chelmsford Lower yard |
| CEC | Carnforth East Jn. - Carnforth Station Jn. |
| CER | Colchester Goods |
| CFM | Church Fenton North Jn. - Micklefield Jn. |
| CFP | Canonbury West Jn. - Finsbury Park |
| CGJ | Crewe - Carlisle |
| CHM | Channelsea North Jn. - High Meads Jn. |
| CHR | Chesterfield (Tapton Jn.) - Rotherham Masborough Stn N. Jn. (Old Road) |
| CHS | Crigglestone Jn. - Horbury Jn. |
| CJC | Clapton Jn. - Chingford |
| CJS | Carcroft Jn. - Stainforth Jn. |
| CNS | Carpenters Road North - Carpenters Road South |
| COC | Colchester - Clacton |
| CPM | Castleford West Jn. - Pontefract West Jn. |
| CPS | Cottam Power Station |
| CRF | Camden Road East Jn. - Freight Terminal Jn. (i/c Kings Cross Yard) |
| CRS | Camden Road Jn. - Camden Jn. |
| CRS | Cromer - Sheringham |
| CST | Carpenters Road North Jn. - Stratford Central Jn. West |
| CTH | Colne Jn. - Hythe Jn. |
| CTL | Calder Bridge Jn. - Turners Lane Jn. |
| CTP | Connington Tip Siding |
| CWJ | Camden Jn. - Watford Jn.(DC lines) |
| CWS | Clipstone West Jn. - Clipstone South Jn. |
| | |
| DAE | Darlington, Parkgate Jn. - Eastgate |
| DDY | Doncaster Down Yard |
| DEX | Derby Extension : Colwick North - Gedling Colliery |
| DJH | Daisyfield Jn. - Hellifield Jn. |
| DOC | Kings Lynn Dock |
| DOL | Doncaster, Marshgate Jn. - Holbeck East Jn. |
| DOW | Doncaster - Wrawby |
| DRA | Drax Power Station |
| DRS | Dewsbury East Jn. - Dewsbury Railway Street |
| DSN | Darlington - Saltburn |
| DUY | Doncaster Up Yard |
| DWS | Dore West - Dore Station Jn. |
| DWW | Dalston Western Jn. - North Woolwich |
| | |
| ECG | Eggborough Power Station |
| ECM | East Coast Main Line: London, Kings Cross - Edinburgh |
| EDE | Eden Valley line: Warcop - Appleby North Jn. |
| EJM | Earsdon Jn. - Morpeth North Jn. |
| ELN | Engine Shed Jn. - Leeds City North Jn. |
| EMP | Ely - March - Peterborough |
| ENT | Enfield Town : Bury St Jn. - Enfield Town |
| ESK | East Suffolk : Ipswich - Lowestoft |
| ETN | Ely - Thetford - Norwich |
| EWC | Ely West Curve : Ely North Jn. - Ely West Jn. |
| | |
| FAS | Fletton Ash Sidings (Peterborough) |
| FED | Felixstowe Dock : Trimley - Felixstowe Dock via N. Freightliner Terminal |
| FEL | Felixstowe Beach : Westerfield Jn. - Felixstowe |
| FEP | Ferryhill - Pelaw |
| FGW | Forest Gate Jn. - Woodgrange Park |
| FKW | Ferrybridge North Jn. - Knottingley West Jn. |
| FOM | Fletton Jn. - Orton Mere |
| FRC | Frickley Colliery branch |
| FSS | London, Fenchurch Street - Shoeburyness |
| FWR | Flyover West Jn. - Rossington Colliery |
| | |
| GCD | Great Chesterford siding |
| GDL | Goole Docks line |
| GFB | Gas Factory Jn. - Bow Jn. |
| GLT | Green lane - Tyne Dock |
| GMS | Grantham Sidings |
| GOJ | Gospel Oak Jn. - Junction Road Jn. |
| GRD | Greetland Jn. - Dryclough Jn. |
| GRE | Graham Road Curve (Hackney) |
| GRS | Grantham : Barkston South Jn. - Skegness |
| GRW | Griffen Wharf (Ipswich) |
| GSM | Kettering North Jn. - Nottingham via Melton |
| GUE | Esholt Jn. - Dockfield Jn. (Shipley) |
| | |
| HAC | Harworth Colliery : Firbeck Jn. - Harworth |
| HAH | Haverton Hill South Branch : Belasis Lane Jn. - Haverton Hill South |
| HAR | Kings Lynn Harbour |
| HAS | Harrogate Goods Siding |
| HAU | Habrough Jn. - Ulceby South Jn. |
| HAY | Harrogate - York |
| HBS | Hull - Bridlington - Seamer |
| HCD | Holmes Chord (Rotherham) |
| HCS | Heaton Carriage Sidings |
| HDB | Hertford Branch : Alexandra Palace - Hertford North - Langley Jn. |
| HDT | Hackney Downs Jn. - Cheshunt Jn. |
| HEB | Hertford East Branch : Broxbourne Jn. - Hertford East |
| HIM | Shirebrook East Jn. - High Marnham |
| HJB | Hexthorpe Jn. - Bentley Jn. (Doncaster Avoiding line) |
| HJM | Hepscott Jn. - Morpeth Jn. |
| HJS | Hessle Road Jn. - Saltend |
| HLD | Hartlepool Docks |
| HLF | Hall Lane Jn. - Foxlow Jn. |
| HLK | High LeveL Bridge Jn. - King Edward Bridge South Jn. |
| HMC | Hatfield Main Colliery ( Stainforth) |
| HNB | Hendon Branch : Ryhope Grange Jn. - Sunderland South Dock |
| HNC | Hambleton North Curve |
| HON | Hopetown Branch (Darlington) |
| HOS | Holgate Jn. - Skelton Jn. via Slow lines |
| HOU | Barnes Jn. - Feltham Jn. via Hounslow (Hounslow Loop) |
| HPC | Hare Park Jn. - Crofton. West Jn. |
| HPQ | Harwich, Parkeston Quay Goods Yard |
| HPW | Harringay Park Jn. - Harringay West |
| HSC | Hambleton South Curve |
| HTY | Heaton Yard (Newcastle) |
| HUE | Hunslet East Goods (Leeds) |
| HUL | Hull - Leeds |
| HYM | Healey Mills Yard (Wakefield) |
| ICS | Ilford Car Sheds |
| ILK | Apperley Jn. - Ilkley |
| IMS | Immingham Storage Co. |
| INW | Immingham Dock North West Entrance |
| IPD | Ipswich Dock : Ipswich Upper Yard - Freight Terminal etc. |
| ISC | Isabella Colliery (Newsham North Jn. - Isabella Colliery) |
| IUP | Ipswich Upper Yard |
| | |
| JAW | Pelaw Jn. - Jarrow Terminal |
| JCA | Joan Croft Jn. - Applehurst Jn. |
| JMM | Ferrybridge Power Station |
| JRT | Junction Road Jn. - Carlton Road Jn. (Tottenham lines) |
| | |
| KBF | Kelloe Bank Foot (Ferryhill) |
| KEB | King Edward Branch East Jn. - North Jn. |
| KES | Knottingley East Jn. - Knottingley South Jn. |
| KGC | Kensal Green Jn. - Willesden Jn. (City lines) |
| KGD | King George Dock (Hull) |
| KGW | Kensal Green Jn. - Willesden LL |
| KIL | Killingholme Branch : Immingham West Jn. - Killingholme |
| KLY | Kings Lynn Yard |
| KWS | Knottingley West Jn. - Shaftholme Jn. |
| | |
| LBE | Leeds, Holbeck WestJn. - Bradford Exchange |
| LCJ | Loversall Jn. - Flyover East Jn. |
| LCR | Loversall Carr Jn. - Rossington Colliery Jn. |
| LEC | London, Euston - Crewe |

| | |
|---|---|
| LEH | Leeds, Wortley Jn. - Harrogate |
| LEN | Leeds - Newcastle East Jn. via Hartlepool (part closed) |
| LFL | Low Fell Sidings (Newcastle) |
| LLG | Willesden, West London Jn. - Sudbury Jn. (Low Level Lines) |
| LLP | Longland Loop Jn. - Boroughbridge Jn. |
| LLS | Lea Jn. - Temple Mills East Jn. |
| LTN | London, Liverpool Street - Norwich via Ipswich |
| LWW | Leeds Station - Whitehall East Jn. |
| MAC | Deepcar - Cleethorpes (Manchester -Cleethorpes) |
| MAH | Manningtree - Harwich Town |
| MAM | Maltby Colliery Branch Jn. - Maltby Colliery |
| MAN | Manton Colliery Branch : Manton Wood - Manton Colliery |
| MAS | Dore South Jn. - Chinley North Jn. (Manchester and Sheffield Mid) |
| MBW | Middlesbrough - Whitby |
| MCG | Carlisle, Currock Jn. - (Forks Jn.) - Rome Street Jn. |
| MCL | London, Moorgate - Carlton Road Jn. (Midland City Line) |
| MDL | Thornhill LNW Jn. - Whitehall West Jn. (Manchester - Diggle - Leeds)(See MVL) |
| MEB | Moorgate Branch : London, Moorgate - Finsbury Park |
| MED | Mile End - Devonshire Street |
| MEW | Methley Jn. - Whitwood Jn. |
| MGW | Milford Jn. - Gascoigne Wood Jn. |
| MII | Mistley Incline |
| MIT | Middleton Towers Branch: Kings Lynn Jn. - Middleton Towers |
| MKB | Monk Bretton Branch: Cudworth - Monk Bretton |
| MLN | Paddington - Penzance via Bristol (Main Line) |
| MMC | Markham Main Colliery: Markham Sidings - Markham Main Colliery |
| MRB | Milner Royd Jn. - Bradford Exchange |
| MUP | March Up and Down Yards |
| MVL | Diggle - Heaton Lodge Jns. (Manchester Victoria - Leeds) (See MDL) |
| MVN | Manchester Victoria - Normanton, Goose Hill Jn. |
| MWJ | Marchey House Jn. - Winning Colliery Jn. |
| MWL | March West Jn. - March Whitemoor Jn. |
| MWN | Marsh West Jn. - Grimsby Docks |
| NAJ | Neasden South Jn. - Aynho Jn |
| NAY | Brundall Jn. - Great Yarmouth |
| NCW | Norwich, Wensum Curve |
| NEC | Newcastle - Carlisle South Jn. |
| NEN | Newcastle West Jn. - Newburn |
| NGC | Netherfie]d Jn. - Colwick North |
| NGD | Carlisle, London Road Jn. - Bog Jn. (Newcastle Goods lines) |
| NHM | Neville Hill Depot and Sidings |
| NJN | Neasden Curve: Neasden Jn. - Neasden South Jn. |
| NKE | New Kew Jn. - Kew East Jn. |
| NLF | Norwood Jn. - Low Fell |
| NOB | Nottingham East Junction - Barnetby |
| NOC | Normanton, Altofts Jn. - Colton Jn. |
| NOE | North Elmham Branch: Wymondham - North Elmham |
| NOG | Nottingham - Grantham |
| NOL | Norwich - Oulton Broad - Lowestoft |
| NOP | Normanby Park Branch (formerly Scunthorpe West Jn. - Normanby Park) |
| NSE | Newark South Jn. - East Jn. |
| NTE | Manningtree North Jn. - East Jn. |
| NUJ | Nunnery Main Line Jn. - Nunnery Jn. |
| NWE | Norton West Jn. - Norton East Jn. |
| OAJ | Oakenshaw South Jn. - Oakenshaw Jn. |
| OSC | Oakenshaw South Jn. - Crofton East Jn. |
| OXO | Oxcroft Opencast: Oxcroft Jn. - Oxcroft Opencast |
| PBS | Pye Bridge Jn. - RTZB MIDLAND/LONDON NORTH EAST |
| PED | Penistone - Doncaster |
| PEF | Pontefract, Monkhill Goods Jn. - Ferrybridge South Jn. |
| PEH | Penistone - Huddersfield |
| PGS | Palace Gates - Seven Sisters |
| PHC | Priory Yard -Hull Central Goods |
| PHS | Peterborough Sidings |
| PLG | Park Lane Jn. - Greensfield Jn. |
| PMJ | Peterborough - Manton Jn. |
| POC | Billingham Jn. - Port Clarence |
| PSE | RTZB MIDLAND/LONDON NORTH EAST - Shireoaks East Jn. |
| PYE | Pyewipe: Immingham East Dock Jn. - Grimsby Docks |
| RBY | Reedham - Berney Arms - Great Yarmouth |
| RDG | London, Waterloo (Windsor lines) - Reading via Richmond |
| REB | Northallerton, Castle Hills Jn. - Redmire |
| RLY | Ripple Lane Yards |
| ROU | Romford - Upminster |
| RUB | Rufford Jn. - Bilsthorpe Colliery |
| RUC | Rufford Colliery Jn. - Rufford Colliery |
| RWS | River Wear Commissioneres (Londonderry - Hendon - Sunderland South Dock) |
| SAC | Settle Jn. - Carlisle, Petteril Bridge Jn. |
| SAN | Santon Ore Branch (Scunthorpe) |
| SAR | South Acton Jn. - Richmond |
| SBF | Shipley East Jn. - Bradford Forster Square |
| SBR | Shepreth Branch: Hitchin, Cambridge Jn. - Shepreth Branch Jn. |
| SCD | Scunthorpe, Trent Jn. - Dawes Lane Jn. |
| SCG | Carlisle, Bog Jn. - Forks Jn. |
| SCW | Scarborough, Gallows Close Goods |
| SDC | Stratford Central Jn. West - Copper Mill North Jn. |
| SEA | Dawdon Jn. - Seabanks |
| SEC | Selby Canal Jn. - Selby West Jn. |
| SEL | Shepcote Lane West Jn. - Tinsley South Jn. |
| SES | Seal Sands Branch (North Tees) |
| SEY | Seymour Colliery Branch (Barrow Hill) |
| SHB | Sheffield - Barnsley |
| SHG | Sherburn Jn. - Gascoigne Wood Jn. |
| SHU | Shoeburyness Sidings |
| SHW | Shireoaks West Jn. - Woodend Jn. |
| SIB | St. Ives Branch (Chesterton Jn. - Fen Drayton) |
| SIC | Silverwood Colliery Branch: Thrybergh Jn. - Silverwood Colliery |
| SIZ | Sizewell Sidings (Saxmundham - Leiston) |
| SJB | St. James Jn. - Bridge Jn. (Doncaster) |
| SJC | Carnforth, Furness & Midland Jn. - Wennington Jn. |
| SJM | Swinton Jn. - Mexborough |
| SKA | Skellow Jn. - Adwick Jn. |
| SKL | Stocksbridge Light Railway |
| SKM | South Kirkby Jn. - Moorthorpe Station Jn. |
| SKS | Skipton Middle Jn.- Grassington |
| SKW | Skipton North Jn. - Wennington Jn. |
| SMJ | Swinton Jn. - Milford Jn. |
| SMP | Stratford Depot |
| SNW | Sleaford North Jn. - West Jn. |
| SOB | Soham Branch (Chippenham Jn. - Ely Dock Jn.) |
| SOL | South Lynn Branch: Kings Lynn Harbour Jn. - South Lynn |
| SOT | Seaton-on-Tees Branch: Seaton Snook Jn. - Seaton-on-Tees |
| SPC | London, St.Pancras - Chesterfield, Tapton Jn. (former Midland Rly) |
| SPD | Spalding South Jn. - Doncaster, Decoy North Jn. |
| SPW | Springbank North Jn. - Walton Street Jn. |
| SSE | Sleaford South Jn. - East Jn. |
| SSG | Sculcoates Goods (Hull) |
| SSH | Scunthorpe Yards |
| SSK | Saltburn West Jn. - Skinningrove |
| SSL | Seven Sisters Loop: South Tottenham West Jn. -Seven Sisters Jn. |
| SSV | Shenfield - Southend Victoria |
| STB | St. Botolph's Branch: Eastgate Jn. - Colchester Town (St. Botolph's) |
| STF | Norton South Jn. - Ferryhill South Jn. (Stillington - Ferryhill) |
| STM | Stratford, Temple Mills Yard |
| SUD | Sudbury Branch: Marks Tey - Sudbury |
| SWP | Shirebrook Jn. - Warsop Jn. |
| TAH | Junction Road Jn. - Barking (Tottenham and Hampstead) |
| TCW | Temple Hirst Jn. - Selby South Jn. (Temple Hirst - Chaloners Whin Jn.) |
| TDE | Tilbury Docks East Side (Grays East Jn. - Northfleet Hope) |
| TEN | Stansted East to North Loop |
| TEY | Tyne Yard |
| TFC | Thornton Fields Carriage Sidings |
| THG | Thorpe Goods (Norwich) |
| THN | Thames Haven Branch |
| TJC | Chesterfield, Tapton Jn. - Old Skipton North Jn. (for Colne) (former Midland Rly) |
| TJG | Thorne Jn. -Gilberdyke |
| TLA | Stansted Airport Link (Third London Airport) |
| TLL | Tilbury Loop Line: Barking, Tilbury Line Jn. West - Pitsea Jn. via Tilbury |
| TMP | Thorpe Marsh Power Station |
| TNC | Treeton North Jn. - Catcliffe Jn. |
| TSE | South Tottenham East Jn. - Tottenham South Jn. |
| TSN | Trent South Jn. - Nottingham East Jn. |
| TSY | Tees Yard |
| TWN | Thorpe-le-Soken - Walton-on-the-Naze |
| TYB | Clarborough Jn. - Cottam Power Station (Torksey Branch) |
| TYC | Thoresby Colliery: Thoresby Colliery Jn. - Thoresby Colliery |
| UCJ | Carlisle, Upperby Jn. - Caldew Jn. (Goods Lines) |
| UDS | Doncaster, Up Decoy Sidings i/c Low Ellers Curve |
| UHL | Wembley Central - Willesden High Level Sidings |
| UPG | Upminster - Grays |
| WAG | Wakefield - Goole |
| WAR | Appleby North Jn. - Appleby West Jn. |
| WAW | Willesdon, Low Level Goods Jn. - Acton Wells Jn. |
| WBC | West Burton Power Station |
| WBH | Westgate Branch (Rotherham) |
| WCI | Wilton ICI Branch (Teesside) |
| WCM | Carlisle - Glasgow Central (West Coast Main Line) |
| WEB | Werrington Branch: Werrington Jn. - Spalding |
| WHC | Whitlingham Jn. - Cromer |
| WHR | Whiskerhill Jn. - Retford Western Jn. |
| WIG | Wisbech Goods Branch: March, Whitemoor Jn. - Wisbech |
| WIS | Wickford -Southminster |
| WKC | Welbeck Colliery Branch: Welbeck Colliery Branch Jn. - Welbeck Colliery |
| WLL | Clapham Jn, Falcon Jn. - Willesden, West London Jn. (West London Line) |
| WMB | Willesden High Level Jn. - Mitre Bridge Jn. |
| WME | Woodburn Jn - Mexborough Jn. |
| WRG | Whitehall Road Goods (Leeds) |
| WSB | West Sleekburn Jn. - North Blyth |
| WTB | West Blythe Staithes: West Blythe Staithes Jn. - West Blythe Staithes |
| WTS | Willesden Through Sidings: Harlesden - Brent |
| WWK | Wakefield Kirkgate, Ings Jn. - Wakefield West Riding Jn. |
| YDS | St. Catherines Jn. - Decoy South Jn. (Doncaster) |
| YMS | York - Malton - Scarborough |

# INDEX TO STATIONS,
# Lines and Selected Other Places

Abbots Ripton 15D
ACKLINGTON 23A
ACLE 8B
Acton Canal Viaduct 1A
Acton Canal Wharf 1A
ACTON CENTRAL 1A
Acton Lane 1A
ACTON MAIN LINE 1A
Acton Wells Jn 1A
Addison LC 21B
Admiralty Sidings (Killingholme) 32B
ADWICK 36B
Adwick Jn 36B
Ainderby LC's 45E
AIRPORT (NEWCASTLE) 52
Ais Gill 45B
Aiskew LC 45E
Albert Hill 20B 47B
Alcan Branch Jn 23C
Aldam Dock (Goole) 40B
Aldersbrook 5A
Aldwarke 33A
ALEXANDRA PALACE 14B
Alexandra Road LC 9B
ALLENS WEST 47C
Allington Jn 25B
ALNMOUTH 23A
ALRESFORD 6A
ALSTON 46D
ALTHORNE 10A
ALTHORPE 34A
Altofts Jn 42A
ANCASTER 25B
Anchor Exchange Sidings (Scunthorpe) 34A
ANDREWS HOUSE 47D
ANGEL ROAD 10B
Angels LC 15C
Anlaby Road Jn 38C
Apperley 43
Apperley Lane Tunnel 43
Appleby (Lincs) 34C
APPLEBY 45C
APPLEBY-FRODINGHAM 34A
Applehurst Jn 18A 33B
Arbour Lane Crossover 5C
Ardleigh 6A
Ardsley Tunnel 36C
Arksey 18A
ARLESEY 15B
ARMATHWAITE 45D
Armley Tunnels 37A
ARRAM 39A
Artengil Viaduct 45B
Arthington Viaduct 42D
Ashington 23C
ASHWELL & MORDEN 24C
Askern 40A
Askew Road Tunnel 22A
Askham Tunnel 17A
ASLOCKTON 25B
Astra Fuels (Immingham) 32A
Attercliffe 29
ATTLEBOROUGH 13B
AUDLEY END (AER) 4C
AUDLEY END 11B
Audley End (Norfolk) LC 6D
Audley End Railway 4C
Aukley LC 17C
Averham Weir Viaduct 27D
Aycliffe 20C
AYLSHAM 54C
Ayrton Terminal 50A
Badgeney Road LC 13C
Badley Viaduct 6C
Baildon Tnls 43
BAILDON 43
Bainton Green LC 24D
Bainton LC 24D
Balby Bridge Tunnel 17C
Balby Carr 17C
Balderton LC 16C
BALDOCK 24C
Balm Road (Leeds) 37A
Balne 18A
Balne Lane 36C
Balne Lowgate 18A
Bank House Tnl 41A
BANKFOOT 52
Barcroft 18A
BARDON MILL 46C
Barham 6C
BARKING 3A
Barking FLT 4A
Barking Sidings (LUL) 3A
Barking Tilbury Line Jns 3A 4A
Barkston Jns 16C 25B
Barlby 38A
Barlby Loops 38A
Barlby North Jn 38A
Barlow 18A
Barlow Road LC 40B
Barmoor North Sdgs 22B
Barnby 16C
Barnby Dun 33B
Barnby Lane LC 16C
Barnby Moor & Sutton LC 17B
Barnet Tunnels 14B
BARNETBY 31C
Barnolds LC 11C
Barnsbury Junction 1A/B
BARNSLEY INTERCHANGE 36A
Barnwell Jn 11C
Baron Wood Tnls 45D
Barrington Light Rly 24C
BARROW HAVEN 32B
Barrow Hill 28E
Barrow Road LC 32B
Barrow Road Sdgs (S Yks Rly) 29
Barton Hill 18C
Barton Road LC 32B
BARTON-ON-HUMBER 32B
Barway Sidings LC 12C
BASF Loop 48A
BASILDON 3B
Bates Staithes 23C
Bathley Lane 16C
BATLEY 41B
BATTERSBY 51B
BATTLESBRIDGE 10A
Batty Moss Vdt 45A
Bawtry 17B
BAYFORD 24A
Baylham LC 6C
Beacon Hill Vdt/Tnl 43
Beal 23B
Beald Drove LC 13C
Bealings LC 9A
Beam Mill Jn 50B
Beamish Open Air Museum 54C
Bearty Fen 26C
Bebside LC 23C
BECCLES 8
Beckingham 27B
BECONTREE 3B
Bedale LC 45E
BEDE 49A 52
Bedlington 23C
Beech Hill LC 27C
Beeston Regis Lc 8
Beighton Jn 28E 29
Beighton Station Jn 29
Belasis Lane 48A
Belaugh Green LC 54C
Belford 23B
Bell Busk Viaduct 44A
Bell's Bank 48A
Belle Isle 14A
Belle Vue Sdgs (Wakefield) 39D
Bellwater Jn 26A
Belmont LC 42D
Belmont Sidings (Doncaster) 17C
Belsize Tunnels 1A
BEMPTON 39C
BEN RHYDDING 43
BENFLEET 3B
Beningborough LC 20A
Bensham Tunnel 21B
BENTHAM 44C
BENTLEY (S. Yorks)* 36B
Bentley Colliery and Jns 18A
Bentley Jn 17C 32A 32B
Bentley LC 6A
Benton Jn 22B 23C
BENTON 52
BERNEY ARMS 8
BERRY BROW 36A
BERWICK-UPON-TWEED 23B
Bessacar Jn/Halt LC 17C
Beswick LC 39A
BETHNAL GREEN 2A
Bevercotes Cly 30B
BEVERLEY 39A
Beverley Parks LC 39A
Beversham LC 9A
BIGGLESWADE 15B
Bill Quay 52
BILLERICAY 10A
Billingham Reach Wf 48A
BILLINGHAM 48A
Billingham-on-Tees 48A
Bilsthorpe 30A
BINGHAM 25A
BINGLEY 43
Birket Tunnel 45B
Birtley 21A
BISHOP AUKLAND 47B
BISHOPS STORTFORD 11B
Bishopsgate Tunnel 2A
Black Bank LC 13C
Black Bush LC 13C
Black Carr Jn 17C
Blackfell 49B
BLACKHAMS 49B
BLACKHORSE ROAD 1B 10B
Blankney 27A
Blaxhall LC 9A
BLAYDON 21B
Blea Moor 45A
BLEASBY 25A
Blenkinsop LC 46A
Blofield Hall LC 9A
Blotoft 26D
Blyth Staithes 23C
Blyth, Cambois 23C
Bog Hall GF 51C
Bog Jn (Carlisle) 46A
Boldon Colliery 49A
Boldon Jns 49A
Boldon LC 49A
Bollo Lane 1A
Bolsover 30A
BOLTON ABBEY 44D
Bolton Hall Vdt 43
BOLTON-ON-DEARNE 33A
Bonsall Lane LC 31C
Bootham LC 19
Boothferry BC Sdg 33B
BOOTHFERRY PARK 38C
Boreham Viaduct 5C
Boroughbridge Road LC 20B
BOSTON 26A
Boston & Spilsby Road LC 26A
Boston Docks 26A
Botanic Gardens 38C
Botany Bay LC 17B
Bothal Viaduct 22B
BOTTESFORD 25B
Bottisham Road LC 11C
Bottom End Sdgs (Carnforth) 44C
Boughton Brake Tnl 30B
Boughton Jn 30B
Boulby Mine 51A
Boultham Crossing 27E
Boultham Jn 27A 27E
Bounds Green 14B
Bow Bridge Loop 44C
BOW CHURCH 3A
Bow Depot 2B
Bow Junction 2B
Bow Road 2B 3A
Bowes Park Jn 14B
BOWES PARK 24A
Bowes Railway 49A
Bowesfield 47C
Bowling Jn/Tnl 43
Bradfield LC 9B
BRADFORD FORSTER SQUARE 43
BRADFORD INTERCHANGE 43
Bradley Jn 41A
Bradley Wood Jn 41A
Bradway Tunnel 28E
Brayford LC 27A
BRAINTREE 5D
Bramfield LC 8
Bramhope Tnl 42C 42D
BRAMLEY 43
BRAMPTON (Cumbria) 46A
BRAMPTON (Suffolk) 8
Brampton Fell 46A
BRAMPTON HALT (Bure Valley) 54C
Bramwith Road LC 33B
Brancliffe East Jn 31A 35A
BRANDON 13A
Branston & W. Cross Rds Tnl 27A
Brayton 18A
Brayton LC 38A
Brent Curve Jn 1A
Brent Sidings (Willesden) 1A
BRENTFORD 1A
BRENTWOOD 5B
Bressingham Steam Museum 7C
Brewery Lane 26D
Brewster Lane LC 26B
Breydon Jn 8
Brick House Crossovers 5C
Brick Pit Sdgs (Grimsby) 32C
Bridge Jn (Doncaster) 17C
Bridges Jn (Hull) 38C
BRIDLINGTON 39B
BRIGG 31C
Brighouse 41A

Brightside 29
BRIMSDOWN 10B
Brinefield LC 48A
Brinkley Road LC 11C
British Dredging Sdgs 4B
BRITISH STEEL REDCAR 50B
Broad Street Tunnel 29
Broadfield Lane LC 26A
Broadwath LC 46A
Broadwood LC 47A
BROCKHOLES 36A
Brocklesby Jn 32A
BROCKLEY WHINS 49A
BROMLEY-BY-BOW 3A
Brompton LC 20B
BRONDESBURY 1A
BRONDESBURY PARK 1A
Brookhouse Viaduct 35A
Brooklands Avenue 11C
BROOKMANS PARK 15A
Broom Hill Viaduct 9A
BROOMFLEET 38B
Brotherton Tnl 35B
Brotton:Skinningrove 51A
BROUGH 38B
Broughton Lane Jn 29
Broughton Road CS 44A
Browick Road 13B
BROXBOURNE 11A
BRUCE GROVE 10B
BRUNDALL 8
BRUNDALL GARDENS 8
Brunton Lane LC 52
BUCKENHAM 8
Buckton Lane LC 39C
Bulcote LC 25A
Bulpit Lane LC 16C
Burdon Road Sdgs 48B
Bure Valley Rly(1991)Ltd 54C
BURES 5E
Burley Jn 43
BURLEY PARK 37A 42C
BURLEY-IN-WHARFDALE 43
Burn Lane LC 18A
BURNHAM-ON-CROUCH 10A
Burnt House Drove LC 13C
Burrs Road LC 6A
Burston LC 6D
Burton Agnes LC 39B
BURTON JOYCE 25A
Burton Lane LC's 25C
Burton Salmon 35B 42B
BURY ST. EDMUNDS 12D
Bury Street Jn 10B
BUSH HILL PARK 10B
Buslingthorpe LC 28E
Butterley Brick Sdg 30B
Butterswood LC 32B
Butterwell 22B
BUXTON 54C
BYKER 52
Bystable Lane LC 32B
Bytham Viaduct 16B

Cadeby Loop 33A
Cadwell 15B
Calder & Hebble Canal Vdt 36A 42A
Calder Bridge 39D
Calder Bridge Jn 42A
CALEDONIAN ROAD & BARNSBURY 1A
CALLERTON PARKWAY 52
Calverley Viduct 43
Cambois LC 23C
CAMBRIDGE 11C
CAMBRIDGE HEATH 1B 2A 10B
Cambridge Jn (Hitchin) 15B 24C
Cambridge South Jn 11C
Camden Jns 1A
CAMDEN ROAD 1A
Camden Road Jn 1A 14A
Camden Viaduct 1A
Campbell Road Jn 3A
Canal Bridge Vdt (Thorne) 33B
Canklow 29
CANNING TOWN 2C
CANONBURY 1B
Canonbury Tunnel 1B 14A
CANTLEY 8
Capernway Viaduct 44C
Carcroft Jn 36B
Cardells LC 15C
Cargo Fleet 50B
Cargo Fleet Road LC 50B
Carlin How 51A
CARLISLE 46A
CARLTON 25A
Carlton and Loops 17A
Carlton Colville 7B
Carlton Road Jn 1A
Carnaby LC 39B
CARNFORTH 44C
Carpenters Road Jns 2B
Carr 17C
Castel Eden viaduct 48B
CASTLE HEDINGHAM 4D
Castle Hills Jns 20B 45E
Castle Sidings GF 22A
CASTLEFORD 39D 42A
Castleford Gates 42A
Castleford Jns 42A
Castleford West Jn 39D
CASTLETON MOOR 51B
Catcliffe Jn 29
CATTALL 42E
Cattawade Viaduct 6A
CAUSEY ARCH 47D
Cave Crossing LC 38B
Cayton 39C
Cemetery North 48A
CENTRAL STATION (NEWCASTLE) (T & W) 52
CHADWELL HEATH 5A
CHAFFORD HUNDRED 3B
Chain Bridge LC 13C
Chalk Lane LC 38C
CHALKWELL 3C
Channelsea Jns 2B
Chantry Road LC 9A
CHAPEL ROAD 7B
Chapel Road LC 8
CHAPELTOWN 29
CHAPPEL & WAKES COLNE 5E
Charlestown Viaduct 43
CHATHILL 23A
Cheal Road LC 26C
CHELMSFORD 5C
Cherrry Hinton LC 11C
Cherry Tree LC 39A
Cherry Willingham LC 28A
Cheshunt Jn 11A
CHESHUNT 11A
CHESTER-LE-STREET 21A
CHESTERFIELD 28E
Chesterton Jn 11C
Chettisham LC 13C
Chevet Viaduct 39D
Chevington 23A
CHICHESTER (T & W) 49A 52
CHILLINGHAM ROAD 22A 52
CHINGFORD 10B
Chippenham Jn 12D
Chitts Hill LC 5E
Chivers LC 13A
Choppington LC 23C
Christian Street Jn 3A
Christon Bank 23A
CHURCH FENTON 35C
Church Lane (Ingat)LC 5C
Church Lane (Norfolk)LC 13B
Church Lane LC 26D
Church Lane LC (Newark) 16C
Church Lane LC (Redcar) 51A
Church St. LC (Hartlepool) 48A
Church Street (Kelvedon)LC 5C
Church Viaduct 45A
Churwell Viaduct 41B
CLACTON 6A
CLAPHAM (N Yorks) 44A
CLAPTON 10B
Clapton Jn 1B 10B
Clapton Tunnel 10B
Clara Vale Viaduct 21C
Clarborough Jn and tunnel 31B
Clarence Road (Hartlepool) 48A
Clarence Yard Jn 14A
Claxby & Usselby LC 28A
Claxby No.24 LC 28A
Claydon 6C
Claypole 16C
CLAYTON WEST 40D
Clayton West Jn 36A 40D
CLEETHORPES 32A
Cleethorpes Coast Lt Rly 28D
Cleveland (Wilton) 50B
Cleveland Bridge Ltd 47C
Cliff Quay 6B
Cliffe House 48A
Cliffe LC 38A
Clifton LC 22B
Clintsfield Viaduct 44C
Clipstone and junctions 30A
Clipstone Colliery and junctions 30A
Clowne Single line 30A
Coal Export Term (Imm) 32B
Coal Import Term (Imm) 32B
Coal Unloading LC (Drax) 40B
Coalfields, Cambridge 11C
Cockspin Road LC 12C
COLCHESTER 6A
Colchester Road LC 6A
COLCHESTER TOWN 6A
Coldham Lane Jn 11C
Coldham LC 13C
COLLINGHAM 27E
Colne Jn 6A
Colne Valley Rly Coy 4D
Colne Viaduct 41A
COLTISHALL 54C
Colton Jns 18B 35C
Colwick 25A
Common Road LC 18C
COMMONDALE 51B
CONISBROUGH 33A
Connington 15D
CONONLEY 44A
Coopers Lane Jn 11B
Coopies Lane LC 22B
Copenhagen Tunnels 14A
Copley Viaduct 41A
Copmanthorpe LC 18B
Coppermill North Jn 10B
CORBRIDGE 46E
Corby Gates 46A
Corby Glen 16B
Corby viaduct 46A
Cornard LC 5E
Corringham Lt. Rly 4B
Cortonwood Halt 38D
Coryton 4B
Cotehill viaduct 45D
Cotgrave 25A
Cottage Lane LC 27E
Cottam Power stn 31B
COTTINGHAM 39A
Cottingham branch 38C
COTTINGLEY 41B
County School 13B
Coupland viaduct 45C
Covered Way (Junction Rd) 1A
Cow Green Crossovers 6C
Cowpen Lane LC 48A
Coxhoe 20C
Crabley Creek LC 38B
Crag Hall 51A
Crag Mill 23B
Crakehall LC 45E
CRAMLINGTON 22B
Crankley Point 27D
Crescent Jn 16A
Crescent Sidings (Peterborough) 16A
CRESSING 5D
CRESWELL 30A
CREWS HILL 24A
Creykes LC 33B
CRICKLEWOOD 1A
Cridling Stubbs LC 40A
Crigglestone Jn 36A
Crimble Viaduct 41A
Crimdon Dene viaduct 48A
Crimple Viaduct 42D
Croft Jn 20B
Croft Viaduct 20B
Crofton Depot 39D
Crofton Jns 39D
CROMER 8
Cromwell Lane LC 16C
Cromwell Road LC 8
Crook Hall GF (Durham) 20C
Crosby Garrett vdt and tunnel 45C
Crosby Mines 34A 34B
Cross Common LC 38A
CROSS GATES 37A
Cross Lane LC 27E
CROSSFLATS 43
Crossgate viaduct 52
CROUCH HILL 1B
Crouch Valley Line 10A
Crowdundle viaduct 45C
CROWLE 33B
Crown Point Depot (Norwich) 7A
Croxdale Viaduct 20C
Croxton LC 13A
CUCKOO'S NEST 40D
CUFFLEY 24A
Culgaith 45D
CULLERCOATES 52
Cumberworth Tunnel 36A
Cumwhinton 46A
Currock Jn 46A
Curry Marsh 4B
CUSTOM HOUSE 2C
Cutsyke Jn 39D

DAGENHAM DOCK 4A
DAGENHAM EAST 3B
DAGENHAM HEATHWAY 3B
Dairycoates 38B
Dairycoates West LC 38B
Dalston Junction 1B
DALSTON KINGSLAND 1B
Dam Dykes LC 22B
DAMENS 54F
DANBY 51B
Danby Wiske 20B
DARLINGTON 20B
DARNALL 29
DARSHAM 8
DARTON 36A
Daw Lane LC 18A
Dawden Dene viaduct 48B
Dawdon 48B
Dawdon Jn 48B
Dawdys LC 8
Dawes Lane Coke Ovens (Scun) 34A
Dawes Lane LC 34A
Dean Street Crossover 22A
Decoy North and South Jns 17C
Decoy Sidings 17C
Deep Wharf LC 4A
Deepcar 29
DEIGHTON 41A
Demaglass 35A
Denaby LC 33A
DENBY DALE 36A
DENT 45b
Dent Head Viaduct 45B
Dent's Wharf 50A
Denton School LC 46B
Denton Village 46B
Denver LC 12A
DERBY ROAD 9A
DEREHAM 13B
Dernford LC 11C
Derwent Valley Lt Rly 19A
Derwenthaugh Crossover 21B
DEVONS ROAD 3A
Devonshire Street 2B
DEWSBURY 41B
Dewsbury East Jn 41B
Dewsbury Railway Street 41B
Digswell 15A
Dilston LC 46E
Dimmocks Cote LC 11C
Dinnington Jn 35A
DINSDALE 47C

DISS 6D
Dock Hills LC 17C 36B
Dock Junction North 1A
Dockfield Jn 43
Doddington Road LC 27E
DODWORTH 36A
DONCASTER 17C
Doncaster Railport 17C
Doncaster RMT 17C
Doncaster Works 17C
DORE 28E
Dormer Green LC 18A
DOVERCOURT 9B
Dowley Gap 43
Downham Bypass LC 12A
DOWNHAM MARKET 12A
Dragonby Sidings 34B
Draughton (Priors Lane) 44D
Drawell GF 4D
Drax Branch Jn 40B
Drax Power Station 40B
DRAYTON PARK 14A
DRIFFIELD 39B
Driffield Trout Stream Vdt 39B
Dringhouses North Jn 18B 19
DRONFIELD 28E
Drybeck Viaduct 45D
Dryclough Jn 41A 43
Ducketts LC 43
Dudding Hill Jn 1A
DULLINGHAM 11C
DUNSTON-ON-TYNE 21B
DURHAM 20C
Durham Warping Drain Vdt 33B
Dutch River Bridge Vdt 40B
Duxford 11B
Duxford LC 11B

Eagle & Thorpe LC 27E
Eagle Barnsdale LC 27E
EAGLESCLIFFE 47C
Earfit Lane LC 18B
Earsden 23C
Easby viaduct 51B
East Anglian Rly Museum 5E
East Anglian Tspt Museum 7B
East Bank Tunnel 28E
EAST BOLDON 49A
East Cowick 40B
East Cowton Crossovers 20B
EAST GARFORTH 37A
East Gate Jn 6A
EAST HAM 3A
East Ham Depot 3A
East Heslerton 18D
East Holmes 27A 27E
East Jn (Northallerton) 20B
East Road LC 15C
East Suffolk Jn 6C 9A
East Suffolk Lt. Rly 7B
EAST TANFIELD 47D
EAST TILBURY 4B
Eastcroft Depot 25A
Eastern Access Road (Hull) 38C
Eastfield 16A
Eastgate-in-Weardale 47A
Eastrea LC 13C
EASTRINGTON 38A
Eastville Lc 26A
Eaton LC 13B
Eaves Lane LC 17A
ECCLES ROAD 13B
Ecclesfield West 29B
EDMONTON GREEN 10B
Edwinstowe 30A
Eggborough LC's 40A
Eggborough Power Stn 40A
Egmanton LC 17A
EGTON 51C
E.I.C.(Immingham) 32B 32C
Elland 41A
ELM PARK 3B
Elm Road LC 13C
Elmsley LC 30A
ELMSWELL 12D
Elmton & Creswell Jn 30A
ELSECAR 35D
Elsecar Steam Rly 38D
ELSENHAM 11B
Elsham 34C
Elswick 22A
ELTON & ORSTON 25B
ELY 12A
Ely Dock Jn 12A 12C
Ely Freight Terminal 12A
Ely North Jn 12A 13A
Ely Station North LC 12A
Ely West Jn 12A
EMBSAY 44D
Embsay & Bolton Abbey Steam Rly 44D
Embsay Jn 44A 44D
EMERSON PARK 5B
ENFIELD CHASE 24A
ENFIELD LOCK 10B
ENFIELD TOWN 10B
Engine Shed Jn (Goole) 40B
Engine Shed Jn (Leeds) 37A
England Lane 40A
Enron LC 48A
Esholt Jn 43
Esholt Tnl,Vdt 43
Essendine 16B
ESSEX ROAD 14A
Essex Road LC 11A
Euro Terminal, Willesden 1A
Everton 15C
Extons Road LC 12B

Faber Prest Terminal (Flix) 34B
Fairburn tunnel 42B
Fairheads LC 11B
Falloden LC 23A
Falsgrave signalbox 18D
FAMBRIDGE 10A
Farmers viaduct 44B
Farnley viaduct 37A
FAWDON 52
FEATHERSTONE 39D
FELIXSTOWE 9A
Felixstowe Beach 9A
Felixstowe Dock Jn 9A
Felixstowe Pier 9A
Felixstowe Port 9A
FELLING 49A 52
Felton Lane LC 22B
Fen Drayton 11C
Fencehouses 20C
FENCHURCH STREET,LONDON 3A
Fenwick LC 18A
Ferme Park Sidings 14B
FERRIBY 38B
Ferry LC (Woodbridge) 9A
FERRY MEADOWS 54A
Ferrybridge 35B 40A
Ferryhill 20C
Field Lane LC 40B
FILEY 39C
FINCHLEY ROAD & FROGNAL 1A
Finghall Lane 45E
Finningley 17C 27C
FINSBURY PARK 14A
Firbeck Jn 35A
Firmin Coates 12C
Firsby East Jn 26B
Fish Dock Road LC 32A
Fish Sidings (Lowestoft) 8A
FISKERTON 25A 27D
FITZWILLIAM 36A
Flagbury LC 9A
Flamborough LC 39B
Flax Mill LC 26C
Flaxton LC 18C
Flemingate LC 39A
Fletton 15D
Fletton Road Jn 16A
Flixborough Wharf 34B
Flockton Sdgs 36A 42A
Flordon Crossover 6D
Flyover East and West Jn's 17C
Fobbing LC 4B
Follingsby 20C 49A
Folly Bank 26C
Folly Bank LC 16A
Ford Motor Coy siding 4A
Ford's Freight Depot 4A
Fordham LC 12C
Foreign Ore Branch Jn (Scun) 34A
FOREST DEEP HALT 4C
FOREST GATE 5A
Forest Gate Jn 3A 5A
Forth Banks 22A
Fossdyke Navigation Canal 27B
FOUR LANE ENDS 52
Foxlow Jn 28E 30A
FOXTON 24C
Frating LC 6A
Freemans LC 23C
Freight Terminal Jn 1A 14A
Friargate LC 32A
Friars Junction 1A
Frickley Colliery 33A
Frinkley Lane LC 25A
FRINTON 6A
FRIZINGHALL 43
Frodingham viaduct 34A
Fulbourn 11C
Fulbourn Old Drift LC 11C
Fullers End LC 11B
Funthams Lane LC 13C
Furnaceway Sidings 23C

GAINSBOROUGH CENTRAL 31B 31C
GAINSBOROUGH LEA ROAD 27B
Gainsborough Oil Terminal 27B
Gainsborough Trent Jn 27B 31B
Gamston Emergency Crossovers 17A
Ganton LC 18D
Garden Street Jn LC 32A
Gardners LC 4B
GARFORTH 37A
GARGRAVE 44A
GARSDALE 45B
Garsdale viaduct 45B
Garvestone LC 13B
Gas Factory Jn 2B 3A
Gas Works Tunnels 14A
Gascoigne Wood 35B 35C 37B
GATESHEAD 52
Gateshead 22A
GATESHEAD STADIUM 52
Gedling 25A
Geldard Road Jn 36C 37A
Gelt viaduct 46A
GIDEA PARK 5B
Gidea Park Sidings 5B
GIGGLESWICK 44B
GILBERDYKE 38A 40C
GILDERDALE 46D
Girton Road LC 11C
Gissing LC 6D
GLAISDALE 51B
Glass Bulbs GF 35A
Gledholt tunnels 36A 41A
Glews Hollow 40B
GOATHLAND 51D
Golcar viaduct 41A
Golden High Hedges 26D
GOLDTHORPE 33A
Gonalston LC 25A
Gonerby tunnel 25B
GOODMAYES 5A
Goodnow Bridge 33B
GOOLE 40B
Goole Bridge 40B 40C
Goole Docks 40B
Goole Yard 40B
Goose Hill Jn 42A
Goose Hill Terminal 42A
GORDON HILL 24A
Gosberton 26D
Gosforth 52
GOSPEL OAK 1A
Goswick LC 23B
Gowdall Lane LC 40B
GOXHILL 32B
Graham Road Curve 1B 10B
Grand Sluice Jn 26A
GRANGE PARK 24A
Grangetown (Tees) 50B
Grangetown LC (Hendon) 48B
Granhams LC 11C
GRANTHAM 16C
Grassthorpe Lane 17A
Gravel Pit LC (Lowes) 8
GRAYS 4B
Graythrop LC 48A
GREAT AYTON 51B
GREAT BENTLEY 6A
Great Catch Water Drain viaduct 12A
GREAT CHESTERFORD 11B
GREAT COATES 32A
Great Coates No.1 signalbox 32C
Great Hale Drove LC's 25C
Great Lime Road viaduct 22B
Great Northern & E. Lincs. Rly 28C
Great Ouse viaduct 15C
Great Plumstead LC 8
GREAT YARMOUTH 8
Greatford LC 16B
Greatham 48A
Greatham Creek Branch 48A
Green Lane Jn 20A 49A
Green Lane LC 23C
Green Oak Goit 40C
Greenbottom tunnel 43
Greens viaduct 44B
Greensfield Jn 22A
Greetland 41A
Greetwell Jn 27A
Griffen Wharf 6B
Grimesthorpe Jn 29
GRIMSBY DOCKS 32A
Grimsby Docks 32C
GRIMSBY TOWN 32A
Gringley Road LC 31B
Grinkle tunnel 51A
Griseburn viaduct 45C
Gristhorpe 39C
GROSMONT 51C 51D
Grove Road 17A
Grove Road LC (Beccles) 8
Guisborough Jn 50B
Guisborough Road LC 51B
GUISELEY 43
Gunhouse 34A
GUNNERSBURY 1A
GUNTON 8
GYPSY LANE 50B

HABROUGH 32A
HACKNEY CENTRAL 1B
HACKNEY DOWNS 1B 10B
Hackney Downs tunnel 10B
HACKNEY WICK 1B
HADDISCOE 8
HADLEY WOOD 15A
HADRIAN ROAD 52
Hagg Lane LC 37B 38A
Hales Street LC 6D
HALESWORTH 8
Halfway (ECML) 20A
HALFWAY (Sheffield) 53
HALIFAX 43
Halifax Jn 6A
Hall Dene 48B
Hall Lane Jn 28E 30A
Hall Lane LC 13B
HALTWHISTLE 46C
Ham Hall LC 45E
Hambleton Jn's 18B 37b
HAMMERTON 42E
Hammerton Road 42E
Hammerton Street 43
HAMPSTEAD HEATH 1A
HARDINGHAM 13B
Hare Park Jn 36C 39D
Harford Bridges 13B
Hargham No.1 LC 13B
HARLESDEN 1A
HARLING ROAD 13B
HARLOW TOWN 11A
HAROLD WOOD 5B
Harperley 47A
HARRINGAY 1B 14B

| | |
|---|---|
| HARRINGAY GREEN LANES | 1B 10B |
| Harringay Jn | 1B 14B |
| Harringay Park Jn | 1B 14B |
| HARROGATE | 42D |
| Harry Moor Lane LC's | 37B |
| Harston LC | 24C |
| Hartburn Jn | 47C |
| HARTLEPOOL | 48A |
| Hartlepool Docks | 48A |
| Hartlepool Power Station | 48A |
| Hartlepool South Works | 48A |
| Hartley LC | 23C |
| Harts Drove LC | 13C |
| HARWICH INTERNATIONAL | 9B |
| Harwich Refinery | 9B |
| HARWICH TOWN | 9B |
| Harwich Train Ferry Span | 9B |
| Harworth Cly | 35A |
| Hassingham Bridge | 8 |
| HATFIELD | 15A |
| HATFIELD & STAINFORTH | 33B |
| Hatfield Main Cly | 33B |
| HATFIELD PEVEREL | 5C |
| Haughley Jn | 6C 12D |
| Haughley LC | 6C 12D |
| Hautbois Loop | 54C |
| Hauxton LC | 24C |
| HAVENHOUSE | 26B |
| Haverton Hill | 48A |
| Haw Bank tunnel | 44A |
| HAWORTH | 54F |
| Hawthorn Bank LC | 26C |
| Hawthorn Dene viaduct | 48A |
| Haxby LC | 19 |
| Haxby Road LC | 19 |
| Haxey & Epworth | 27C |
| Haxey LC | 27C |
| HAYDON BRIDGE | 46E |
| Hayes LC | 24C |
| HAYMARKET | 52 |
| Hays Distribution (Dagenham) | 4A |
| Haywards LC | 9A |
| Haywood LC | 40A |
| HEADINGLEY | 42C |
| Headingley tunnel | 37A |
| Headley Grove | 7B |
| Healey Mills | 41B |
| HEALING | 32A |
| Heath LC's | 13B |
| Heaton Depots etc | 22A |
| Heaton Lodge Jn's | 41A |
| HEBBURN | 49A 52 |
| HEBDON BRIDGE | 41A |
| Heck | 18A |
| Heck Ings | 40A 40B |
| Heck Lane | 40A |
| HECKINGTON | 25C |
| Hedingham North (CVR) | 4D |
| Hedon Road Bridge | 38C |
| Hedon Road Sidings | 38C |
| Heeley | 28E |
| HEIGHTON | 47B |
| HELLIFIELD | 44B |
| Helm tunnel | 45C |
| Helpston Jn | 16B |
| Hemingfield tunnel | 35D |
| Hemmingfield (ESR) | 38D |
| Hemsworth | 36B |
| HENSALL | 40A |
| Henwick Hall | 18A |
| Hepscott Jn | 22B 23C |
| Hepscott LC | 23C |
| HERDINGS PARK | 53 |
| HERTFORD EAST | 11A |
| HERTFORD NORTH | 24A |
| Hertford viaduct | 24A |
| Heslerton LC | 18D |
| Hessay | 42E |
| HESSLE | 38B |
| Hessle East Jn | 38B |
| Hessle Road Jn | 38C |
| Hethersett | 13B |
| Hett Mill LC | 20C |
| HEWORTH | 49A 52 |
| HEXHAM | 46E |
| Hexthorpe Depot & sdgs | 17C |
| Hexthorpe Jn | 33A |
| Heyworth LC | 18A |
| Hibaldstow LC | 31C |
| Hickleton | 33A |
| High Dyke Jn | 16B |
| High Eggborough | 40A |
| High Ferry Lane LC | 26A |
| High Ferry LC | 26A |
| High Jn (Northallerton) | 20B |
| High Level Bridge (Newcastle) | 22A |
| High Marnham Power Stn | 30B |
| High Meads Jn | 2B |
| High Scampston | 18D |
| High Stand viaduct | 45D |
| High Street (Lincoln) | 27A 27E |
| High Street Jn (Newcastle) | 22A |
| HIGHAMS PARK | 10B |
| HIGHBURY & ISLINGTON | 1B 14A |
| Highbury Vale Jn | 14A |
| Highgate Road viaduct | 1A |
| Hilgay LC | 12A |
| Hillam Gates LC | 35B 42B |
| Hinxton LC | 11B |
| Hipperholme tunnel | 43 |
| Hirst Lane LC | 23C |
| Histon LC | 11C |
| HITCHIN | 15B |
| HOCKLEY | 10A |
| Hoe LC | 13B |
| Hoe Street tunnel | 10B |
| Holbeck Depot | 37A |
| Holbeck East Jn | 37A |
| Holbeck West Jn | 37A |
| Holderness Road viaduct | 38C |
| Holgate Jn | 19 |
| Holgate Recep. Sdgs | 19 |
| Holgate Works | 19 |
| Holloway Jn's | 14A |
| Holme | 15D |
| Holme Green LC | 15C |
| Holme Lode | 15D |
| Holmes Jn | 29 |
| Holmes Lane sdg | 29 |
| HOLT | 54B |
| Holton Gatehouse LC | 28A |
| Holton-le-Moor | 28A |
| HOLYWELL HALT | 44D |
| Holywell LC | 23C |
| HOMERTON | 1B |
| Honington | 25B |
| HONLEY | 36A |
| Hopetown Jn | 20B 47B |
| Horbury Jn | 36A 42A |
| Horbury Sidings | 42A |
| HORNBEAM PARK | 42D |
| HORNCHURCH | 3B |
| Horns Bridge | 28E |
| HORNSEY | 14B |
| Hornsey Carr. Sdgs | 14B |
| Hornsmill viaduct | 24A |
| Horsemoor LC | 13C |
| HORSFORTH | 42C |
| HORTON-IN-RIBBLESDALE | 45A |
| HOVETON & WROXHAM | 8 |
| HOVETON (WROXHAM) (BVR) | 54C |
| How Mill LC | 46A |
| HOWDEN | 38A |
| HOWDEN (T & w) | 52 |
| Howe & Co's Siding | 45D |
| Howsham | 18C |
| Howsham LC | 28B |
| HUBBERTS BRIDGE | 25C |
| HUDDERSFIELD | 41A |
| Huddersfield Jn | 36A |
| Huddersfield tunnels | 36A |
| HULL | 38C |
| Hull Paragon signalbox | 38C |
| Hull River Swing Bridge | 38C |
| Hull Speedlink Yard | 38B |
| Humber Refinery (Conoco) | 32B |
| Humber Road Jn | 32B |
| Humber Terminals (Grimsby) | 32C |
| HUNMANBY | 39C |
| Hunslet | 37A |
| Hunslet East | 37A |
| HUNTINGDON | 15C |
| HUTTON CRANSWICK | 39A |
| Hutton LC | 39A |
| Huttons Ambo bridge | 18C |
| Hydrocracker LC | 4B |
| HYKEHAM | 27E |
| Hylton Street Depot | 52 |
| HYTHE | 6A |
| Hythe Jn | 6A |
| Ickles | 29 |
| Ickleton Road LC | 11B |
| ILFORD | 5A |
| Ilford Depot | 5A |
| Ilford Flyover | 5A |
| ILFORD ROAD | 52 |
| ILKLEY | 43 |
| Immingham | 32B |
| Immingham East and West Jns | 32B |
| Immingham Refineries | 32B |
| Ingate Street LC | 8 |
| INGATESTONE | 5C |
| Ingrave Summit | 5B |
| INGROW WEST | 54F |
| Inkerswell LC | 30A |
| Intwood LC | 13B |
| IPSWICH | 6C |
| Ipswich Freight Term. | 6A |
| Ipswich Goods Jn | 6C |
| Ipswich Lower Yard | 6B |
| Ipswich tunnel | 6A |
| Ipswich Upper Yard | 6C |
| Ipswich West Bank | 6B |
| Isabella LC | 23C |
| Ivy Farm LC | 24C |
| Jack Lane viaduct | 41B |
| Jacky Duffin Wood LC | 40B |
| JARROW | 49A 52 |
| Jarrow Sidings | 49A |
| JESMOND | 52 |
| Joan Croft Jn | 18A 33B |
| John Kennedy Road LC | 12B |
| Jubilee Carr. Sdgs. (Norwich) | 7A |
| Jumble Lane | 36A |
| Jurgens LC | 4A |
| Keadby bridges | 34A |
| Keadby Canal | 34A |
| KEIGHLEY | 43 54F |
| Keighley Road viaduct | 44A |
| Keighly & Worth Valley Rly Ltd | 54F |
| Kelby Lane LC | 25C |
| KELLING HEATH PARK | 54B |
| Kellingley Cly | 40A |
| Kelloe Bank Foot | 20C |
| KELVEDON | 5C |
| KENNETT | 12D |
| KENSAL GREEN | 1A |
| Kensal Green Jn | 1A |
| KENSAL RISE | 1A |
| KENTISH TOWN | 1A |
| Kentish Town viaduct | 1A |
| KENTISH TOWN WEST | 1A |
| Kesteven LC | 27B |
| Keswick LC | 13B |
| Kettleby LC | 31C |
| Ketton | 24D |
| Ketton Cement Works | 24D |
| KEW BRIDGE | 1A |
| Kew East Jn | 1A |
| KEW GARDENS | 1A |
| KILBURN HIGH ROAD | 1A |
| Kilburn Loop | 1A |
| KILDALE | 51B |
| Kildwick | 44A |
| Killingholme | 32B |
| Killingworth LC | 22B |
| Kiln Lane LC | 12A 32B |
| Kilnhurst | 33A |
| Kilnhurst West | 33A |
| Kilnwick LC | 39A |
| Kimberley Park LC | 13B |
| King Edward Bridge | 22A |
| King George Dock (Hull) | 38C |
| King's Cross Goods Jn | 1A |
| KING'S CROSS, LONDON | 14A |
| KING'S LYNN | 12B |
| King's Lynn Docks | 12B |
| King's Lynn Harbour | 12B |
| King's Lynn Jn | 12B |
| Kings Dyke | 13C |
| Kings Sdgs GF | 12C |
| Kingston Bulk Terminal (Hull) | 38C |
| KINGSTON PARK | 52 |
| Kingston-upon-Hull | 38C |
| KINGSWAY | 28D |
| KIRBY CROSS | 6A |
| Kirby Laythorpe | 25C |
| KIRK SANDALL | 33B |
| KIRKBY STEPHEN | 45B |
| Kirkby Summit | 30A |
| Kirkby Thore | 45C |
| Kirkham Abbey | 18C |
| KIRKHAUGH | 46D |
| Kirklees Light Rly Coy | 40D |
| Kirkstall Forge viaduct | 43 |
| Kirkstall Loops and viaduct | 37A |
| Kirton Lane LC | 33B |
| Kirton Lime Sidings | 31C |
| Kirton Lindsey | 31C |
| Kirton tunnel | 31C |
| Kitroyd viaduct | 35D |
| KIVETON BRIDGE | 31A |
| KIVETON PARK | 31A |
| Klondyke Yard | 19 |
| Knapton LC | 18D |
| KNARESBOROUGH | 42D |
| KNEBWORTH | 15B |
| Knodishall LC | 9A |
| KNOTTINGLEY | 40A |
| Knottingley junctions | 35B 40A |
| Kvaerner Ltd | 47C |
| Lackenby Steel Works | 50B |
| LAINDON | 3B |
| Laisterdyke | 43 |
| Lakenham | 6D 7A |
| Lakenham viaduct | 6D 7A |
| Lakenheath | 13A |
| Lakenheath No.8 LC | 13A |
| LAKESIDE | 28D |
| Lamesley Crossover | 21B |
| Landing Lane bridge | 19 |
| Lane Head | 46B |
| Langford LC | 27D |
| Langley Jn's | 15B 24B |
| Langley Moor viaduct | 20C |
| LANGWATHBY | 45D |
| LANGWITH WHALEY THORNS | 30A |
| Langworth | 28A |
| Larpool viaduct | 51C |
| Laundry Lane LC | 11C |
| LAZONBY & KIRKOSWALD | 45D |
| Lazonby tunnel | 45D |
| Lea Jn | 2B |
| Lea Valley viaduct | 1B 10B |
| LEAHOLM | 51B |
| Leamside | 20C |
| Lebberston Road LC | 39C |
| LEEDS | 37A |
| Leeds FLT | 37A |
| Leeds ORT | 37A |
| Leeds East, North, West Jn's | 37A |
| Leeds, Neville Hill Depot | 43A |
| Leeman Road Yard (York) | 19B |
| Leeming Bar LC | 45E |
| LEIGH-ON-SEA | 3B |
| Leiston | 9A |
| Lenton Jn's | 25A |
| Leston | 42A |
| LETCHWORTH | 24C |
| Leverton LC | 31B |
| Levington No.6 LC | 9A |
| LEVISHAM | 51D |
| Lexden viaduct | 5E |
| Ley Street Yard sidings | 5A |
| Leyburn | 45E |
| LEYTON MIDLAND ROAD | 3A 10B |
| LEYTONSTONE HIGH ROAD | 3A |
| Lightcliffe tunnel | 43 |
| Lime Kiln LC (Woodbridge) | 9A |
| LIMEHOUSE | 3A |
| Limekiln Road LC | 52 |
| LINCOLN | 27A 27E |

Lincoln Road LC (Enfield) 10B
Lindsey Oil Refineries 32B
LING FARM HALT 7C
LINGWOOD 8
Linsells LC 15C
Linwith Lane viaduct 40B
Lismore Circus Umbrella 1A
Lissingley LC 28A
Litlington LC 24C
Little Barford 15C
Little Bytham 16B
Little London LC 32A
Little Mill 23A
Little Ouse viaduct 13A
Little Salkeld 45D
Little Steeping LC 26A
Littlebury tunnel 11B
Littlefield Lane LC 32A
LITTLEPORT 12A
Littlewood viaduct 30A
Littleworth 26C
LIVERPOOL STREET, LONDON 2A
Lockington LC 39A
LOCKWOOD 36A
Lolham LC 16B
LONDON FIELDS 1B 10B
London Intnl. Freight Term 2B
London Road (Ipswich) 6C
London Road Jn's (Carlisle) 46A
London Road LC (Beccles) 8
London Road LC (Boston) 26A
London Road LC (Spalding) 26C
London Road viaduct (Sheffield) 28C
LONDON, FENCHURCH STREET 3A
LONDON, KING'S CROSS 14A
LONDON, LIVERPOOL STREET 2A
Londonderry Sidings 48B
Long Bridge viaduct 11A
Long Byre LC 46B
Long Green LC 5E
Long Lane 20B
Long Marton 45C
Long Meg viaduct 45D
LONG PRESTON 44B
Long Stanton LC 11C
LONGBECK 51A
LONGBENTON 52
Longhirst LC 22B
Longlands Jn 20B
Longueville Jn 15D 54A
Loversall Carr Jn 17C
Low Bentham viaduct 44C
Low Ellers Curve 17C
Low Fell 21B
Low Gates 20B
Low House Crossing 45D
Low Jn (Northallerton) 20B
Low Moor 43
Low Row 46B
Low Scampston 18D
Low Street LC 4B
LOWDHAM 25A
LOWESTOFT 8A
Lowestoft Harbour 8A
Lowthorpe LC 39B
Lucker LC 23A
Lucks Road LC 26C
LUDBOROUGH 28C
Luffenham LC 24D
Lunds viaduct 45B
Lune viaducts 44C
Lymn Bank LC 26B
Lynemouth 23C
Lyswood viaduct 46E

Magdalen Road 12B
Maidendale 47C
Maltby Cly 35A
Malting Lane LC 26D
MALTON 18C
MANEA 13C
Mangapps Farm Rly Museum 54E
MANNINGTREE 6A
Manningtree Jn's 6A 9B
MANOR PARK 5A
Manor Sidings 4A
Manor Way LC 4A
MANORS 22A 52
Mansfield 30A
Mansfield Jn (Nottingham) 25A
Mansfield Road LC 31B
Manston LC 37A
Manton Cly 31A
Manton Jn's etc 24D
Manton Wood 31A
MARCH 13C
March Jn's 13C
Marcheys House 23C
Margaretting LC 5C
Maria Street LC 9B
MARKET RASEN 28A
Markham 17A
Markham Main Cly 17C
MARKS TEY 5E
MARLEY HILL 47D
MARSDEN 41A
Marsh Farm LC (Imm) 32B
Marsh Jn (Grimsby) 32A
Marsh Lane (Leeds) 37A
Marsh Lane LC (Imm) 32C
Marsh West Jn 32A
Marsh Yards 13C
Marshall Meadows 23B
Marshfield viaduct 45A
Marshgate Jn 17C
Marshgate Sidings 2B 17C
MARSKE 51A
Marston Hall LC 9A
Marston Moor 42E
MARTON 50B
Marton Carr LC 50B
Marton Lane LC 50B
MARYLAND 2B
Maryland East Jn 2B
Masborough Sorting Sdgs S. Jn 29B
Masborough Station Jn's 29B
Matt Pitts Lane LC 26B
Maud Foster LC 26A
Maxey LC 16B 24D
MEADOW WELL 52
MEADOWHALL 29B
MEADOWHALL INTERCHANGE 53
Meadows Exch. Sidings 24D
Medge Hall 33A
MELDRETH 24C
Melkridge Disposal Point 46C
Melling tunnel 44C
Mellis LC 6D
MELTON (SUFFOLK) 9A
Melton Lane 38B
MENSTON 43
Mere Way LC 11C
METHERINGHAM 27A
Methley Jn 37A
Methley North LC 37A
METROCENTRE 21B
MEXBOROUGH 33A
MICKLEFIELD 37B
Mickley LC 21C
Mid-Norfolk Rly 13B
Middle Drove LC 13C
Midden 54D
Middlemere LC 12C
MIDDLESBOROUGH 50A 50B
Middlesborough Goods Yd 50A
Middleton LC 8
MIDDLETON PARK 37A
Middleton Rly. Ltd 37A
Middleton Towers 12B
MIDDLEWOOD 53
Midland Jn (Dewsbury) 41B
Mile End 2B
Mile End LC (Ely) 13A
Milford 35B
Milford Jn 35B 42B
Milford sidings 35B
Milford signalbox 42B
Milford West sidings 37B
Mill Drove LC 12C
Mill Green LC 26C
Mill Lane Jn 43
Mill Race Jn 29B
Millfield 47C
Millmoor 29B
Milne viaduct 41A
Milner Royd Jn 41A
Milton Fen LC 11C
Milton Road LC 11C
Milton Village 46A
Mineral Quay (Immingham) 32B
MIRFIELD 41A
Misterton 27B
MISTLEY 9B
Mistley Quay 9B
Mitre Bridge 1A
Mitre tunnel 1A
Moat Hills LC 17C 18A
Molewood tunnel 24A
Monk Bretton 39D
MONKSEATON 52
Monkwearmouth 48B
Monsanto Jn/LC 48A
MONUMENT 52
Moody Lane LC's 32C
Moorcock tunnel 45B
MOORGATE 14A
MOORTHORPE 33A 35B 36B
Moortown LC 28B
MORLEY 41B
Morley tunnel 41B
MORPETH 22B
Mortimer Street Jn 1A
Mortimer Street viaduct 1A
Moss 18A
Moulton LC 6D
Mount Bures LC 5E
Mountnessing Jn 10A
Mucking LC 4B
MURTON (D.V.L.Rly) 19A
MUSEUM (N.T.S.R.) 52
Museum GF 5E
Muskham viaduct 16C
Muston LC 39C
Mytholmes tunnel 54F
MYTHOLMROYD 41A

NAFFERTON 39B
National Railway Museum 19
Navarino Road Jn 1B 10B
Naworth LC 46A
Nearleigh Works 28D
NEASDEN 1A
Neasden Freight Term 1A
Neasden Jn 1A
Neasden South Jn 1A
Neatherd Road LC 13B
NEEB LC 48A
NEEDHAM MARKET 6C
Nene Carriage Sidings (Pet) 16A
Nene Valley Rly 54A
Nether Lane LC 39B
Nether Poppleton LC 42E
NETHERFIELD 25A
Neville Hill Depot 37A 43A
NEW BARNET 15A
New Barnetby LC 31C
New Biggin 45C
NEW CLEE 32A
New England North Jn 16A
New England Sidings 16A
New Furnace tunnel 43
New Ground sidings 48A
NEW HOLLAND 32B
New Kew Jn 1A
New LC (Imm) 32B
New Moor LC 23C
NEW PUDSEY 43
New Sidings (Hull) 38C
NEW SOUTHGATE 14B
New Swinton Curve 33A
NEWARK CASTLE 27D
Newark Crossing 16C 27D
NEWARK NORTH GATE 16C
NEWCASTLE 22A
Newham LC 23A
NEWMARKET 11C
NEWPORT (Essex) 11B
Newport East Jn 49C 50A
Newport viaduct 11B
Newsham 23C
NEWTON AYCLIFFE 47B
Newton Flotman LC 6D
Newton Hall 21B
NEWTONDALE 51D
Nickstream branch 47B
Niffany viaduct 44A
Noblethorpe LC 18A
Normanby Park 34B
NORMANTON 42A
Normanton LC (Bottesford) 25B
Norsk Hydro (Imm) 32B
North Blyth 23C
North Carr LC 27C
North Crossing LC (Drax) 40B
North Elmham 13B
North Fen LC 13C
North FLT (Felixstowe) 9A
North Green LC 8
North Kelsey LC 28B
North Lincoln Jn 34A
North Norfolk Rly 54B
North Pole Intl. Depot 1A
North Pole Jn 1A
North Quay branch 9A
NORTH ROAD (Darl) 20B 47B
North Seaton viaduct 23C
NORTH SHIELDS 52
NORTH STATION (Southend Pier) 3D
North Tees LC 48A
North Tyneside Steam Rly 52
NORTH WALSHAM 8
North Western Ent. LC (Imm) 32B
NORTH WOOLWICH 2C
North Yorkshire Moors Rly 51D
North/South Access LC 48A
NORTHALLERTON 20B
Northfleet Hope Term. 4B
Northorpe 31C
NORTHUMBERLAND PARK 10B
Norton 40A
Norton-on-Tees 48A
Norton-on-Tees Jn's 47C
Norwell Lane LC 16C
NORWICH 7A
Norwich Road LC 8
Norwich Road LC (Mid. Norfolk) 13B
Norwood Junction 21B
Norwood LC (Shirebrook) 30A
Norwood Road LC 13C
NOTTINGHAM 25A
Nottingham Branch Jn (Gran) 16C
Nunnery Depot 53
Nunnery Jn 29B
Nunnery Jn (C.V.R.) 4D
Nunnery Main Line Jn 29B
NUNTHORPE 50B

Oakenshaw Jn's 39D
Oakington LC 11C
OAKLEIGH PARK 14B
OAKWORTH 54F
OCKENDEN 3B
Offord & Buckden 15C
OLD HEATH 54E
Old Kew Jn 1A
Old Leake LC 26A
Old Oak Common Sidings 1A
Old Oak Jn 1A
Old Oak Sidings (Willesden) 1A
OLD STREET 14A
Old Trent Dyke viaduct 27D
Ollerton Cly signalbox 30B
One Mile Bridge 7A
Ore Terminal (Imm) 32B
Ormside viaduct 45C
Orston Lane LC 25B
ORTON MERE 54A
Orton Mere 15D
Osterfen LC 16C
OULTON BROAD NORTH 8
Oulton Broad North Jn 8 8A
OULTON BROAD SOUTH 8
Oulton Swing Bridge 8
Ouseburn viaduct 22A
Ouston crossovers 21A

OUTWOOD 36C
Oxbridge sidings 47C
Oxcroft Disposal Point 30A
Oxcroft Jn 30A
OXENHOPE 54F
Oxmardyke 38A
Oxmarsh 32B
Oxspring tunnel 36A
Oxspring viaduct 36A
Oxwellgate 22A

Paddock viaduct 36A
Palace Gates 14B
Palgrave LC 6D
PALMERS GREEN 24A
PALMERSVILLE 52
PANNAL 42D
Park Drain LC 27C
PARK HALT 37A
Park Lane LC 10B
Park Lane Sdgs (Darl) 20B
Park Road LC (Spalding) 26C
Parkeston Container Term. 9B
Parkeston Goods Jn 9B
Parkeston LC's 9B
Parkeston Yard 9B
Parkgate & Rawmarsh 33A
Parkgate Jn 20B 47b
Parkside Farm LC 23C
Parkside Jn 37A
Pasture Road LC (Barton-on-H) 32B
Pasture Street LC (Grim) 32A
Peascliffe tunnel and crossovers 16C
25B
Peckfield crossover 37B
PEGSWOOD 22B
PELAW 49A 52
Pelaw Jn 49A
Pelham Street 27A 27E
PENISTONE 36A
Penshaw 20C
PERCY MAIN 52
PERCY MAIN (N.T.S.R) 52
PETERBOROUGH 16A
PETERBOROUGH (Nene Valley) 54A
Peterborough East 16A
Peterborough North Depot 16A
Petteril Bridge Jn 46A
Philip Lane LC 18B 37B
Phillips LC's 48A
PICKERING 51D
Picton LC 47C
Pig's Bay 3C
Pile sdg (Heaton) 22A
Pilleys Lane LC 26A
Pilmoor 20A
Pipers Wood 17B
Pitmore viaduct 5E
PITSEA 3B 3C 4B
Pitsea Hall LC 3B 4B
PLAISTOW 3A
Plants LC 16B
Plawsworth viaduct 21A
Pleasants LC 12A
Plenmeller 46C
Plessey crossovers etc 22B
Plessey Road LC 23C
Pockerley Waggonway 54G
PONDERS END 10B
Ponsbourne tunnel 24A
PONTEFRACT BAGHILL 35B
Pontefract M. Goods Jn 35B
PONTEFRACT MONKHILL 39D 40A
PONTEFRACT TANSHELF 39D
Pontefract West Jn 40A
Poplar Farm LC 13B
POPPLETON 42E
Pork Lane LC 6A
Port Clarence 48A
Port of Parkeston Quay 9B
Portrack Sidings 48A
Post Office Lane LC 40A
Potland 23C
Potteric Carr Jn 17C
POTTERS BAR 15A
Potters Grange Jn 40B
Powell Duffryn sdgs (Purfleet) 4A
Primrose Hill 1A
Prince of Wales 39D
Prince of Wales Cly 39D
Prince of Wales tunnel 47B
Prison siding (Wake.) 36C
PRITTLEWELL 10A
Proctor & G. Sdg (Grays) 4B
PRUDHOE 21C
PUDDING MILL LANE 2B
Punch Bowl viaduct 44C
PURFLEET 4A
Purfleet Long Siding 4A
Pyewipe Road LC (Grim) 32C

Quadring LC 26D
Quarrington LC 25C
Quarry Jn 36A
Queen Adelaide LC's 12A 13A
Queen Elizabeth Dock (Hull) 38C
Queen Elizabeth II Bridge 52
Queen's Road tunnel 10B
QUEENS PARK 1A
Queens Road (Shef) 28E

Raby sdg (Imm) 32B
Rackheath Road LC 8
RADCLIFFE 25A
Railway Dock (Goole) 40B
Rainbow Bridge viaduct 33A
RIANHAM 4A
Raisby Hill 20C
Ramsey Road LC 13C
Ranelagh Road LC 6B 6C
Ranskill Loops 17B
RAUCEBY 25C
RAVENSTHORPE 41B
RAWCLIFFE 40B
RAYLEIGH 10A
Reading Lane Jn 1B 10B
Rectory Jn 25A
RECTORY ROAD 10B
Rectory Road LC (Diss) 6D
Red Barns tunnel 22A
Red Cap Lane LC 26A
Red Lane LC 39D
REDCAR CENTRAL 51A
REDCAR EAST 51A
Redcar Mineral Terminal 50B
Redcar Ore Terminal 50B
Redcar Ore Terminal Jn 50B
Redcar Works 50B
Redmire 45E
Redmire Reversing Line 20B 45E
Redmoor LC 13C
REEDHAM (Norfolk) 8
Reedham Swing Bridge 8
Reedhams:Shell 4B
Reepham LC 28A
REGENT CENTRE 52
Regent Street LC 6C
Relly Mill viaduct 20C
Rendlesham viaduct 24A
Renishaw Park 28E
RETFORD 17A 31B
Reyrolles 52
RIBBLEHEAD 45A
RICHMOND 1A
Richmond Hill tunnel 37A
RIDING MILL 46E
Ridley Hall viaduct 46E
Rigton 42D
Rillington LC 18D
Ripple Lane yards 4A
Risehill tunnel 45B
River Aln viaduct 23A
River Bedford viaducts 13C
River Blythe viaduct 8
River Calder viaduct 36A
River Cann viaduct 5C
River Chelmer viaduct 5C
River Coquet viaduct 23A
River Derwent viaduct 21B
River Devon viaduct 27D
River Fynn viaduct 9A
River Idle viaduct (RETFORD) 17A 31B
River Nene viaduct 16A
River Ouse viaduct 12A
River Rother viaduct 29
River Ryton viaduct 31A
River Skerne viaduct 20C
River Stour viaduct (Mann.) 6A
River Swale viaduct 45E
River Ter viaduct 5C
River Trent vdt. (Gains) 27B 31B
River Waveney viaduct 6D
River Wear viaduct 47A
River Wear viaduct (Sund) 48B
River Went viaduct 35B
River Wharfe viaduct 35C
River Wiske viaduct (Northallerton) 45E
River Wiske viaduct (Rounton) 47C
River Wissey viaduct 12A
River Worth viaduct 43
Robbery Lane viaduct 15B
Robin Hood tunnel 36A
ROCHFORD 10A
ROCKINGHAM 38C
ROLLESTON 27D
Romanby Road LC 20B
ROMFORD 5B
Rossington Cly. 17C
Rossington LC 17B 17C
Rotherham CentraL 29
Rotherham Masborough 29
Rotherham Thrybergh 33A
Roughton Road 8
Roughton Road Jn 8
Roundwood Chord 33A
Rounton Gates LC 47C
Routes No.8 LC 9A
Rowland Hall LC 38A
ROWLEY 54G
Rowston 26D
Roxby 34B
Roxton Siding 32A
Royal Border Bridge 23B
Royal Mail- Doncaster 17C
Royal Mail- Tyneside 21B
Royal Mint St.Jn 3A
Royal Oak LC 39C
ROYAL VICTORIA 2C
ROYDON 11A
ROYSTON 24C
Royston Branch viaduct 36A
Royston Drift Mine 39D
Royston Jn 39D
Rufford Cly etc 30A
Runton East Jn 8
Rushey Sidings LC 31B
RUSKINGTON 26D
Ruston's Tip LC 27A 27E
RUSWARP 51C
RYE HOUSE 11A
Ryhope Grange 48B
Rylstone 44A
Ryther viaducts 18B

SALHOUSE 8
SALTAIRE 43
SALTBURN (by-the-Sea) 51A
Saltend 38C
Salterhebble tunnels 41A
SALTMARSHE 40C
Sand Bank Jn 17C
SANDALL & AGBRIGG 36C
Sandhill Lane 37B
Sandhill LC 12A
SANDY 15C
Santon LC (Norfolk) 13A
SAWBRIDGEWORTH 11A
Sawston LC 11C
SAXILBY 27B
SAXMUNDHAM 9A
Saxmundham Jn 8 9A
Saxmundham Road LC 9A
Scalm Lane LC 18B 37B
SCARBOROUGH 18D
Scarborough bridge (York) 19
Scarrington Lane LC 25B
Scopwick 27A
Scorborough LC 39A
Scremerston 23B
Scruton LC 45E
Sculcoates 38C
SCUNTHORPE 34A
Seabrook Sidings 4B
SEABURN 48B
SEAHAM 48B
Seal Sands 48A
SEAMER 18D
Seamer West 18D 39C
SEATON CAREW 48A
Seaton Snook Jn 48A
Seaton-on-Tees 48A
Second Drove LC 13C
Seghill North LC 23C
SELBY 38A
Selby Canal Jn 38A
Selby Canal viaduct 18A
Selby Mine Sidings 37B
Selby Road LC 40A
Selby South Jn 38A
Selby Swing Bridge 38A
Selby West 37B 38A
SETTLE 45A
Settle Jn 44B 45A
SEVEN KINGS 5A
SEVEN SISTERS 1B 10B
Severus Jn 19
Sewerby LC 39B
Sewerston Lane LC 25B
Seymour Jn 30A
Seymour sidings 30A
SHADWELL 3A
Shaftholme Jn 18A 33B 40A
Sharlston Cly. 39D
Shay Lane viaduct 36C
Sheepwash viaduct 30A
SHEFFIELD 28E
SHELFORD 11C
Shell (UK) Thameshaven 4B
Shell Jn 50B
SHELLEY (Copley Lane) 40D
Shelley Woodhouse tunnel 40D
SHENFIELD 5B
Shepcote Lane Jn's 29
SHEPLEY 36A
SHEPRETH 24C
Shepreth Branch Jn 11C
Sherburn Jn 35C
SHERBURN-IN-ELMET 35C
Sherif Brow viaduct 45A
SHERINGHAM 8
SHERINGHAM (N.N.R) 54B
Sherriff LC 15C
Shield Well GF 46D
Shields Road tunnel 52
SHILDON 47B
SHIPLEY 43
SHIPPEA HILL 13A
SHIREBROOK 30A
Shirebrook Jn's 30A
SHIREMOOR 52
SHIREOAKS 31A
SHOEBURYNESS 3C
SHOREDITCH 2A
Shotlock Hill tunnel 45B
Sibsey 26A
SILKSTONE COMMON 36A
Silkstone Jn 36A
SILVER STREET 10B
SILVERTOWN & LONDON CITY
AIRPORT 2C
Silvertown tunnel 2C
Silverwood Cly. 33A
Simon House LC 26A
Simon Storage (Imm) 32B
Simon Storage West LC 32B
Sincil Bank LC 27A 27E
Six Mile Bottom LC 11C
Sizewell LC 9A
Sizewell Power Stn 9A
SKEGNESS 26B
Skellow Jn 36B
SKELMANTHORPE 40D
Skelton Bridge Jn 19 20A
Skelton bridge 19 20A

Skelton Jn 19 42E
Skibeden siding 44D
Skiers Spring 35D
Skinningrove 51A
SKIPTON 44A
Slaggyford 46D
SLAITHWAITE 41A
Slater Quarry 23B
SLEAFORD 25C 26D
SLEIGHTS 51C
Sloley Lane LC 8
Smardale viaduct 45C
Smeafield LC 23B
Smithfield Road LC 28B
Snailwell Jn 12C 12D
Snailwell Sidings 12C
SNAITH 40B
Snaith & Pont. H. LC 40A
Snaith Road LC 40B
Sneinton Jn 25A
Snelland LC 28A
Soham Jn 12C
SOMERLEYTON 8
Sopers Farm viaduct 24A
SOUTH ACTON 1A
SOUTH BANK 50B
South Crossing LC (Drax) 40B
South Drove LC 26C
SOUTH ELMSALL 36B
South FLT (Felixstowe) 9A
SOUTH GOSFORTH 52
SOUTH HAMPSTEAD 1A
South Kirkby Jn 35B 36A
South Lynn 12B
SOUTH MILFORD 37B
South Scarle LC 27C
SOUTH SHIELDS 52
SOUTH STATION (S.P.R.) 3D
SOUTH TOTTENHAM 1B 10B
South Tottenham Jn's 10B
South Tyne viaduct 46E
South Tynedale Rly 46D
South West Sidings (Willesden) 1A
South Yorks. Supertram 53
South Yorkshire Jn 17C
South Yorkshire Rly 29A
SOUTHBURY 10B
SOUTHEND CENTRAL 3C
SOUTHEND EAST 3C
Southend Pier Railway 3D
SOUTHEND VICTORIA 10A
SOUTHMINSTER 10A
SOWERBY BRIDGE 41A
SPALDING 26C
Speeton LC 39C
Spellbrook 11A
Spinks Lane LC 13B
Spital sidings 16A
Spittal LC 23B
Splash Dyke viaduct 54A
SPOONER ROW 13B
Spring Lodge LC 40A
Springbank Jn's 38C
Springhead South Bch. 38C
Springs Jn 43
Springs tunnel 43
SPRINGWELL 49B
Springwell Lane LC 20B
Springwood Jn 36A 41A
Spronces LC 13B
St. Catherines Jn 17C 35A
St. Georges Road LC (Hull) 38C
St. Germans LC 12B
ST. JAMES 52
St. James' Jn's 17C
St. James Bridge Jn (Necastle) 22A
St. James Deeping 26C
ST. JAMES STREET 10B
ST. MARGARETS 11A
ST. NEOTS 15C
Staggs Sidings 38A
Stainforth Jn 33B
Stainforth Road 33B
Stainforth tunnel 45A
Stainton LC 28A
STALLINGBOROUGH 32A
STAMFORD 24D
STAMFORD HILL 10B
Stamford LC 23A
Standedge tunnels 41A
STANFORD-LE-HOPE 4B
Stanhope 47A
Stanhope Dock (Goole) 40B
Stanningley tunnel/viaduct 43
Stannington LC 22B
STANSTED AIRPORT 4E 11B
Stansted Airport People-mover 4E
Stansted Airport tunnel 11B
Stansted Jn's 11B
STANSTED MOUNTFICHET 11B
STARBECK 42D
Staveley North Curve 30A
Staythorpe Crossing 27D
Steamtown 44C
STEETON & SILSDEN 44A
STEVENAGE 15B
Stifford viaduct 3B
Stillington 20C
Stilton Fen 15D
Stocksbridge 29B
STOCKSFIELD 21C
STOCKSMOOR 36A
STOCKTON 47C
Stockton Cut Jn 47C
Stoddart Street sdgs. 52
Stoke Bridge LC 6B
Stoke Lane LC 25A
STOKE NEWINGTON 10B
Stoke summit/tunnel 16B
Stonea 13C
Stoneacre loop 44D
Stoneyhurst Road 52
Stora siding 4A
Stourton 37A
Stow Bardolph LC 12B
Stow Park 27B
Stowgate LC 26C
STOWMARKET 6C
Stranton 48A
STRATFORD 2B
STRATFORD Low Level 2B
Stratford Central Jn 2B
Stratford Country End Jn 2B
Stratford Depots 2B
Stratford FLT 2B
Stratford LL tunnel 2B
Stratford Market Depot (LUL) 2B
Stratford Old Yard 2B
STREETHOUSE 39D
Strensall 19
Strumpshaw LC 8
Stubbs Waldens LC's 40A
Sudbrook Lane LC 25B
SUDBURY 5E
Sudforth Lane 40A
Sugar Factory GF 38A
Summer Lane 36A
Sun Wharf LC 9A
SUNDERLAND 48B
Sunderland South Dk. 48B
Sunderland tnls. 48B
SUNNISIDE 47D
Sussex Street LC 50A 50B
Suton LC 13B
Swainsthorpe LC 6D
Swaithe viaduct 35D
Swalwall Jn 21B
Swanton Road LC 13B
Swavesey LC 11C
SWINDERBY 27E
Swinderby Road 27E
Swinedyke LC 31C
SWINESHEAD 25C
Swing Bridge Jn 7A
SWINTON (S. Yorks) 33A
Sykes LC 27B

Tallington 16B
Tanfield Rly 47D
Tankersley tunnel 29 35D
Tapton Jn 28E
Tattershall Road LC 26A
Tees Bridge 49C
Tees Dock 50B
Tees Works siding 50B
Tees Yard 49C
TEES-SIDE AIRPORT 47C
Temple Hirst Jn 18A
Temple Mills East Jn 2B 10B
Temple Mills West 10B
Temple Mills Yard 10B
Templeborough Works 29
Tempsford LC 15C
Ten Mile Bottom LC 13A
Tennyson Avenue LC 12B
Terminus GF 4B
Terrace Sidings (Lincoln) 27A
Teversham LC 11C
Thackley tunnels 43
Thames Board Mills LC 4A
Thames Haven 4B
Thames Haven Jn 4B
Tharston viaduct 6D
THEOBALDS GROVE 10B
THETFORD 13A
Third Drove LC 13C
THIRSK 20A
Thompsons LC 17B
Thoresby Cly 30A
THORNABY 49C
Thorne Jn 33B
Thorne LC's 33B
Thorne Moor LC 33B
THORNE NORTH 33B
THORNE SOUTH 33B
Thornhill Jn 41B
Thornhill LNW Jn 41B
THORNTON ABBEY 32B
Thornton Fields Carr. sdgs 2B
THORPE BAY 3C
THORPE CULVERT 26B
Thorpe Gates 37B
Thorpe Jn 6A
Thorpe Lane LC 9A
Thorpe LC 40A
Thorpe Marsh 33B
Thorpe Road LC 33B
Thorpe Yard 7A
THORPE-LE-SOKEN 6A
Thorpe-on-the-Hill LC 27E
Thorrington LC 6A
Three Horse Shoes 13C
Thrislington Quarry 20C
Thrumpton and Jn's 31B
Thrybergh Jn 33A
THURGATON 25A
THURNSCOE 33A
THURSTON 12D
Thurstonland tunnel 36A
THUXTON 13B
Thwaite Gates LC 39A
Ti-Oxide Europe 32C
Tickhill viaduct 35A
Tilbury Dock 4B
Tilbury IRFT 4b
Tilbury RCT 4B
TILBURY TOWN 4B
Tile Shed LC 49A
Tiled House Farm LC 12C
Tinsley Jn's 29
Tinsley Yard 29
Tivetshall LC 6D
Tollerton 20A
Tolney Lane viaduct 27D
Tong Park viaduct 43
Torworth LC 17B
Totley tunnel 28E
Tottenham GF 10B
TOTTENHAM HALE 1B 10B
Tottenham North Curve tnls 1A
Tottenham South Jn 1B 10B
Tottenham West Jn 10B
TOWER GATEWAY 3A
Transit Quays (Imm) 32B
Trees LC 11B
Treeton Jn's 29
Trent East Jn (Gains) 27B 31B
Trent Fields viaduct 25A
Trent Jn (Scun) 34A
Trent Sidings (Scun) 34A
Trent West Jn (Gains) 27B 31B
TRIMLEY 9A
Trinity Lane LC 10B 11A
TROWSE 7A
Trowse Lower Jn 7A
Trowse Swing Bridge 7A
TUNSTALL ROAD (Hunslet Moor) 37A
Tunstead Mkt. St. LC 8
TURKEY STREET 10B
Turners Lane Jn 42A
Tursdale Jn 20C
Tuxford 30B
Tuxford crossovers 17A
Tweedmouth 23B
Tye Green Jn 11B
Tyne & Wear Metro 52
Tyne Coal Terminal 49A
TYNE DOCK 49A 52
Tyne Dock Bottom 49A
Tyne Dock Loop 49A
Tyne Yard 21B
TYNEMOUTH 52
Tyneside Signalling Centre 22A

Uffington 24D
Ufford LC 9A
ULCEBY 32B
Ulceby North Jn 32B
Ulceby South Jn 32A 32B
Ulgham Grange LC 22B
Ulgham Lane LC 22B
ULLESKELF 35C
Unstone viaduct 28E
Unthank LC 47A
UPMINSTER 3B 5B
UPMINSTER BRIDGE 3B
Upminster East Jn 3B
UPNEY 3A 3B
Upney Jn 3A
Upper Denton LC 46B
UPPER HOLLOWAY 1A 1B
Upperby Bridge Jn 46A
Upperby Jn 46A
UPTON PARK 3A
Urlay Nook 47C
Usworth 20C

Van Ommeran Tank Farm 4A
Van Siding GF 48B
Vange Wharf LC 3B 4B
Victoria Park 1B
Victoria Road Covered Way 42D
Victoria Road LC 8
Victoria Sdgs (Norwich) 7A
Victoria viaduct 20C
Uffington 24D
Ufford LC 9A
ULCEBY 32B
Ulceby North Jn 32B
Ulceby South Jn 32A 32B
Ulgham Grange LC 22B
Ulgham Lane LC 22B
ULLESKELF 35C
Unstone viaduct 28E
Unthank LC 47A
UPMINSTER 3B 5B
UPMINSTER BRIDGE 3B
Upminster East Jn 3B
UPNEY 3A 3B
Upney Jn 3A
Upper Denton LC 46B
UPPER HOLLOWAY 1A 1B
Upperby Bridge Jn 46A
Upperby Jn 46A
UPTON PARK 3A
Urlay Nook 47C
Usworth 20C

Van Ommeran Tank Farm 4A
Van Siding GF 48B
Vange Wharf LC 3B 4B
Victoria Park 1B
Victoria Road Covered Way 42D
Victoria Road LC 8

Victoria Sdgs (Norwich) 7A
Victoria viaduct 20C

WADSLEY BRIDGE 29
WAINFLEET 26B
Wakefield Europort 42A
Wakefield K. West Jn 36C
WAKEFIELD KIRKGATE 42A
Wakefield Road tunnel 43
Waldersea LC 13C
Walesby LC 28A
WALKERGATE 22A 52
WALLSEND 52
Walpole LC 8
WALSINGHAM 54D
WALTHAM CROSS 10B
WALTHAMSTOW CENTRAL 10B
WALTHAMSTOW QUEENS ROAD 1B 3A 10B
Walton Street 38C
WALTON-ON-THE-NAZE 6A
WANSBECK ROAD 52
WANSFORD 54A
Wansford Road LC 39B
WANSTEAD PARK 3A
Warcop 45C
Warden LC 46E
Wardley 49A
WARE 11A
Warehouse line 19
Warham 54D
Warksworth LC 23A
Warren Hill tunnel 12D
Warsop 30A
Warsop Jn 30A
Warsop Yard 30A
Washington 20C
Wassicks LC 6C
Waste Bank tunnel 45D
Water Drove LC 26C
WATERBEACH 11C
Waterbeach Spur 11C
Wath Road Jn 33A
WATLINGTON 12B
Watlington Road LC 12B
Watton LC 39A
WATTON-AT-STONE 24B
Wear Valley Jn 47A
Weardale Rly 47A
Weasel Hall tunnel 41A
Weasenham Lane LC 13C
Weaverthorpe 18D
WEELEY 6A
WEETON 42D
Welbeck Cly 30A
Welbeck Cly Jn 30A
Welbeck Discharge Bunker 42A
Welbury LC 20B
WELHAM GREEN 15A
Wellhouse tunnel 36A
Wellowgate LC 32A
Wells & Walsingham Rly 54D
WELLS-ON-SEA 54D
Welney Road LC 13C
Welton Depot 28A
Welton LC 38B
WELWYN GARDEN CITY 15A
WELWYN NORTH 15B
WENNINGTON 44C
Wensley LC 45E
Wensum Depot 7A
Wensum Jn 7A
Werrington Jn 16A 26C
Wescoehill tunnel 42D
West Bank Hall LC 40B
West Burton Power Stn 31B
West Cornforth LC 20C
West Cowick LC 40B
West Gate viaduct 16C
WEST HAM 2C 3A
WEST HAMPSTEAD 1A
WEST HAMPSTEAD THAMESLINK 1A
West Heslerton LC 18D
West Holmes 27A 27E
WEST HORNDEN 3B
West House LC 9A
WEST JESMOND 52
West London Jn (Willes) 1A
West Marsh sidings 32C
WEST MONKSEATON 52
West Parade Jn 38C
West Parade North Jn 38C
West River LC 12A
WEST RUNTON 8
West Sleekburn Jn 23C
West Street Jn 26A
West Thurrock Jn 4B
Westbrecks LC 31B
Westbrook Lane LC 27E
WESTCLIFF 3C
WESTERFIELD 9A
Western Entrance LC (Imm) 32B
Western Storage (Imm) 32B
Westgate South Jn 36B 42A
Westhall LC 8
Westley Road LC 11C
Weston LC 8
Westwood sidings 16A
WETHERAL 46A
WEYBOURNE 54B
Wharf Road LC 11A
Wheeler Street Jn 2A
Wherstead Road 6A
Whiley Hill LC 47B
WHITBY 51C
Whitchester tunnel 46C
WHITE HART LANE 10B
WHITE NOTLEY 5D
Whitehall Jn's 37A
Whitehall Rd. Depot 37A
Whitehouse 50B
Whitemoor Drove LC 13C
Whitemoor Jn 13C
WHITLEY BAY 52
WHITLEY BRIDGE 40A
Whitley viaduct 46D
Whitlingham Jn 7A 8
Whitting Moor Road vdt. 28E
WHITTLESEA 13C
WHITTLESFORD 11B
Whittlesford crossover 11C
WHITWELL 30A
Whitwell LC 20C
Whitwood Jn 42A
Whixley 42E
Wick Lane 2B
Wick Lane LC 10A
Wickenby 28A
WICKFORD 10A
Wickford Jn 10A
WICKHAM MARKET 9A
WIDDRINGTON 22B
Wighton 54D
WILLESDEN JUNCTION HL/LL 1A
Willesden Jn's/Sdgs 1A
Willesden Subn.signalbox 1A
Willesden signalbox 1A
Willoughby Road LC 26A
Willow Marsh LC 8
Willows Lane LC 26A
Wilsford LC 25C
Wilstrop 42E
Wilton ICI 50B
WINCHMORE HILL 24A
Wincobank Jn 29
Wincobank viaduct 29
Windmill Lane LC 11A
Winning 23C
Winsover Road LC 26C
Wintersett 36B
Winthorpe LC 27D
Wisbech 13C
Wisterley Hall LC 47A
WITHAM 5C 5D
Withams 42A
Witton Park 47B
Witton-le-Wear 47A
WIVENHOE 6A
Woad Lane LC 32C
Wolsingham 47A
WOMBWELL 35D
Womersley LC 40A
Wood Ditton LC 11C
Wood Green GF's, Jn's,tnls 14B
WOOD STREET 10B
Wood Yard (Doncaster) 17C
Wood Yard (Worksop) 31A
WOODBRIDGE 9A
Woodburn Jn 29
Woodcroft LC 16A
Wooden Gate LC 23A
Woodend Jn 31A
WOODGRANGE PARK 3A 5A
Woodgrange Park Jn 3A 5A
Woodhall Lane LC 38A
WOODHAM FERRERS 10A
WOODHOUSE 29
WOODLESFORD 37A
WOODSIDE 7B
Woodthorn 23C
Woolley Coal Siding 36A
Woolley tunnels 36A
Woolmer Green 15B
WORKSOP 31A
WORSTEAD 8
Worthing LC 13B
Wortley Jn 37A
Wortley South Jn 37A
Wortley West 37A
WRABNESS 9A
Wrawby Jn 28B 31C 34C
Wrekenton 49B
Wrenthorpe sidings 36C
WRESSLE 38A
Wroot Road LC 27C
Wroxham viaduct 8
Wyberton LC 26A
Wyke tunnel 43
WYLAM 21C
WYMONDHAM 13B

Yafforth LC 45E
YARM 47C
Yarm tunnel/viaduct 47C
Yarmouth Vauxhall 8
Yarwell Mill 54A
YAXHAM 13B
Yaxham Road LC 13B
Yaxley 15D
YORK 19

NORTH LONDON LINE ● TOTTENHAM & HAMPSTEAD LINE

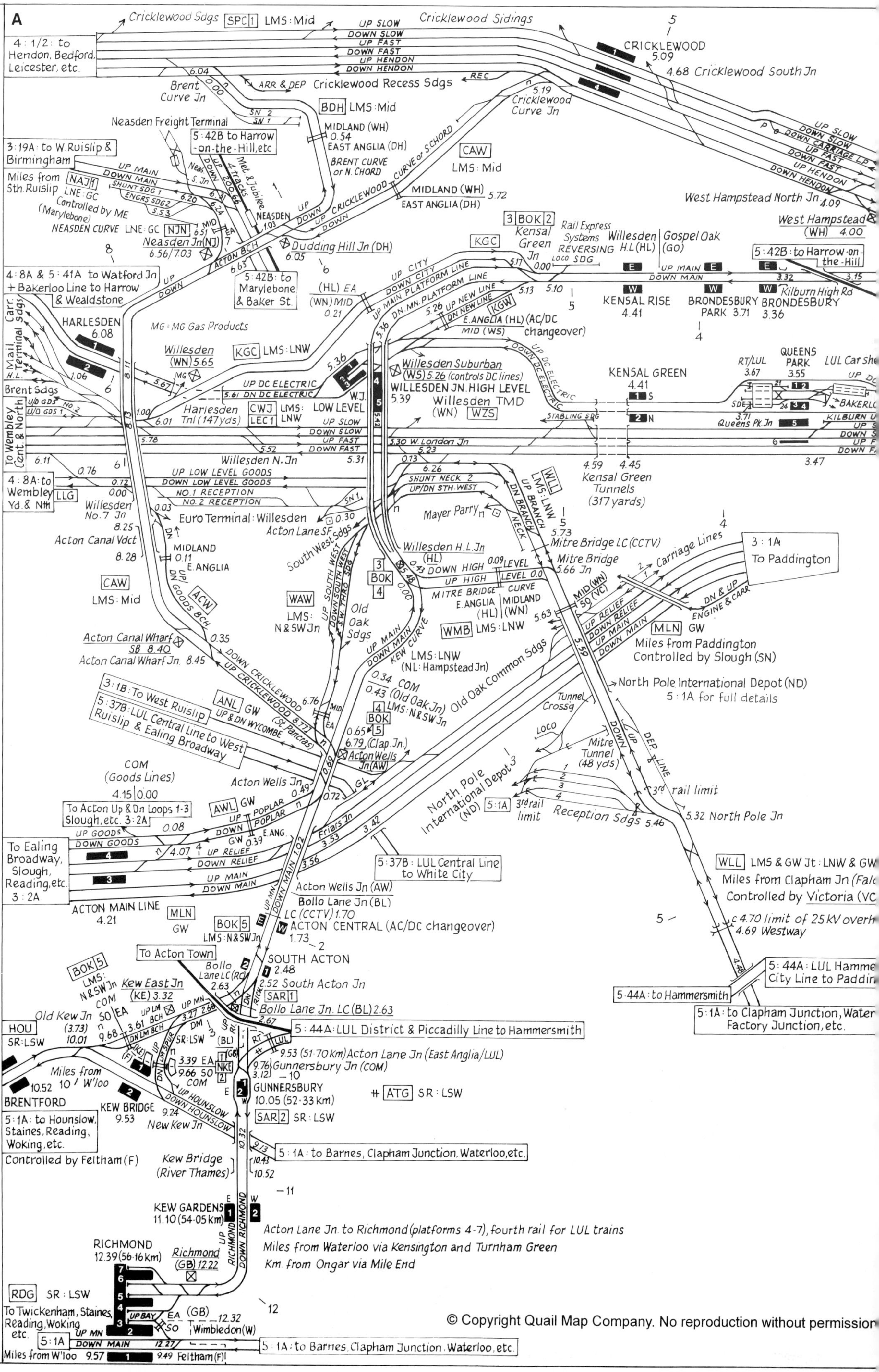

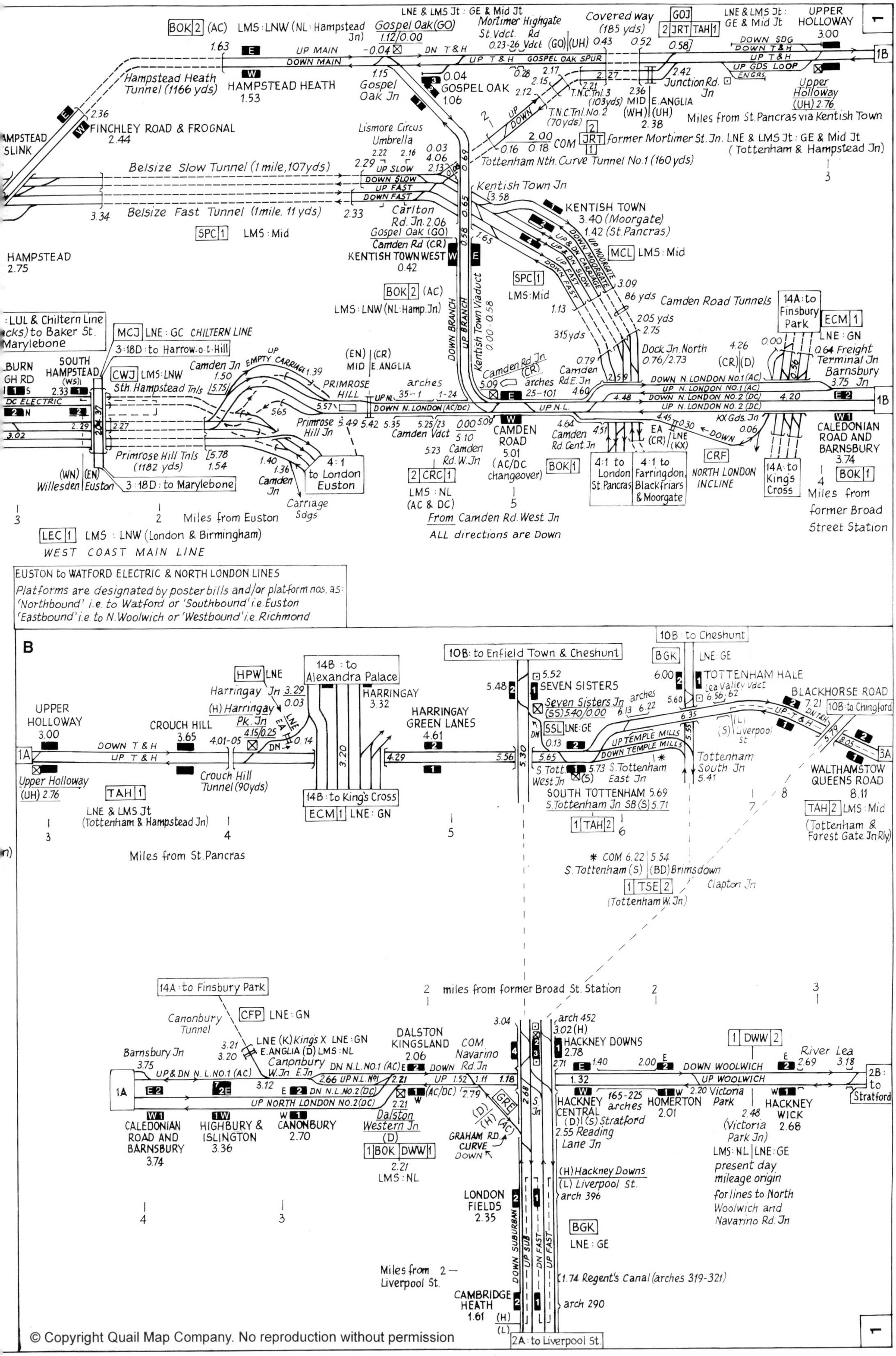
1
BOK 2 (AC) LMS: LNW (NL: Hampstead Jn)
LNE & LMS Jt: GE & Mid Jt
Gospel Oak (GO) 1.12/0.00
Mortimer Highgate St. Vdct. Rd 0.23-26 Vdct (GO)|(UH)
Covered way (185 yds) 0.43 0.52
GOJ 2 JRT TAH 1
LNE & LMS Jt: GE & Mid Jt
UPPER HOLLOWAY 3.00
1B
UP MAIN
DOWN MAIN
DN T&H
UP T&H
GOSPEL OAK SPUR
DOWN SDG
DOWN T&H
UP T&H
UP GDS LOOP
ENGRS
Hampstead Heath Tunnel (1166 yds)
HAMPSTEAD HEATH 1.53
Gospel Oak Jn
GOSPEL OAK 1.06
T.N.C. Tnl. 3 (103yds)
T.N.C. Tnl. No. 2 (70yds)
MID (WH) E. ANGLIA (UH) 2.38
Junction Rd. Jn
Upper Holloway (UH) 2.76
Miles from St. Pancras via Kentish Town
FINCHLEY ROAD & FROGNAL 2.44
HAMPSTEAD SLINK
Lismore Circus Umbrella
2.00 COM 2 JRT 1 former Mortimer St. Jn. LNE & LMS Jt: GE & Mid Jt (Tottenham & Hampstead Jn)
Tottenham Nth. Curve Tunnel No. 1 (160 yds)
Belsize Slow Tunnel (1 mile, 107 yds)
Belsize Fast Tunnel (1 mile, 11 yds)
UP SLOW
DOWN SLOW
UP FAST
DOWN FAST
Carlton Rd. Jn. 2.06
Kentish Town Jn 3.58
KENTISH TOWN 3.40 (Moorgate) 1.42 (St. Pancras)
SPC 1 LMS: Mid
Gospel Oak (GO) Camden Rd (CR)
KENTISH TOWN WEST 0.42
HAMPSTEAD 2.75
MCL LMS: Mid
UP MOORGATE
DOWN MOORGATE
UP & DN CARRIAGE
UP & DN SLOW
UP FAST
DOWN FAST
BOK 2 (AC) LMS: LNW (NL: Hamp. Jn)
SPC 1 LMS: Mid
86 yds Camden Road Tunnels
205 yds
315 yds
DOWN BRANCH
UP BRANCH
Kentish Town Viaduct 0.00-0.58
14A: to Finsbury Park
ECM 1 LNE: GN
: LUL & Chiltern Line tracks) to Baker St. Marylebone
MCJ LNE: GC CHILTERN LINE 3:18D: to Harrow-o-t-Hill
Dock Jn. North 0.76/2.73
0.64 Freight Terminal Jn
Barnsbury 3.75 Jn
SOUTH HAMPSTEAD
KILBURN HIGH RD
CWJ LMS: LNW Sth. Hampstead Tnls
Camden Jn 1.50
EMPTY CARRIAGE
(EN) MID (CR) E. ANGLIA
PRIMROSE HILL
arches 35-1 1-24
Camden Rd. Jn (CR)
arches 25-101
Camden Rd. E. Jn
DOWN N. LONDON NO. 1 (AC)
UP N. LONDON NO. 1 (AC)
DOWN N. LONDON NO. 2 (DC)
UP N. LONDON NO. 2 (DC)
DOWN N. LONDON (AC/DC)
UP N.L.
DC ELECTRIC
Primrose Hill Jn
Camden Vdct
CAMDEN ROAD 5.01 (AC/DC changeover)
Camden Rd. Cent. Jn
KX Gds. Jn
CALEDONIAN ROAD AND BARNSBURY 3.74
Primrose Hill Tnls (1182 yds)
4:1 to London Euston
Camden Jn
Camden Rd. W. Jn
2 CRC 1 LMS: NL (AC & DC)
BOK 1
4:1 to London St. Pancras
4:1 to Farringdon, Blackfriars & Moorgate
EA (CR) LNE (KX)
CRF NORTH LONDON INCLINE
14A: to Kings Cross
BOK 1
Miles from former Broad Street Station
(WN) Willesden (EN) Euston
3:18D: to Marylebone
Carriage Sdgs
Miles from Euston
From Camden Rd. West Jn
ALL directions are Down
LEC 1 LMS: LNW (London & Birmingham)
WEST COAST MAIN LINE
EUSTON to WATFORD ELECTRIC & NORTH LONDON LINES
Platforms are designated by poster bills and/or platform nos. as: 'Northbound' i.e. to Watford or 'Southbound' i.e. Euston 'Eastbound' i.e. to N. Woolwich or 'Westbound' i.e. Richmond
B
UPPER HOLLOWAY 3.00
1A
DOWN T&H
UP T&H
Upper Holloway (UH) 2.76
CROUCH HILL 3.65
Crouch Hill Tunnel (90yds)
TAH 1 LNE & LMS Jt (Tottenham & Hampstead Jn)
Miles from St. Pancras
HPW LNE
Harringay Jn 3.29 0.03
(H) Harringay Pk. Jn 4.15/0.25
14B: to Alexandra Palace
HARRINGAY 3.32
HARRINGAY GREEN LANES 4.61
14B: to King's Cross
ECM 1 LNE: GN
10B: to Enfield Town & Cheshunt
SEVEN SISTERS 5.52
Seven Sisters Jn (SS) 5.40/0.00
SSL LNE: GE
10B: to Cheshunt
BGK LNE: GE
TOTTENHAM HALE
Lea Valley Vdct 6.56/.62
BLACKHORSE ROAD 7.21
10B: to Chingford
UP TEMPLE MILLS
DOWN TEMPLE MILLS
(L) Liverpool St
S. Tott. West Jn
S. Tottenham East Jn
Tottenham South Jn 5.41
SOUTH TOTTENHAM 5.69
S. Tottenham Jn SB (S) 5.71
1 TAH 2
WALTHAMSTOW QUEENS ROAD 8.11
TAH 2 LMS: Mid (Tottenham & Forest Gate Jn Rly)
3A
* COM 6.22 5.54 S. Tottenham (S) (BD) Brimsdown
1 TSE 2 (Tottenham W. Jn)
Clapton Jn
14A: to Finsbury Park
miles from former Broad St. Station
Canonbury Tunnel
CFP LNE: GN
LNE (K) Kings X LNE: GN E. ANGLIA (D) LMS: NL
Barnsbury Jn 3.75
Canonbury W. Jn E. Jn
DALSTON KINGSLAND 2.06
COM Navarino Rd. Jn
UP & DN N. L. NO. 1 (AC)
DN N.L. NO. 1 (AC)
DOWN
UP N.L. NO. 1
DN N.L. NO. 2 (DC)
UP NORTH LONDON NO. 2 (DC)
UP
arch 452 3.02 (H)
HACKNEY DOWNS 2.78
1 DWW 2
River Lea
DOWN WOOLWICH
UP WOOLWICH
2B: to Stratford
CALEDONIAN ROAD AND BARNSBURY 3.74
HIGHBURY & ISLINGTON 3.36
CANONBURY 2.70
Dalston Western Jn (D)
1 BOK DWW 1
LMS: NL
GRAHAM RD. CURVE DOWN
HACKNEY CENTRAL (D) (S) Stratford
165-225 arches
HOMERTON 2.01
Victoria Park
HACKNEY WICK 2.68
2.55 Reading Lane Jn
(Victoria Park Jn)
LMS: NL LNE: GE present day mileage origin for lines to North Woolwich and Navarino Rd. Jn
(H) Hackney Downs (L) Liverpool St. arch 396
LONDON FIELDS 2.35
BGK LNE: GE
DOWN SUBURBAN
UP SUB
DN FAST
UP FAST
Miles from Liverpool St.
1.74 Regent's Canal (arches 319-321)
CAMBRIDGE HEATH 1.61
arch 290
2A: to Liverpool St.

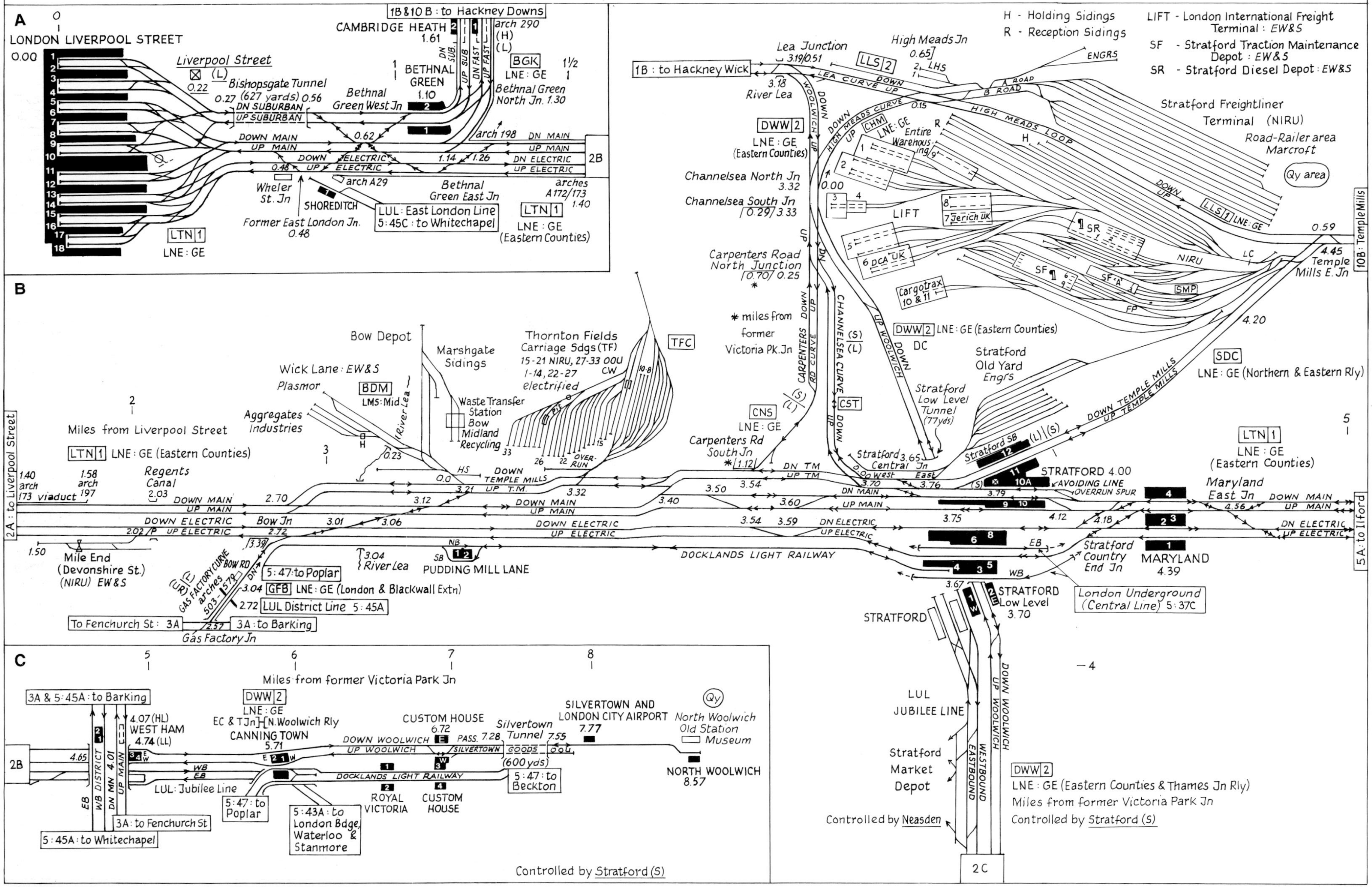
A
LONDON LIVERPOOL STREET 0.00
Liverpool Street (L) 0.22
Bishopsgate Tunnel 0.27 (627 yards) 0.56
DN SUBURBAN
UP SUBURBAN
DOWN MAIN
UP MAIN
DOWN ELECTRIC
UP ELECTRIC
Wheler St. Jn
SHOREDITCH
Former East London Jn. 0.48
LUL: East London Line 5: 45C: to Whitechapel
arch A29
Bethnal Green West Jn
BETHNAL GREEN 1.10
Bethnal Green East Jn
CAMBRIDGE HEATH 1.61
1B & 10 B: to Hackney Downs
arch 290 (H) (L)
BGK LNE: GE
Bethnal Green North Jn. 1.30
arch 198
arches A172/173 1.40
LTN 1 LNE: GE (Eastern Counties)
LTN 1 LNE: GE
2B
H - Holding Sidings
R - Reception Sidings
LIFT - London International Freight Terminal: EW&S
SF - Stratford Traction Maintenance Depot: EW&S
SR - Stratford Diesel Depot: EW&S
1B: to Hackney Wick
Lea Junction 3.19/0.51
3.18 River Lea
LLS 2
High Meads Jn 0.65
LEA CURVE
HIGH MEADS CURVE
HIGH MEADS LOOP
A ROAD
B ROAD
ENGRS
CHM LNE: GE Entire Warehousing
Stratford Freightliner Terminal (NIRU)
Road-Railer area Marcroft
Qy area
LLS 1 LNE: GE
10B: Temple Mills
4.45 Temple Mills E. Jn
LIFT
Jerich UK
DCA UK
Cargotrax 10 & 11
SMP
NIRU
DWW 2 LNE: GE (Eastern Counties)
Channelsea North Jn 3.32
Channelsea South Jn 0.29/3.33
Carpenters Road North Junction 0.70/0.25
* miles from former Victoria Pk. Jn
CARPENTERS RD CURVE
CHANNELSEA CURVE
CST
CNS LNE: GE
Carpenters Rd South Jn 1.12
DWW 2 LNE: GE (Eastern Counties) DC
Stratford Low Level Tunnel (77 yds)
Stratford Old Yard Engrs
Stratford Central Jn 3.65
SDC LNE: GE (Northern & Eastern Rly)
DOWN TEMPLE MILLS
UP TEMPLE MILLS
Stratford SB
STRATFORD 4.00
AVOIDING LINE
OVERRUN SPUR
LTN 1 LNE: GE (Eastern Counties)
Maryland East Jn
MARYLAND 4.39
Stratford Country End Jn
London Underground (Central Line) 5: 37C
5A: to Ilford
STRATFORD Low Level 3.70
STRATFORD
LUL JUBILEE LINE
Stratford Market Depot
Controlled by Neasden
DWW 2 LNE: GE (Eastern Counties & Thames Jn Rly)
Miles from former Victoria Park Jn
Controlled by Stratford (S)
2C
B
2A: to Liverpool Street
Miles from Liverpool Street
LTN 1 LNE: GE (Eastern Counties)
1.40 arch 173 viaduct
1.58 arch 197
Regents Canal 2.03
Mile End (Devonshire St.) (NIRU) EW&S
Bow Jn 2.72
Aggregates Industries
Plasmor
Wick Lane: EW&S
Bow Depot
BDM LMS: Mid
River Lea
Marshgate Sidings
Waste Transfer Station
Bow Midland Recycling
Thornton Fields Carriage Sdgs (TF) 15-21 NIRU, 27-33 OOU CW 1-14, 22-27 electrified
TFC
DOWN TEMPLE MILLS
UP T.M.
DOCKLANDS LIGHT RAILWAY
PUDDING MILL LANE
3.04 River Lea
5: 47: to Poplar
GFB LNE: GE (London & Blackwall Extn)
LUL District Line 5: 45A
GAS FACTORY CURVE
To Fenchurch St: 3A
3A: to Barking
Gas Factory Jn
C
Miles from former Victoria Park Jn
3A & 5: 45A: to Barking
WEST HAM 4.07 (HL) 4.74 (LL)
2B
WB DISTRICT
DN MN 4.01
UP MAIN
LUL: Jubilee Line
3A: to Fenchurch St
5: 45A: to Whitechapel
DWW 2 LNE: GE
EC & TJn | N. Woolwich Rly
CANNING TOWN 5.71
5: 47: to Poplar
5: 43A: to London Bdge, Waterloo & Stanmore
DOWN WOOLWICH
UP WOOLWICH
CUSTOM HOUSE 6.72
PASS. 7.28
ROYAL VICTORIA
CUSTOM HOUSE
Silvertown Tunnel 7.55 (600 yds)
5: 47: to Beckton
SILVERTOWN AND LONDON CITY AIRPORT 7.77
North Woolwich Old Station Museum
NORTH WOOLWICH 8.57
Controlled by Stratford (S)

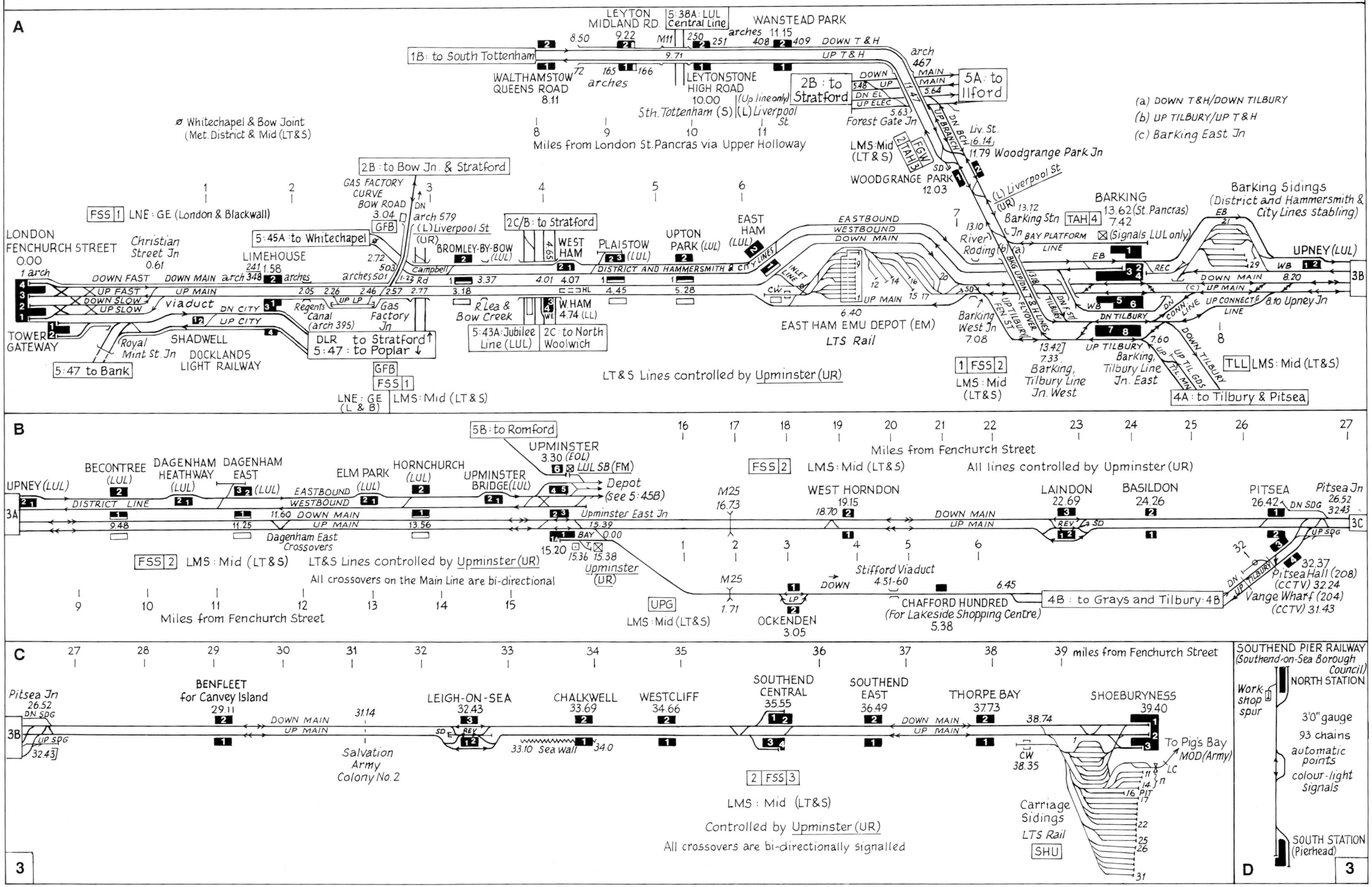
A
LONDON FENCHURCH STREET 0.00
1 arch
TOWER GATEWAY
Christian Street Jn 0.61
LIMEHOUSE 1.58
SHADWELL
DOCKLANDS LIGHT RAILWAY
Royal Mint St. Jn
5:47 to Bank
FSS 1 LNE : GE (London & Blackwall)
ø Whitechapel & Bow Joint (Met. District & Mid (LT&S))
5:45A to Whitechapel
DOWN FAST
UP FAST
DOWN SLOW
UP SLOW
DOWN MAIN
UP MAIN
viaduct
DN CITY
UP CITY
Regents Canal (arch 395)
Gas Factory Jn
DLR to Stratford ↑
5:47 : to Poplar ↓
GFB
FSS 1
LNE : GE (L & B)
LMS : Mid (LT & S)
2B : to Bow Jn. & Stratford
GAS FACTORY CURVE
BOW ROAD 3.04
arch 579
(L) Liverpool St (UR)
BROMLEY-BY-BOW (LUL)
Campbell Rd
2C/B : to Stratford
WEST HAM 4.65
R. Lea & Bow Creek
W.HAM 4.74 (LL)
5:43A: Jubilee Line (LUL)
2C : to North Woolwich
PLAISTOW (LUL)
UPTON PARK (LUL)
EAST HAM (LUL)
DISTRICT AND HAMMERSMITH & CITY LINES
INLET LINE
EASTBOUND
WESTBOUND
DOWN MAIN
UP MAIN
EAST HAM EMU DEPOT (EM)
LTS Rail
6.40
LT&S Lines controlled by Upminster (UR)
1B : to South Tottenham
WALTHAMSTOW QUEENS ROAD 8.11
LEYTON MIDLAND RD. 9.22
5:38A : LUL Central Line
arches
LEYTONSTONE HIGH ROAD 10.00
WANSTEAD PARK 11.15
DOWN T & H
UP T & H
2B : to Stratford
(Up line only) (L) Liverpool St.
Sth. Tottenham (S)
Miles from London St. Pancras via Upper Holloway
5A : to Ilford
Forest Gate Jn 5.63
LMS: Mid (LT & S)
FGW
2 TAH 3
WOODGRANGE PARK 12.03
11.79 Woodgrange Park Jn
(L) Liverpool St (UR)
13.12 Barking Stn Jn
13.10 River Roding
BAY PLATFORM LINE
BARKING 13.62 (St. Pancras) 7.42
TAH 4
⊠ (Signals LUL only)
BKG UP/DN T & H LINES
FLYOVER
UP TILBURY FEN. ST
Barking West Jn 7.08
1 FSS 2
LMS : Mid (LT&S)
13.42 7.33 Barking, Tilbury Line Jn. West
UP TILBURY
DN TILBURY
Barking, Tilbury Line Jn. East 7.60
DOWN TILBURY
UP TIL. GDS
TLL LMS: Mid (LT&S)
4A : to Tilbury & Pitsea
(a) DOWN T&H/DOWN TILBURY
(b) UP TILBURY/UP T&H
(c) Barking East Jn
Barking Sidings (District and Hammersmith & City Lines stabling)
UP CONNECT & LINE
8.10 Upney Jn
UPNEY (LUL)
3B
B
3A
UPNEY (LUL)
BECONTREE (LUL)
DAGENHAM HEATHWAY (LUL)
DAGENHAM EAST (LUL)
DISTRICT LINE
EASTBOUND
WESTBOUND
Dagenham East Crossovers
ELM PARK (LUL)
HORNCHURCH (LUL)
UPMINSTER BRIDGE (LUL)
5B : to Romford
UPMINSTER 3.30 (EOL)
LUL SB (FM)
Depot (see 5:45B)
Upminster East Jn
Upminster (UR)
FSS 2 LMS : Mid (LT&S)
LT&S Lines controlled by Upminster (UR)
All crossovers on the Main Line are bi-directional
Miles from Fenchurch Street
M25 16.73
WEST HORNDON 19.15
LAINDON 22.69
BASILDON 24.26
PITSEA 26.42
Pitsea Jn 26.52 32.43
DN SDG
UP SPG
All lines controlled by Upminster (UR)
UPG
LMS : Mid (LT&S)
M25 1.71
OCKENDEN 3.05
Stifford Viaduct 4.51-60
CHAFFORD HUNDRED (For Lakeside Shopping Centre) 5.38
4B : to Grays and Tilbury : 4B
Pitsea Hall (208) (CCTV) 32.24
Vange Wharf (204) (CCTV) 31.43
3C
C
3B
Pitsea Jn 26.52
BENFLEET for Canvey Island 29.11
DOWN MAIN
UP MAIN
Salvation Army Colony No. 2
LEIGH-ON-SEA 32.43
33.10 Sea wall 34.0
CHALKWELL 33.69
WESTCLIFF 34.66
SOUTHEND CENTRAL 35.55
SOUTHEND EAST 36.49
THORPE BAY 37.73
SHOEBURYNESS 39.40
39 miles from Fenchurch Street
2 FSS 3
LMS : Mid (LT&S)
Controlled by Upminster (UR)
All crossovers are bi-directionally signalled
To Pig's Bay MOD (Army)
Carriage Sidings
LTS Rail
SHU
D
SOUTHEND PIER RAILWAY (Southend-on-Sea Borough Council)
NORTH STATION
Work shop spur
3'0" gauge
93 chains
automatic points
colour-light signals
SOUTH STATION (Pierhead)
3

A

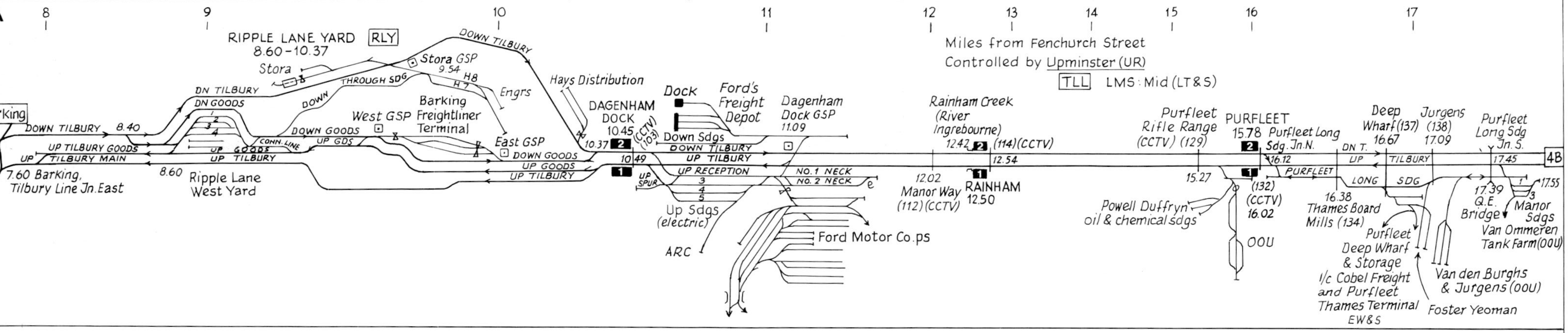


B

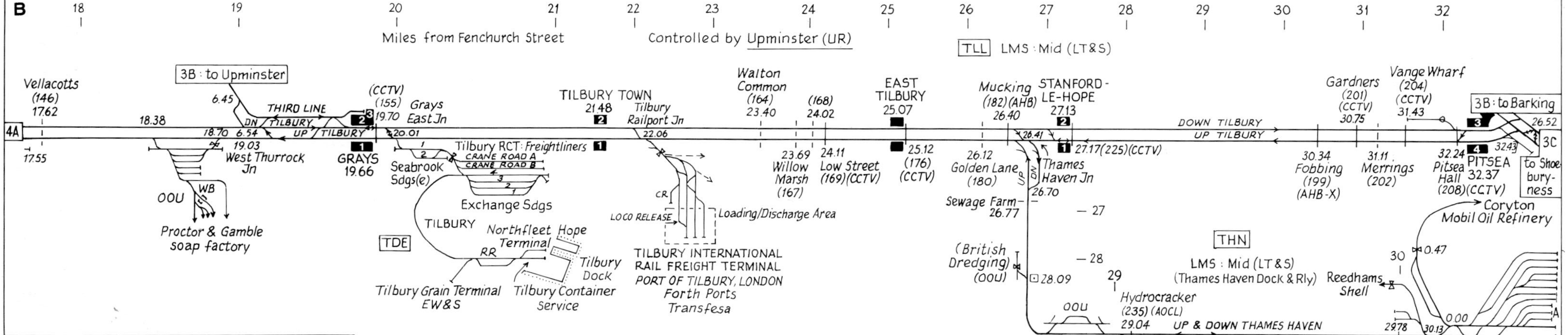


C

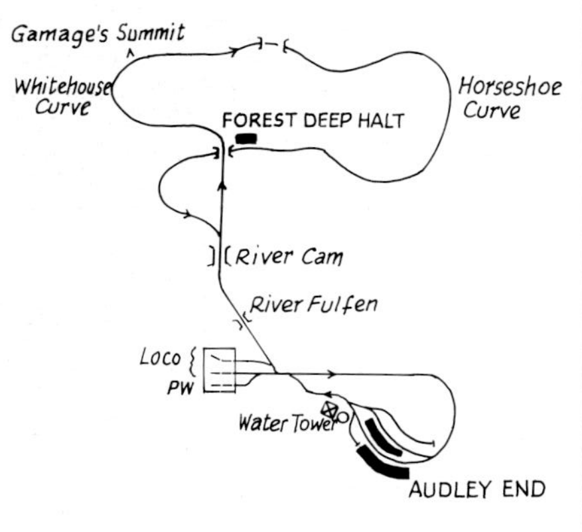


AUDLEY END RAILWAY 10¼" gauge - 96 chains

D

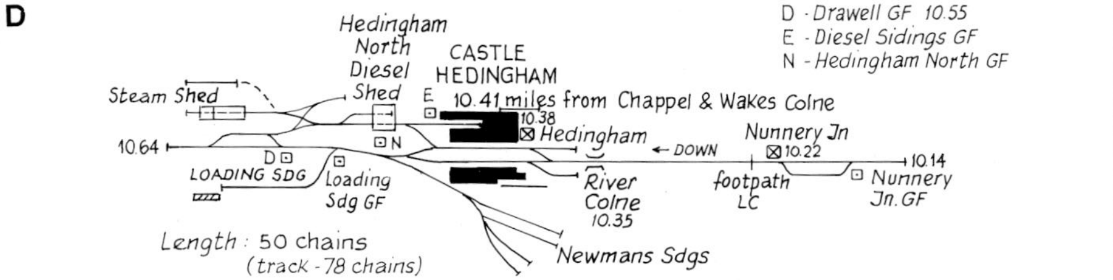


COLNE VALLEY RAILWAY CO. LTD : Colne Valley Railway Preservation Society Ltd.

E

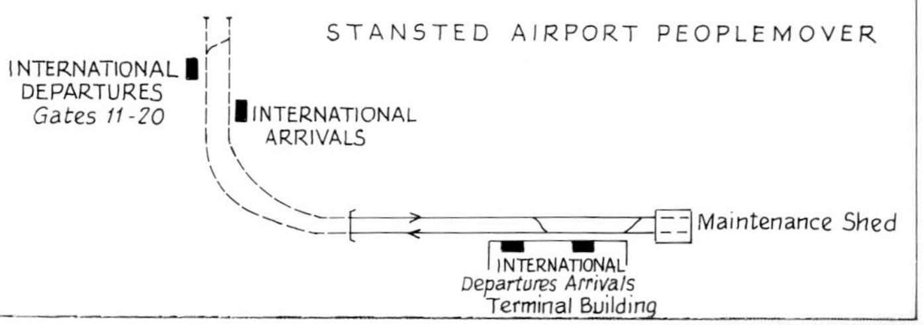

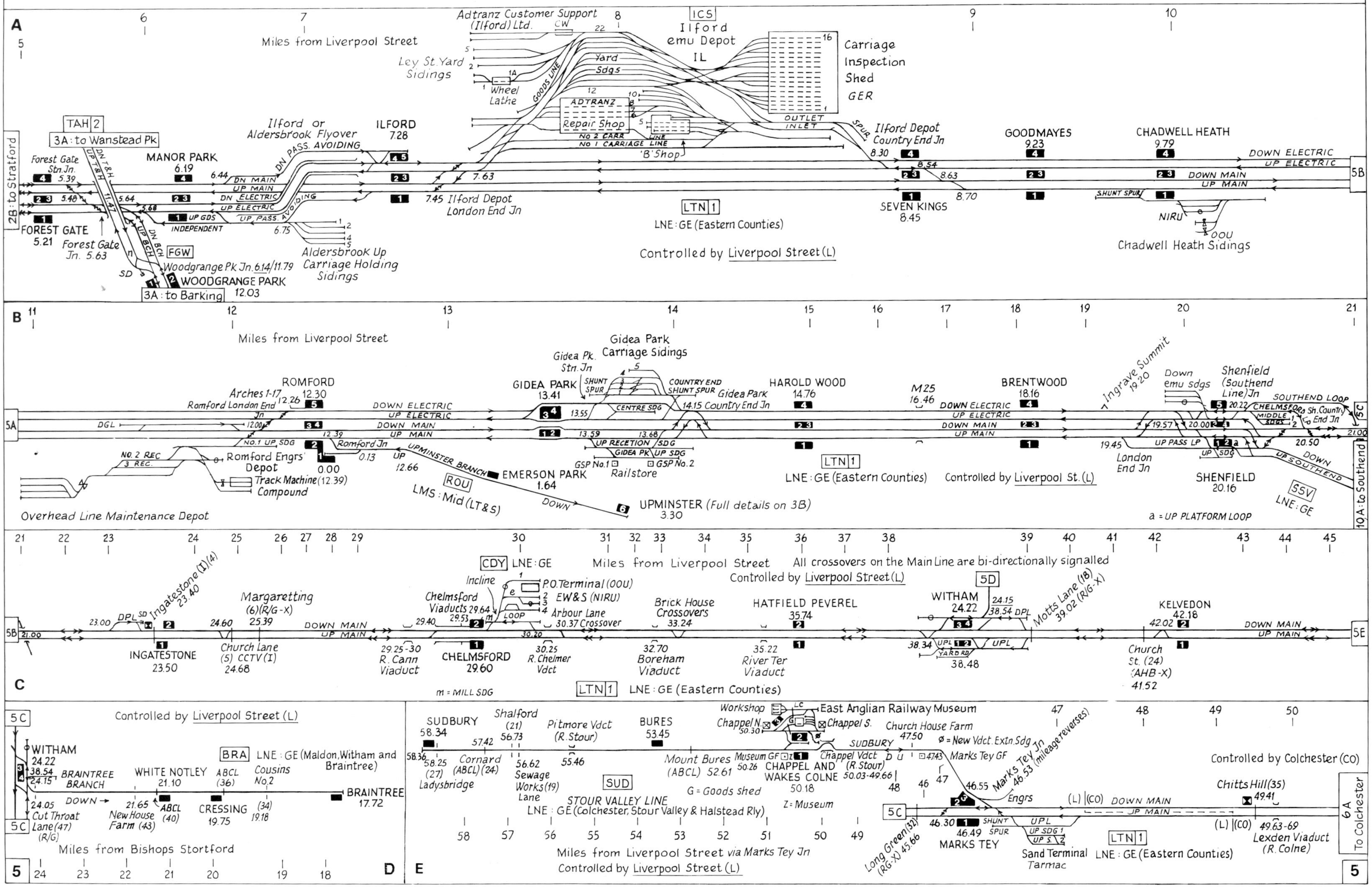
A
Miles from Liverpool Street
Adtranz Customer Support (Ilford) Ltd.
ICS
Ilford emu Depot IL
Carriage Inspection Shed GER
Ley St. Yard Sidings
Wheel Lathe
GOODS LINE
Yard Sdgs
ADTRANZ Repair Shop
'B' Shop
OUTLET
INLET
NO 2 CARR
NO 1 CARRIAGE LINE
TAH 2
3A: to Wanstead Pk
2B: to Stratford
Forest Gate Str. Jn. 5.39
FOREST GATE 5.21
Forest Gate Jn. 5.63
MANOR PARK 6.19
Ilford or Aldersbrook Flyover
DN PASS. AVOIDING
ILFORD 7.28
DN MAIN
UP MAIN
DN ELECTRIC
UP ELECTRIC
UP PASS
UP GDS
INDEPENDENT
FGW
Woodgrange Pk Jn. 6.14/11.79
WOODGRANGE PARK 12.03
3A: to Barking
Aldersbrook Up Carriage Holding Sidings
7.45 Ilford Depot London End Jn
Ilford Depot Country End Jn 8.30
SEVEN KINGS 8.45
GOODMAYES 9.23
CHADWELL HEATH 9.79
SHUNT SPUR
NIRU
OOU
Chadwell Heath Sidings
DOWN ELECTRIC
UP ELECTRIC
DOWN MAIN
UP MAIN
5B
LTN 1
LNE: GE (Eastern Counties)
Controlled by Liverpool Street (L)
B
Miles from Liverpool Street
5A
DGL
Romford London End Jn
Arches 1-17
ROMFORD 12.30
NO.1 UP SDG
NO. 2 REC
3 REC.
Romford Engrs' Depot 0.00
Track Machine (12.39) Compound
Overhead Line Maintenance Depot
Romford Jn 0.13
UPMINSTER BRANCH
ROU
LMS: Mid (LT&S)
EMERSON PARK 1.64
UPMINSTER (Full details on 3B) 3.30
Gidea Pk. Str. Jn
Gidea Park Carriage Sidings
GIDEA PARK 13.41
SHUNT SPUR
CENTRE SDG
COUNTRY END SHUNT SPUR
Gidea Park 14.15 Country End Jn
UP RECETION SDG
GIDEA PK UP SDG
GSP No.1
GSP No.2
Railstore
HAROLD WOOD 14.76
M25 16.46
BRENTWOOD 18.16
Ingrave Summit 19.20
Down emu sdgs
Shenfield (Southend Line) Jn
SOUTHEND LOOP
CHELMSFORD
MIDDLE
SDGS
Sh. Country End Jn
London End Jn 19.45
UP PASS LP
SHENFIELD 20.16
UP SOUTHEND
DOWN
SSV
LNE: GE
10A: to Southend
5C
LNE: GE (Eastern Counties)
Controlled by Liverpool St. (L)
a = UP PLATFORM LOOP
C
CDY LNE: GE
Miles from Liverpool Street
All crossovers on the Main Line are bi-directionally signalled
Controlled by Liverpool Street (L)
5B
Ingatestone (I)(4) 23.40
DPL
INGATESTONE 23.50
Margaretting (6)(R/G-X) 25.39
Church Lane (5) CCTV (I) 24.68
29.25-30 R. Cann Viaduct
Chelmsford Viaducts 29.64
Incline
P.O. Terminal (OOU)
EW&S (NIRU)
Arbour Lane 30.37 Crossover
LOOP
CHELMSFORD 29.60
30.25 R. Chelmer Vdct
m = MILL SDG
Brick House Crossovers 33.24
32.70 Boreham Viaduct
HATFIELD PEVEREL 35.74
35.22 River Ter Viaduct
5D
WITHAM 24.22
24.15
38.54 DPL
38.34 UPL
YARD RD
38.48
Motts Lane (18) 39.02 (R/G-X)
KELVEDON 42.18
42.02
Church St. (24) (AHB-X) 41.52
DOWN MAIN
UP MAIN
5E
LTN 1 LNE: GE (Eastern Counties)
5C
Controlled by Liverpool Street (L)
WITHAM 24.22
38.54
24.15
BRAINTREE BRANCH
DOWN
24.05 Cut Throat Lane (47) (R/G)
WHITE NOTLEY 21.10
21.65 New House Farm (43)
ABCL (40)
BRA
LNE: GE (Maldon, Witham and Braintree)
ABCL (36)
Cousins No.2
CRESSING 19.75
(34) 19.18
BRAINTREE 17.72
Miles from Bishops Stortford
5
D
E
SUDBURY 58.34
58.36
58.25 (27) Ladysbridge
57.42
Cornard (ABCL) (24)
Shalford (21) 56.73
56.62 Sewage Works (19) Lane
Pitmore Vdct (R. Stour)
55.46
BURES 53.45
SUD
STOUR VALLEY LINE
LNE: GE (Colchester, Stour Valley & Halstead Rly)
Mount Bures (ABCL) 52.61
Workshop
Chappel N. 50.30
LC
East Anglian Railway Museum
Chappel S.
Museum GF 50.26
CHAPPEL AND WAKES COLNE 50.18
G = Goods Shed
Z = Museum
SUDBURY 47.50
Chappel Vdct (R. Stour) 50.03-49.66
Church House Farm
ø = New Vdct. Extn. Sdg
47.43 Marks Tey GF
Marks Tey Jn 46.53 (mileage reverses)
46.55
Engrs
5C
46.30
SHUNT SPUR
46.49 MARKS TEY
Long Green (32) (RG-X) 45.66
UPL
UP SDG 1
UP S 2
Sand Terminal Tarmac
(L) (CO) DOWN MAIN
UP MAIN
Chitts Hill (35) 49.41
(L) (CO) 49.63-69 Lexden Viaduct (R. Colne)
Controlled by Colchester (CO)
LTN 1 LNE: GE (Eastern Counties)
6A To Colchester
Miles from Liverpool Street via Marks Tey Jn
Controlled by Liverpool Street (L)
5

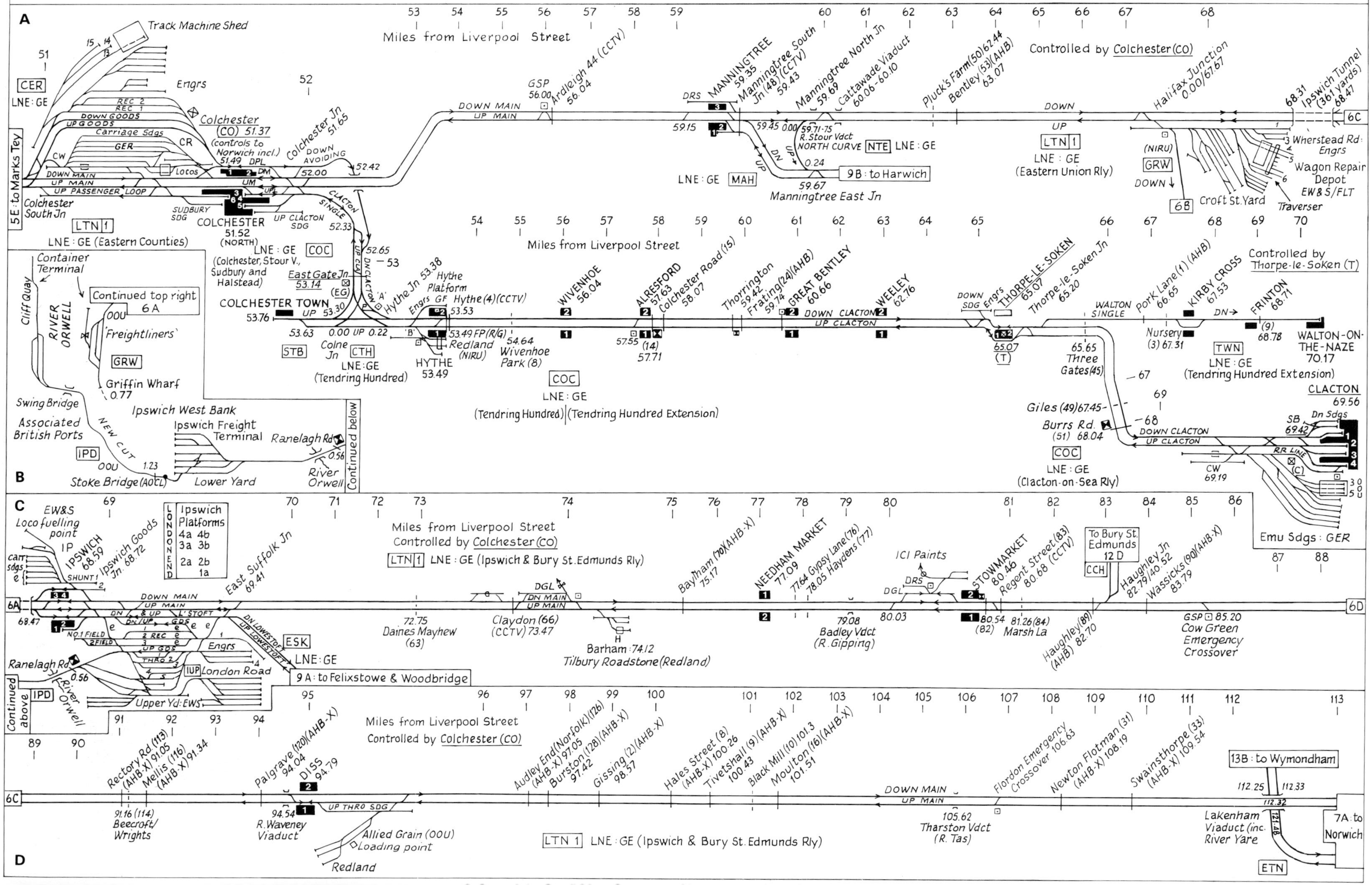
A
Miles from Liverpool Street
Controlled by Colchester (CO)
Track Machine Shed
CER
LNE : GE
Engrs
Colchester (CO) 51.37 (controls to Norwich incl.)
Colchester Jn 51.65
DOWN AVOIDING
52.42
52.00
Carriage Sdgs
GER
CR
Lotos
DOWN MAIN
UP MAIN
UP PASSENGER LOOP
DOWN GOODS
UP GOODS
5E: to Marks Tey
Colchester South Jn
LTN 1
LNE : GE (Eastern Counties)
SUDBURY SDG
COLCHESTER 51.52 (NORTH)
UP CLACTON SDG
CLACTON SINGLE
52.33
GSP 56.00
Ardleigh 44 (CCTV) 56.04
DRS
MANNINGTREE 59.35
Manningtree South Jn (48) (CCTV) 59.43
Manningtree North Jn 59.69
Cattawade Viaduct 60.06-60.10
Pluck's Farm (50) 62.44
Bentley (53) (AHB) 63.07
Halifax Junction 0.00/67.67
Ipswich Tunnel (361 yards)
68.31
68.47
6C
59.15
59.45 0.00
59.71-75 R. Stour Vdct NORTH CURVE
NTE LNE : GE
0.24
9B : to Harwich
59.67 Manningtree East Jn
LNE : GE
MAH
LTN 1
LNE : GE (Eastern Union Rly)
GRW
DOWN
Croft St. Yard
6B
Wherstead Rd : Engrs
Wagon Repair Depot EW&S/FLT
Traverser
B
Miles from Liverpool Street
LNE : GE
COC
(Colchester, Stour V., Sudbury and Halstead)
East Gate Jn 53.14 (EG)
COLCHESTER TOWN 53.76
53.30
53.63
0.00 UP 0.22
Colne Jn
STB
CTH
LNE : GE (Tendring Hundred)
52.65
53
Hythe Jn 53.38
Hythe Platform
Hythe (4) (CCTV) 53.53
53.49 FP (R/G)
Redland (NIRU)
HYTHE 53.49
54.64 Wivenhoe Park (8)
WIVENHOE 56.04
COC
LNE : GE
(Tendring Hundred) | (Tendring Hundred Extension)
ALRESFORD 57.63
Colchester Road (15) 58.07
57.55 (14) 57.71
Thorrington 59.42
Frating (24) (AHB) 59.74
GREAT BENTLEY 60.66
DOWN CLACTON
UP CLACTON
WEELEY 62.76
DOWN SDG
Engrs
THORPE-LE-SOKEN 65.07
Thorpe-le-Soken Jn 65.20
65.07 (T)
65.65 Three Gates (45)
WALTON SINGLE
Pork Lane (1) (AHB) 66.65
Nursery (3) 67.31
KIRBY CROSS 67.53
FRINTON 68.71
(9) 68.78
WALTON-ON-THE-NAZE 70.17
TWN
LNE : GE (Tendring Hundred Extension)
Controlled by Thorpe-le-Soken (T)
CLACTON 69.56
Giles (49) 67.45
Burrs Rd. (51) 68.04
COC
LNE : GE (Clacton-on-Sea Rly)
SB 69.42
Dn Sdgs
RR LINE
CW 69.19
Container Terminal
Cliff Quay
RIVER ORWELL
Continued top right 6A
OOU
'Freightliners'
GRW
Griffin Wharf 0.77
Swing Bridge
Associated British Ports
IPD
Ipswich West Bank
NEW CUT
Ipswich Freight Terminal
Ranelagh Rd
0.56
River Orwell
Continued below
OOU 1.23
Stoke Bridge (AOCL)
Lower Yard
C
EW&S Loco fuelling point
IP
IPSWICH 68.59
Ipswich Goods Jn 68.72
Ipswich Platforms
4a 4b
3a 3b
2a 2b
1a
LONDON END
East Suffolk Jn 69.41
Miles from Liverpool Street
Controlled by Colchester (CO)
LTN 1 LNE : GE (Ipswich & Bury St. Edmunds Rly)
72.75 Daines Mayhew (63)
Claydon (66) (CCTV) 73.47
DGL
DN MAIN
UP MAIN
Barham 74.12
Tilbury Roadstone (Redland)
Baylham (70) (AHB-X) 75.17
NEEDHAM MARKET 77.09
77.64 Gypsy Lane (76)
78.05 Haydens (77)
79.08 Badley Vdct (R. Gipping)
ICI Paints
DRS
80.03
STOWMARKET 80.46
Regent Street (83) 80.68 (CCTV)
80.54 (82)
81.26 (84) Marsh La
To Bury St. Edmunds 12 D
CCH
Haughley Jn 82.79/40.52
Haughley (89) (AHB) 82.70
Wassicks (90) (AHB-X) 83.79
GSP 85.20 Cow Green Emergency Crossover
Emu Sdgs : GER
6A
6D
68.47
NO.1 FIELD
2 FIELD
2 REC
UP GDS
THRO
DN LOWESTOFT
UP LOWESTOFT
ESK
LNE : GE
Engrs
1UP London Road
9 A : to Felixstowe & Woodbridge
Ranelagh Rd
0.56
River Orwell
IPD
Continued above
Upper Yd : EWS
D
Miles from Liverpool Street
Controlled by Colchester (CO)
Rectory Rd (113) (AHB-X) 91.05
Mellis (116) (AHB-X) 91.34
91.16 (114) Beecroft/Wrights
Palgrave (120) (AHB-X) 94.04
DISS 94.79
94.54 R. Waveney Viaduct
UP THRO SDG
Allied Grain (OOU) Loading point
Redland
LTN 1 LNE : GE (Ipswich & Bury St. Edmunds Rly)
Audley End (Norfolk) (126) (AHB-X) 97.05
Burston (128) (AHB-X) 97.42
Gissing (2) (AHB-X) 98.57
Hales Street (8) (AHB-X) 100.26
Tivetshall (9) (AHB-X) 100.43
Black Mill (10) 101.3
Moulton (16) (AHB-X) 101.51
DOWN MAIN
UP MAIN
105.62 Tharston Vdct (R. Tas)
Flordon Emergency Crossover 106.63
Newton Flotman (31) (AHB-X) 108.19
Swainsthorpe (33) (AHB-X) 109.54
13B : to Wymondham
112.25
112.33
112.32
121.48
Lakenham Viaduct (inc. River Yare
7A : to Norwich
ETN
6C

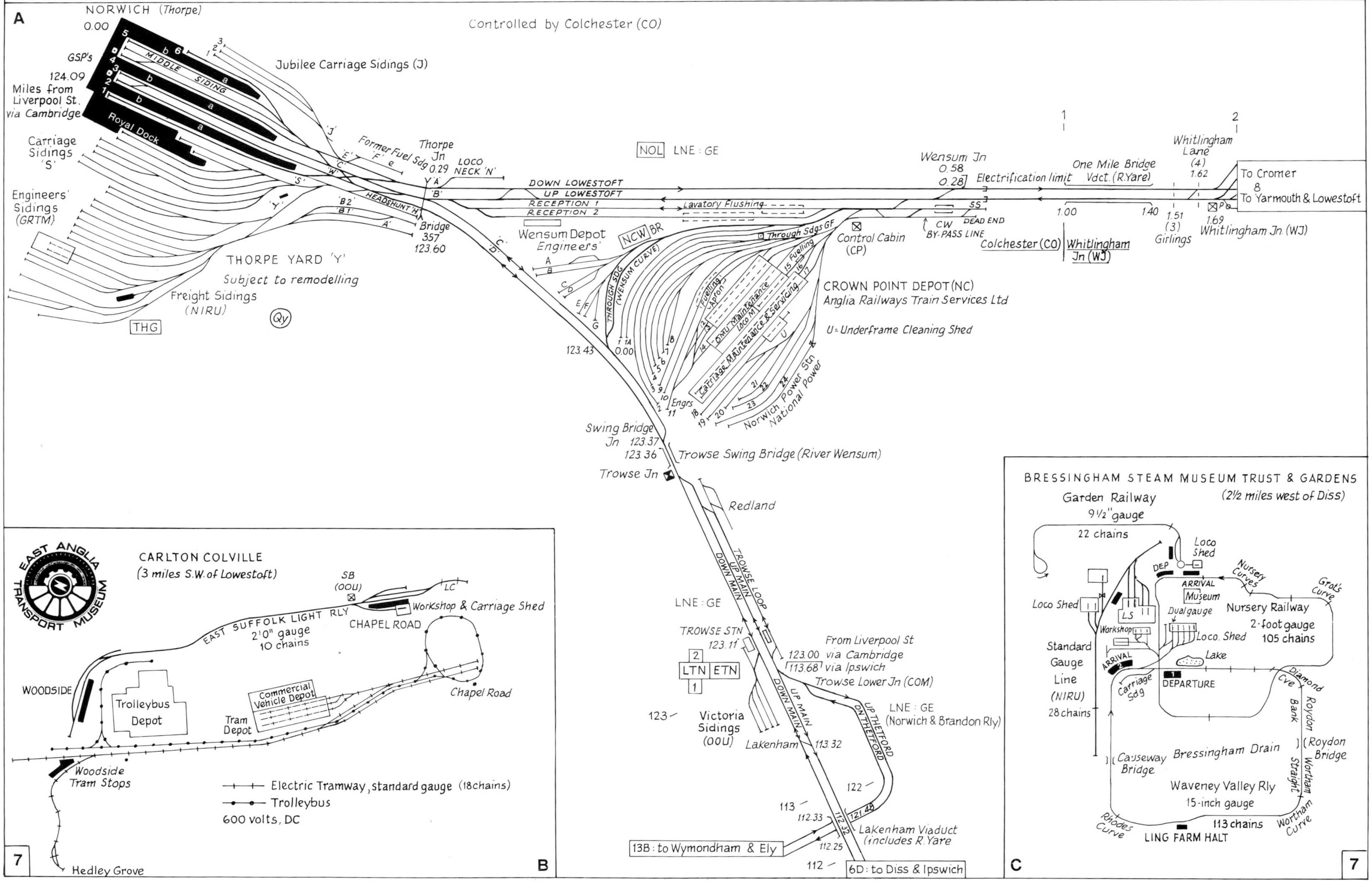
A
NORWICH (Thorpe)
0.00
Controlled by Colchester (CO)
Jubilee Carriage Sidings (J)
GSP's
124.09
Miles from Liverpool St. via Cambridge
MIDDLE SIDING
Royal Dock
Carriage Sidings 'S'
Engineers' Sidings (GRTM)
Former Fuel Sdg
Thorpe Jn 0.29
LOCO NECK 'N'
HEADSHUNT 'H'
Bridge 357 123.60
THORPE YARD 'Y'
Subject to remodelling
Freight Sidings (NIRU)
THG
Qy
NOL LNE : GE
DOWN LOWESTOFT
UP LOWESTOFT
RECEPTION 1
RECEPTION 2
Lavatory Flushing
Wensum Depot Engineers'
NCW BR
THROUGH SDG (WENSUM CURVE)
Through Sdgs GF
Control Cabin (CP)
CROWN POINT DEPOT (NC)
Anglia Railways Train Services Ltd
U=Underframe Cleaning Shed
Fuelling Apron
DMU Maintenance Loco M
Carriage Maintenance & Servicing
15 Fuelling
Engrs
Norwich Power Stn National Power
123.43
Wensum Jn 0.58 0.28
Electrification limit
One Mile Bridge Vdct. (R.Yare)
CW BY-PASS LINE
DEAD END
Colchester (CO)
Whitlingham Jn (WJ)
1.00
1.40
1.51 (3) Girlings
Whitlingham Lane (4) 1.62
1.69 Whitlingham Jn (WJ)
To Cromer
8
To Yarmouth & Lowestoft
Swing Bridge Jn 123.37
123.36
Trowse Swing Bridge (River Wensum)
Trowse Jn
Redland
TROWSE LOOP
UP MAIN
DOWN MAIN
LNE : GE
TROWSE STN 123.11
LTN ETN
Victoria Sidings (OOU)
Lakenham
123.00 via Cambridge
113.68 via Ipswich
From Liverpool St
Trowse Lower Jn (COM)
LNE : GE (Norwich & Brandon Rly)
UP THETFORD
DN THETFORD
113.32
122
121.48
113
112.33
112.32
112.25
112
Lakenham Viaduct (includes R.Yare)
13B : to Wymondham & Ely
6D : to Diss & Ipswich
B
EAST ANGLIA TRANSPORT MUSEUM
CARLTON COLVILLE
(3 miles S.W. of Lowestoft)
SB (OOU)
LC
Workshop & Carriage Shed
CHAPEL ROAD
EAST SUFFOLK LIGHT RLY
2'0" gauge
10 chains
WOODSIDE
Trolleybus Depot
Tram Depot
Commercial Vehicle Depot
Chapel Road
Woodside Tram Stops
Hedley Grove
Electric Tramway, standard gauge (18chains)
Trolleybus
600 volts, DC
C
BRESSINGHAM STEAM MUSEUM TRUST & GARDENS
(2½ miles west of Diss)
Garden Railway
9½" gauge
22 chains
Loco Shed
DEP
ARRIVAL
Museum
Nursery Curves
Grot's Curve
Nursery Railway
2-foot gauge
105 chains
Dual gauge
Loco. Shed
Lake
Workshop
LS
Standard Gauge Line (NIRU)
28 chains
ARRIVAL
Carriage Sdg
DEPARTURE
Diamond Cve
Roydon Bank
Roydon Bridge
Causeway Bridge
Bressingham Drain
Wortham Straight
Waveney Valley Rly
15-inch gauge
Rhodes Curve
113 chains
LING FARM HALT
Wortham Curve

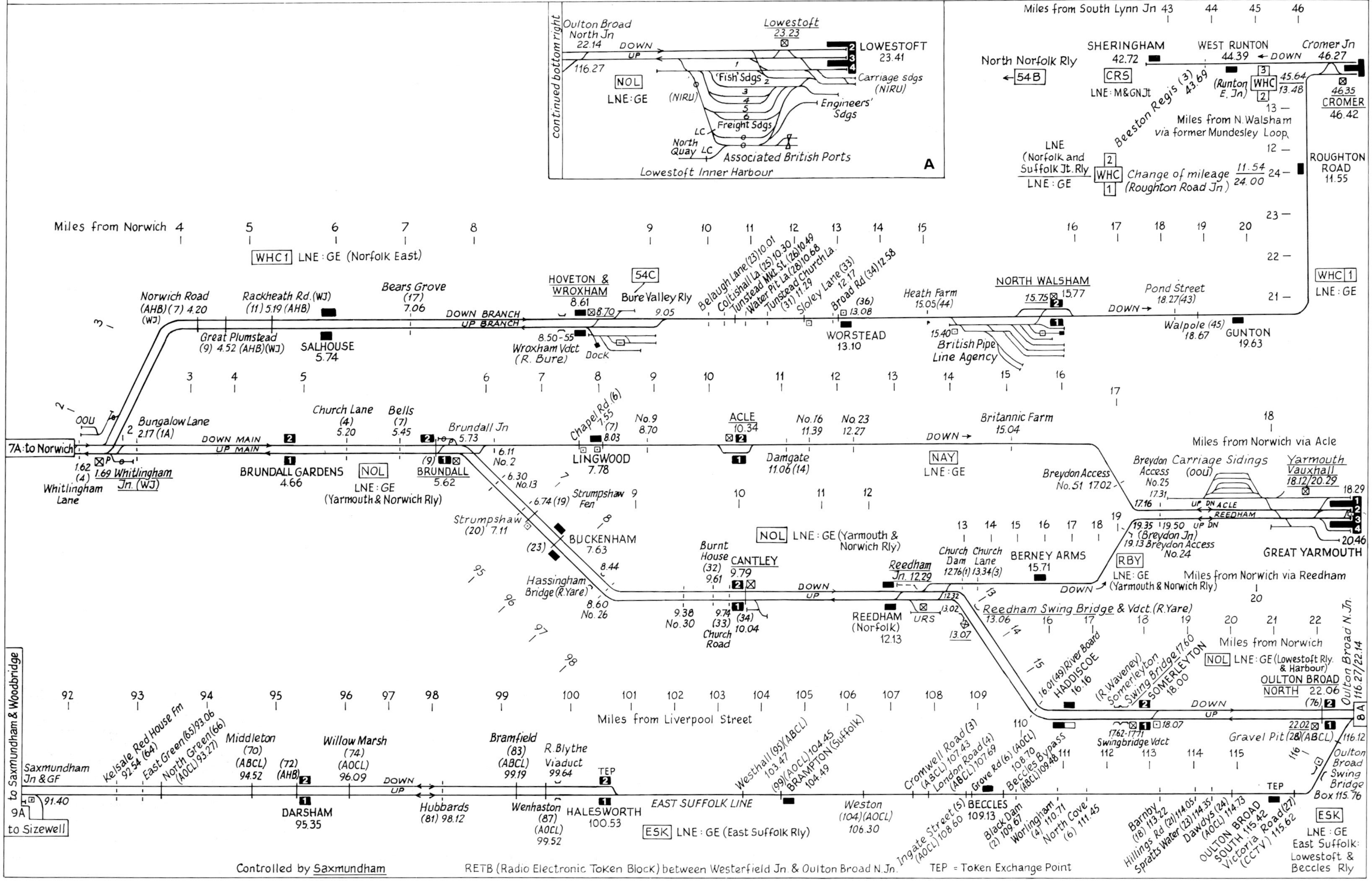
Oulton Broad North Jn 22.14
Lowestoft 23.23
LOWESTOFT 23.41
116.27
NOL
LNE: GE
(NIRU)
'Fish' Sdgs
Carriage sdgs (NIRU)
Engineers' Sdgs
Freight Sdgs
North Quay LC
Associated British Ports
Lowestoft Inner Harbour
continued bottom right
A
Miles from South Lynn Jn 43 44 45 46
North Norfolk Rly
54B
SHERINGHAM 42.72
CRS
LNE: M&GNJt
WEST RUNTON 44.39
Cromer Jn 46.27
DOWN
Beeston Regis (3) 43.69
(Runton E. Jn)
WHC
45.64 / 13.48
46.35
CROMER 46.42
Miles from N. Walsham via former Mundesley Loop
LNE (Norfolk and Suffolk Jt. Rly) LNE: GE
Change of mileage 11.54 / 24.00 (Roughton Road Jn)
ROUGHTON ROAD 11.55
Miles from Norwich
WHC1 LNE: GE (Norfolk East)
WHC1 LNE: GE
Norwich Road (AHB) (7) 4.20 (WJ)
Rackheath Rd. (WJ) (11) 5.19 (AHB)
Great Plumstead (9) 4.52 (AHB)(WJ)
SALHOUSE 5.74
Bears Grove (17) 7.06
DOWN BRANCH
UP BRANCH
HOVETON & WROXHAM 8.61
8.70
54C
Bure Valley Rly
9.05
8.50-55 Wroxham Vdct (R. Bure)
Dock
Belaugh Lane (23) 10.01
Coltishall La. (25) 10.30
Tunstead Mkt. St. (26) 10.49
Water Pit La (28) 10.68
Tunstead Church La. (31) 11.29
Sloley Lane (33) 12.17
Broad Rd (34) 12.58
(36) 13.08
WORSTEAD 13.10
Heath Farm 15.05 (44)
15.40 British Pipe Line Agency
NORTH WALSHAM 15.75 15.77
Pond Street 18.27 (43)
DOWN
Walpole (45) 18.67
GUNTON 19.63
7A: to Norwich
OOU
Bungalow Lane 2.17 (1A)
1.62 (4) Whitlingham Lane
1.69 Whitlingham Jn. (WJ)
DOWN MAIN
UP MAIN
BRUNDALL GARDENS 4.66
Church Lane (4) 5.20
Bells (7) 5.45
NOL LNE: GE (Yarmouth & Norwich Rly)
Brundall Jn 5.73
(9) BRUNDALL 5.62
6.11 No. 2
6.30 No. 13
6.74 (19)
Strumpshaw (20) 7.11
Strumpshaw Fen
Chapel Rd (6) 7.55 (7) 8.03
LINGWOOD 7.78
No. 9 8.70
BUCKENHAM 7.63
(23)
8.44
Hassingham Bridge (R. Yare)
8.60 No. 26
ACLE 10.34
Damgate 11.06 (14)
No. 16 11.39
No. 23 12.27
Britannic Farm 15.04
NAY LNE: GE
Breydon Access No. 51 17.02
Miles from Norwich via Acle
Breydon Access No. 25 17.31
Carriage Sidings (OOU)
Yarmouth Vauxhall 18.12/20.29
18.29
17.16
UP DN ACLE
REEDHAM
19.35 19.50 (Breydon Jn)
19.13 Breydon Access No. 24
20.46
GREAT YARMOUTH
RBY LNE: GE (Yarmouth & Norwich Rly)
Miles from Norwich via Reedham
Burnt House (32) 9.61
CANTLEY 9.79
9.38 No. 30
9.74 (33) (34) Church Road 10.04
NOL LNE: GE (Yarmouth & Norwich Rly)
DOWN UP
REEDHAM (Norfolk) 12.13
Reedham Jn. 12.29
URS
12.32
13.02
13.07
Church Dam 12.76 (1)
Church Lane 13.34 (3)
BERNEY ARMS 15.71
Reedham Swing Bridge & Vdct. (R. Yare) 13.06
16.01 (49) River Board
HADDISCOE 16.16
(R. Waveney) Somerleyton Swing Bridge 17.60
SOMERLEYTON 18.00
Miles from Norwich
NOL LNE: GE (Lowestoft Rly. & Harbour)
OULTON BROAD NORTH 22.06
(76)
Oulton Broad N. Jn. 116.27/22.14
8A
17.62-17.71 Swingbridge Vdct
18.07
22.02
Gravel Pit (28) (ABCL)
116.12
Oulton Broad Swing Bridge Box 115.76
TEP
ESK LNE: GE East Suffolk: Lowestoft & Beccles Rly
to Saxmundham & Woodbridge
9A
to Sizewell
Saxmundham Jn & GF
91.40
Kelsale Red House Fm 92.54 (64)
East Green (65) 93.06
North Green (66) (AOCL) 93.27
Middleton (70) (ABCL) 94.52
(72) (AHB)
DARSHAM 95.35
Willow Marsh (74) (AOCL) 96.09
Hubbards (81) 98.12
Bramfield (83) (ABCL) 99.19
R. Blythe Viaduct 99.64
Wenhaston (87) (AOCL) 99.52
HALESWORTH 100.53
Miles from Liverpool Street
EAST SUFFOLK LINE
ESK LNE: GE (East Suffolk Rly)
Westhall (95) (ABCL) 103.47
(99) (AOCL) 104.45 BRAMPTON (Suffolk) 104.49
Weston (104) (AOCL) 106.30
Cromwell Road (3) (ABCL) 107.43
London Road (4) (ABCL) 107.69
Grove Rd (6) (AOCL) 108.70
Ingate Street (5) (AOCL) 108.60
BECCLES 109.13
Beccles Bypass (ABCL) 109.48
Black Dam (2) 109.67
Worlingham (4) 110.71
North Cove (6) 111.45
Barnby (18) 113.22
Hillings Rd (21) 114.05
Spratts Water (23) 114.35
Dawdys (24) (AOCL) 114.73
OULTON BROAD SOUTH 115.42
Victoria Road (27) (CCTV) 115.62
Controlled by Saxmundham
RETB (Radio Electronic Token Block) between Westerfield Jn. & Oulton Broad N. Jn.
TEP = Token Exchange Point

# (IPSWICH) – SAXMUNDHAM – LEISTON / FELIXSTOWE ● HARWICH BRANCH



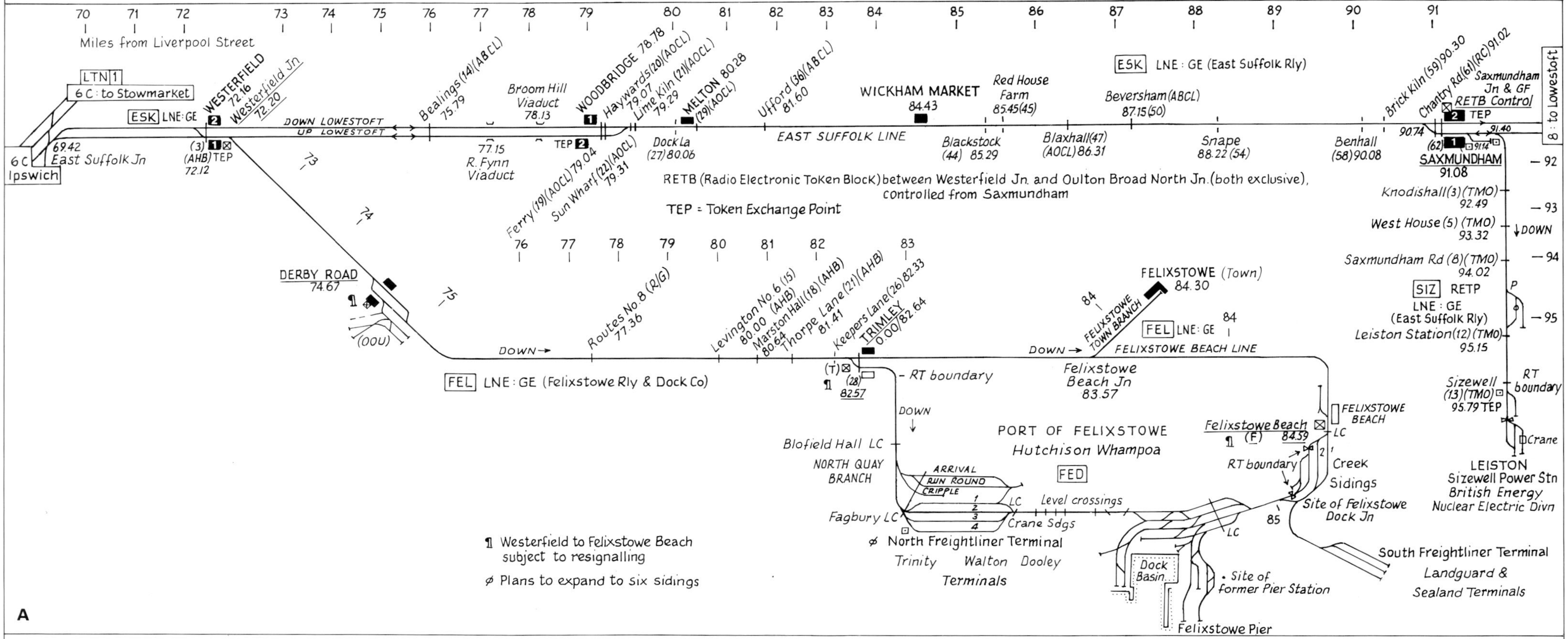


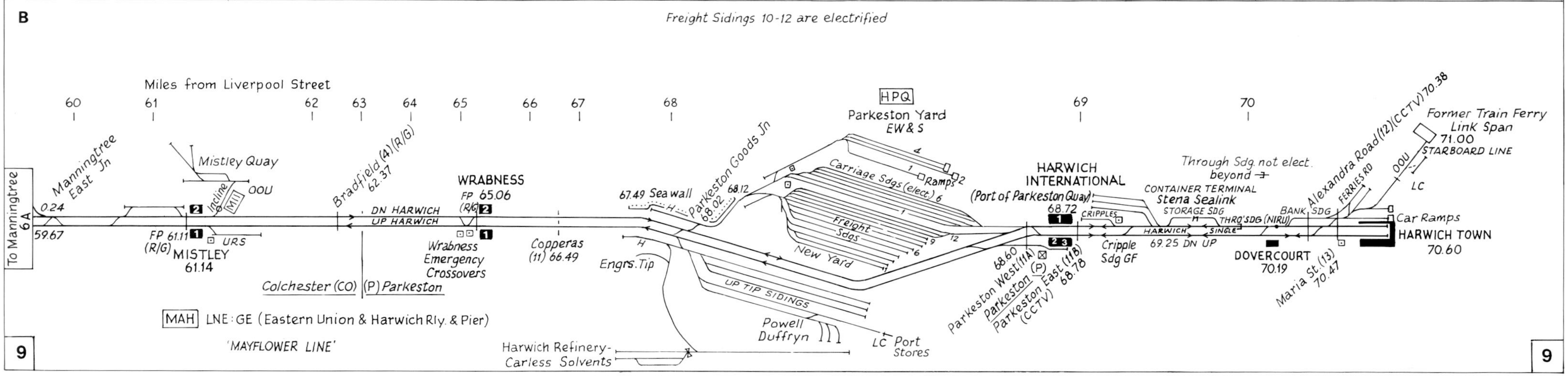

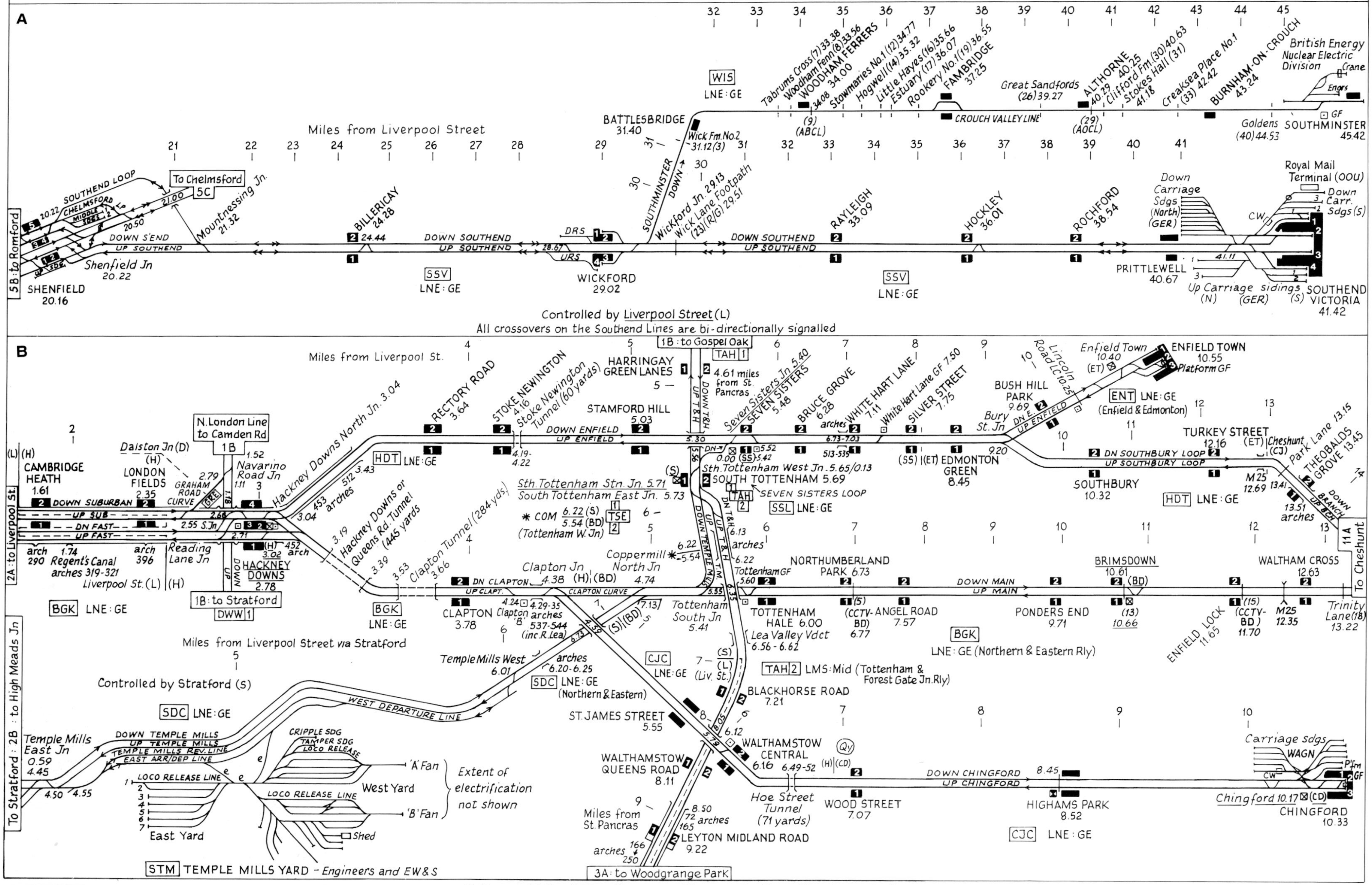
A
Miles from Liverpool Street
SHENFIELD 20.16
Shenfield Jn 20.22
5B: to Romford
SOUTHEND LOOP
To Chelmsford 5C
Mountnessing Jn. 21.32
DOWN S'END
UP SOUTHEND
BILLERICAY 24.28
24.44
DOWN SOUTHEND
UP SOUTHEND
SSV LNE: GE
DRS
URS
WICKFORD 29.02
28.67
BATTLESBRIDGE 31.40
Wick Fm. No.2 31.12(3)
SOUTHMINSTER DOWN
Wickford Jn. 29.13
Wick Lane Footpath (23)(R/G) 29.51
WIS LNE: GE
Tabrums Cross (7) 33.38
Woodham Fenn (8) 33.56
WOODHAM FERRERS 34.00
34.08
(9) (ABCL)
Stowmaries No.1 (12) 34.77
Hogwell (14) 35.32
Little Hayes (16) 35.66
Estuary (17) 36.07
Rookery No.1 (19) 36.55
FAMBRIDGE 37.25
CROUCH VALLEY LINE
Great Sandfords (26) 39.27
ALTHORNE 40.29 40.25
(29) (AOCL)
Clifford Fm. (30) 40.63
Stokes Hall (31) 41.18
Creaksea Place No.1 (33) 42.42
BURNHAM-ON-CROUCH 43.24
Goldens (40) 44.53
SOUTHMINSTER 45.42
British Energy Nuclear Electric Division
Crane
Engrs
GF
RAYLEIGH 33.09
HOCKLEY 36.01
ROCHFORD 38.54
PRITTLEWELL 40.67
41.11
Down Carriage Sdgs (North) (GER)
Royal Mail Terminal (OOU)
Down Carr. Sdgs (S)
CW
Up Carriage sidings (N) (GER) (S)
SOUTHEND VICTORIA 41.42
Controlled by Liverpool Street (L)
All crossovers on the Southend Lines are bi-directionally signalled
B
Miles from Liverpool St.
2A: to Liverpool St.
(L) (H)
CAMBRIDGE HEATH 1.61
DOWN SUBURBAN
UP SUB
DN FAST
UP FAST
arch 290
1.74
Regent's Canal arches 319-321
Liverpool St. (L) (H)
BGK LNE: GE
Dalston Jn (D) (H)
LONDON FIELDS 2.35
GRAHAM ROAD CURVE
2.79
2.55 S. Jn
arch 396
Reading Lane Jn
N. London Line to Camden Rd 1B
1.52
Navarino Road Jn
1.11
1.18
2.68
2.71
HACKNEY DOWNS 2.78
3.02 arch
452
1B: to Stratford DWW 1
DOWN UP
Hackney Downs North Jn. 3.04
453 arches
512 3.43
3.04
Hackney Downs or Queens Rd. Tunnel (445 yards)
3.19
3.39
3.53
Clapton Tunnel (284 yds)
3.66
HDT LNE: GE
RECTORY ROAD 3.64
STOKE NEWINGTON 4.16
Stoke Newington Tunnel (60 yards)
4.19-4.22
DOWN ENFIELD
UP ENFIELD
STAMFORD HILL 5.03
HARRINGAY GREEN LANES
1B: to Gospel Oak
TAH 1
4.61 miles from St. Pancras
DOWN T&H
UP T&H
5.30
Seven Sisters Jn 5.40
SEVEN SISTERS 5.48
BRUCE GROVE 6.28
arches
6.73-7.03
WHITE HART LANE 7.11
White Hart Lane GF 7.50
SILVER STREET 7.75
(SS) (ET) EDMONTON GREEN 8.45
9.20
Bury St. Jn
BUSH HILL PARK 9.69
DN E.
UP ENFIELD
Lincoln Road LC 10.25
Enfield Town 10.40 (ET)
ENFIELD TOWN 10.55
Platform GF
ENT LNE: GE (Enfield & Edmonton)
DN SOUTHBURY LOOP
UP SOUTHBURY LOOP
SOUTHBURY 10.32
HDT LNE: GE
TURKEY STREET 12.16
(ET) Cheshunt (CJ)
M25 12.69
13.41
13.51 arches
Park Lane 13.15
THEOBALDS GROVE 13.45
DOWN BRANCH
UP BCH
11A To Cheshunt
(S)
Sth. Tottenham Stn. Jn. 5.71
South Tottenham East Jn. 5.73
0.00 (SS) 5.42
5.52
513-535
Sth. Tottenham West Jn. 5.65/0.13
SOUTH TOTTENHAM 5.69
TAH 2
SEVEN SISTERS LOOP
SSL LNE: GE
✱ COM 6.22 (S) 5.54 (BD) (Tottenham W. Jn)
TSE 1 2
Coppermill North Jn 4.74
6.22
5.54
6.13 arches
DOWN TEMPLE MILLS
UP T&H
Clapton Jn 4.38 (H) (BD)
DN CLAPTON
UP CLAPT.
CLAPTON CURVE
CLAPTON 3.78
4.24
4.29-35
Clapton arches 'B' 537-544 (inc. R. Lea)
BGK LNE: GE
Tottenham GF 5.60
5.55
6.22
TOTTENHAM HALE 6.00
Lea Valley Vdct 6.56-6.62
NORTHUMBERLAND PARK 6.73
(5) (CCTV-BD) 6.77
ANGEL ROAD 7.57
DOWN MAIN
UP MAIN
PONDERS END 9.71
BRIMSDOWN 10.61 (BD)
(13) 10.66
ENFIELD LOCK 11.65
(15) (CCTV-BD) 11.70
M25 12.35
WALTHAM CROSS 12.63
Trinity Lane (18) 13.22
BGK LNE: GE (Northern & Eastern Rly)
Tottenham South Jn 5.41
7.13
4.39
6.13
(S) (BD)
CJC LNE: GE
(S) (L) (Liv. St.)
TAH 2 LMS: Mid (Tottenham & Forest Gate Jn. Rly)
BLACKHORSE ROAD 7.21
Temple Mills West 6.01
arches 6.20-6.25
SDC LNE: GE (Northern & Eastern)
ST. JAMES STREET 5.55
8.05
6.12
5.79
WALTHAMSTOW CENTRAL 6.16
6.49-52
(H) (CD)
Qy
WALTHAMSTOW QUEENS ROAD 8.11
Hoe Street Tunnel (71 yards)
WOOD STREET 7.07
DOWN CHINGFORD
UP CHINGFORD
8.45
HIGHAMS PARK 8.52
CJC LNE: GE
Carriage sdgs
WAGN
CW
P'fm GF
Chingford 10.17 (CD)
CHINGFORD 10.33
Miles from Liverpool Street via Stratford
Controlled by Stratford (S)
SDC LNE: GE
WEST DEPARTURE LINE
2B: to High Meads Jn
To Stratford
Temple Mills East Jn 0.59 4.45
4.50
4.55
DOWN TEMPLE MILLS
UP TEMPLE MILLS
TEMPLE MILLS REV. LINE
EAST ARR/DEP LINE
LOCO RELEASE LINE
CRIPPLE SDG
TAMPER SDG
LOCO RELEASE
'A' Fan
West Yard
'B' Fan
Shed
East Yard
Extent of electrification not shown
STM TEMPLE MILLS YARD - Engineers and EW&S
Miles from St. Pancras
8.50 72 arches 165
LEYTON MIDLAND ROAD 9.22
arches 166 250
3A: to Woodgrange Park

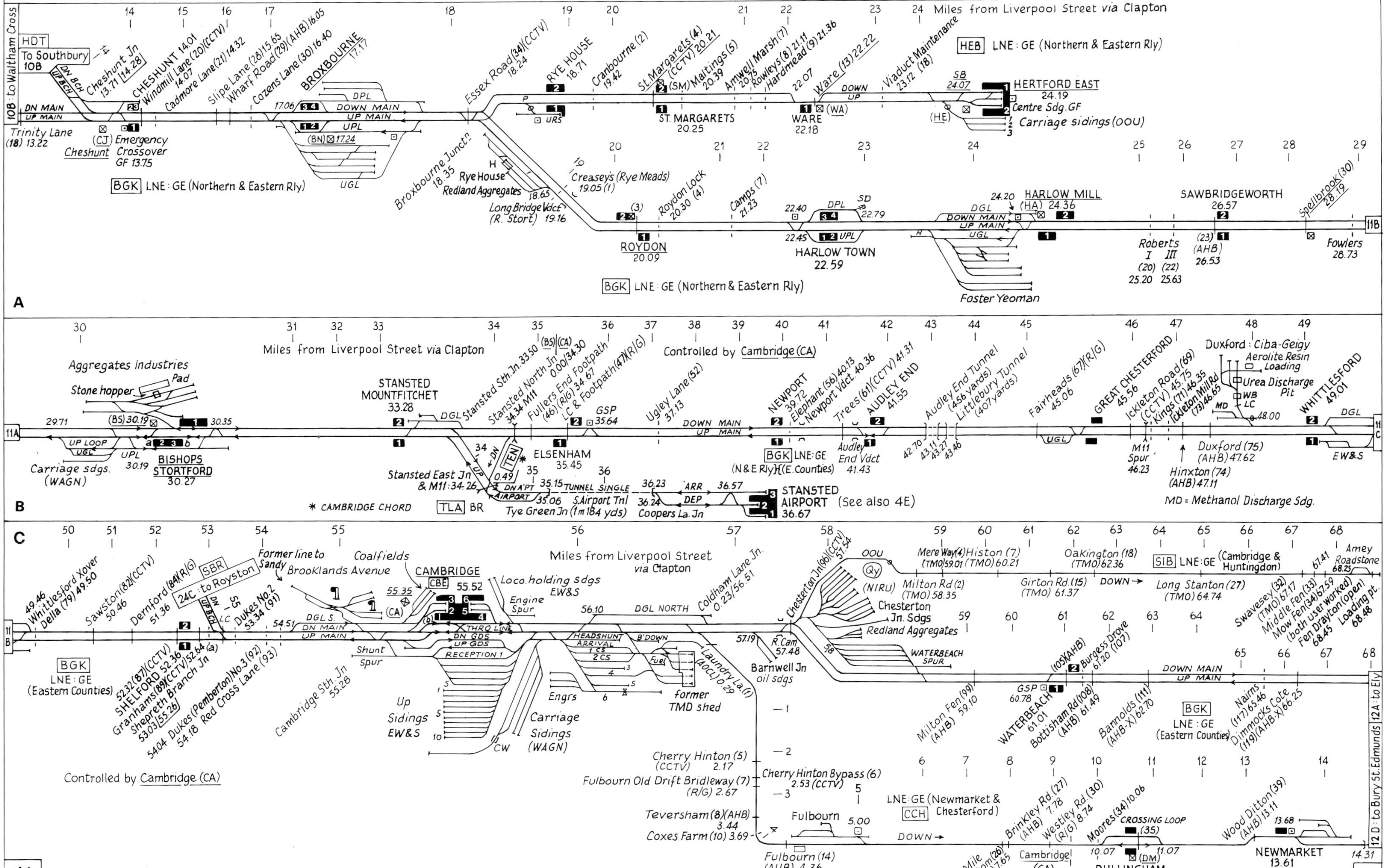




(a) - Websters (90) 53.00 (b) - PLATFORM LINE

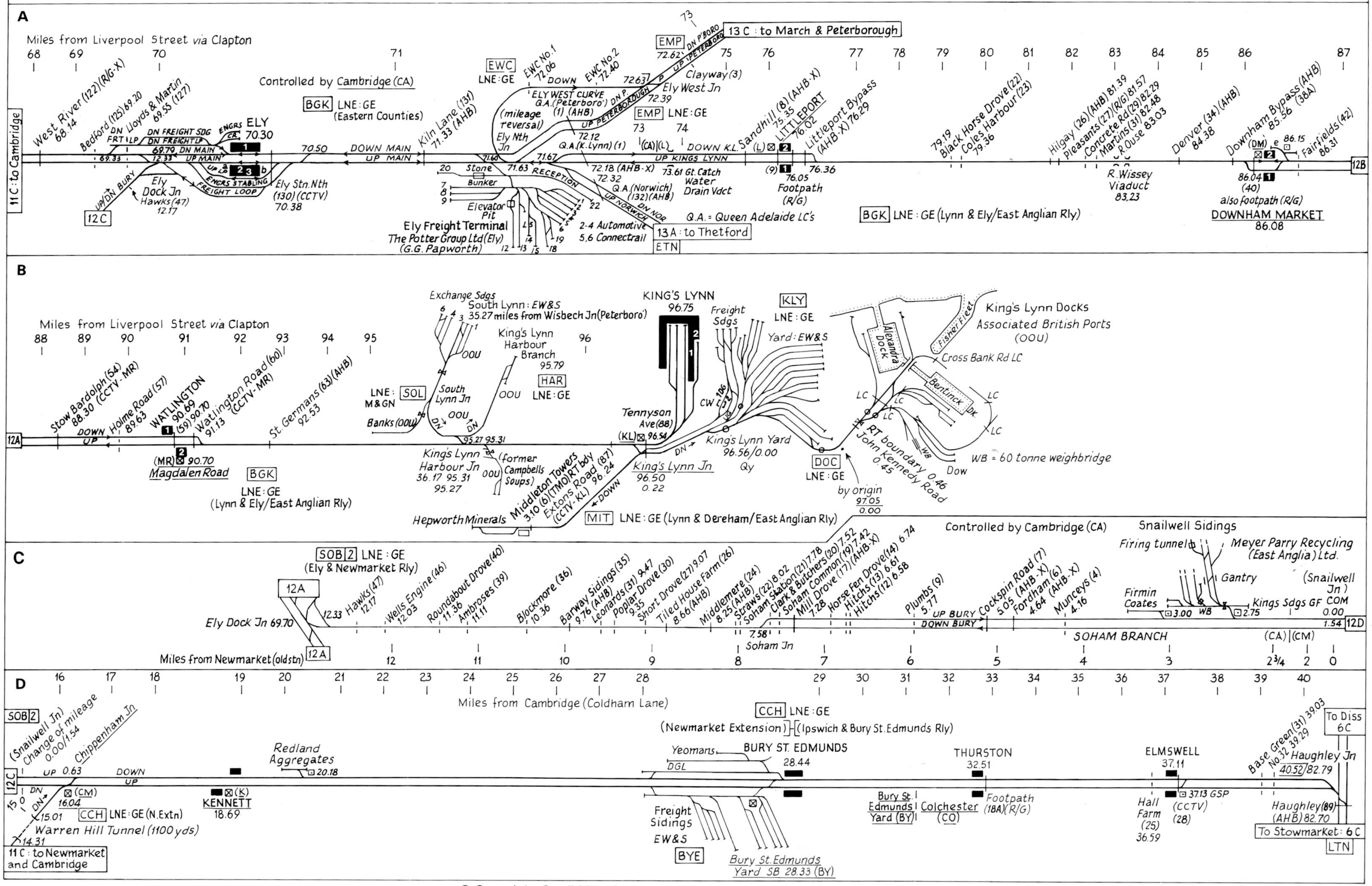
A
Miles from Liverpool Street via Clapton
11 C : to Cambridge
West River (122)(R/G-X) 68.14
Bedford (125) 69.20
Lloyds & Martin 69.55 (127)
DN FREIGHT SDG
DN FREIGHT LP
69.79 DN MAIN
UP MAIN
ELY 70.30
Ely Dock Jn
Hawks (47) 12.17
12 C
ENGRS STABLING
FREIGHT LOOP
Ely Stn.Nth (130) (CCTV) 70.38
70.50
Controlled by Cambridge (CA)
BGK LNE : GE (Eastern Counties)
DOWN MAIN
UP MAIN
Kiln Lane (131) 71.33 (AHB)
EWC LNE : GE
EWC No.1 72.06
EWC No.2 72.40
ELY WEST CURVE
Q.A. (Peterboro') (1) (AHB)
(mileage reversal)
Ely Nth Jn
Stone Bunker
Elevator Pit
Ely Freight Terminal
The Potter Group Ltd (Ely)
(G.G. Papworth)
RECEPTION
2-4 Automotive
5,6 Connectrail
Q.A. (K.Lynn) (1)
72.12
72.18 (AHB-X)
72.32
Q.A. (Norwich) (132) (AHB)
73.61 Gt. Catch Water Drain Vdct
Q.A. = Queen Adelaide LC's
13 A : to Thetford
ETN
EMP 72.62
EMP LNE : GE
13 C : to March & Peterborough
Clayway (3)
Ely West Jn
72.39
DOWN K.L.
UP KINGS LYNN
Sandhill (8) (AHB-X) 75.35
LITTLEPORT 76.02
Littleport Bypass (AHB-X) 76.29
76.05
76.36
Footpath (R/G)
Black Horse Drove (22) 79.19
Coles Harbour (23) 79.36
BGK LNE : GE (Lynn & Ely/East Anglian Rly)
Hilgay (26) (AHB) 81.39
Pleasants (27) (R/G) 81.57
Concrete Rd (29) 82.29
Martins (31) 82.48
R.Ouse 83.03
R.Wissey Viaduct 83.23
Denver (34) (AHB) 84.38
Downham Bypass (AHB) 85.56 (38A)
86.15
Fairfields (42) 86.31
86.04 (40)
also footpath (R/G)
DOWNHAM MARKET 86.08
12B
B
Miles from Liverpool Street via Clapton
12A
Stow Bardolph (54) 88.30 (CCTV-MR)
Holme Road (57) 89.63
WATLINGTON 90.69
(59) 90.70
Watlington Road (60) 91.13 (CCTV-MR)
(MR) 90.70
Magdalen Road
BGK
LNE : GE (Lynn & Ely/East Anglian Rly)
St. Germans (63) (AHB) 92.53
Exchange Sdgs
South Lynn : EW&S
35.27 miles from Wisbech Jn (Peterboro')
LNE : M&GN
SOL
South Lynn Jn
Banks (OOU)
King's Lynn Harbour Jn 36.17 95.31 95.27
(former Campbells Soups)
King's Lynn Harbour Branch 95.79
HAR LNE : GE
Hepworth Minerals
Middleton Towers 3.10 (6) (TMO) RT bdy
Extons Road (87) 96.24 (CCTV-KL)
MIT LNE : GE (Lynn & Dereham/East Anglian Rly)
Tennyson Ave (88)
(KL) 96.54
KING'S LYNN 96.75
Freight Sdgs
KLY LNE : GE
Yard : EW&S
King's Lynn Yard 96.56/0.00
King's Lynn Jn 96.50 0.22
Qy
DOC LNE : GE
by origin 97.05 0.00
RT boundary 0.46
John Kennedy Road 0.45
King's Lynn Docks
Associated British Ports (OOU)
Alexandra Dock
Fisher Fleet
Cross Bank Rd LC
Bentinck Dk.
WB = 60 tonne weighbridge
Dow
C
SOB 2 LNE : GE (Ely & Newmarket Rly)
12A
Ely Dock Jn 69.70
12.33
Hawks (47) 12.17
Wells Engine (46) 12.03
Roundabout Drove (40) 11.36
Ambroses (39) 11.11
Blockmore (36) 10.36
Barway Sidings (35) 9.76 (AHB)
Leonards (31) 9.47
Poplar Drove (30) 9.35
Short Drove (27) 9.07
Tiled House Farm (26) 8.66 (AHB)
Middlemere (24) 8.25 (AHB)
Straws (22) 8.02
Soham Station (21) 7.78
Clark & Butchers (20) 7.52
Soham Common (19) 7.42
Mill Drove (17) (AHB-X) 7.28
Horse Fen Drove (14) 6.74
Hitchs (13) 6.61
Hitchs (12) 6.58
7.58
Soham Jn
Plumbs (9) 5.77
UP BURY
DOWN BURY
Cockspin Road (7) 5.05 (AHB-X)
Fordham (6) 4.64 (AHB-X)
Munceys (4) 4.16
Miles from Newmarket (old stn)
SOHAM BRANCH
Controlled by Cambridge (CA)
Snailwell Sidings
Firing tunnel
Meyer Parry Recycling (East Anglia) Ltd.
Gantry
Firmin Coates
3.00
WB
2.75
Kings Sdgs GF
(Snailwell Jn) COM 0.00
1.54
12D
(CA) (CM)
D
Miles from Cambridge (Coldham Lane)
SOB 2
(Snailwell Jn) Change of mileage 0.00/1.54
Chippenham Jn
12C
UP 0.63
DOWN
UP
(CM) 16.04
15.01
CCH LNE : GE (N.Extn)
Warren Hill Tunnel (1100 yds)
14.31
11 C : to Newmarket and Cambridge
Redland Aggregates 20.18
(K) KENNETT 18.69
CCH LNE : GE
(Newmarket Extension) (Ipswich & Bury St. Edmunds Rly)
Yeomans
DGL
BURY ST. EDMUNDS 28.44
Freight Sidings
EW&S
BYE
Bury St. Edmunds Yard SB 28.33 (BY)
Bury St. Edmunds Yard (BY)
Colchester (CO)
THURSTON 32.51
Footpath (18A) (R/G)
ELMSWELL 37.11
37.13 GSP
Hall Farm (25) 36.59
(CCTV) (28)
Base Green (31) 39.03
No.32 39.29
Haughley Jn 40.52/82.79
Haughley (89) (AHB) 82.70
To Diss 6C
To Stowmarket : 6C
LTN

# BRECKLAND LINE : ELY – (NORWICH) ● NORTH ELMHAM BRANCH ● (PETERBOROUGH) – MARCH – (ELY)



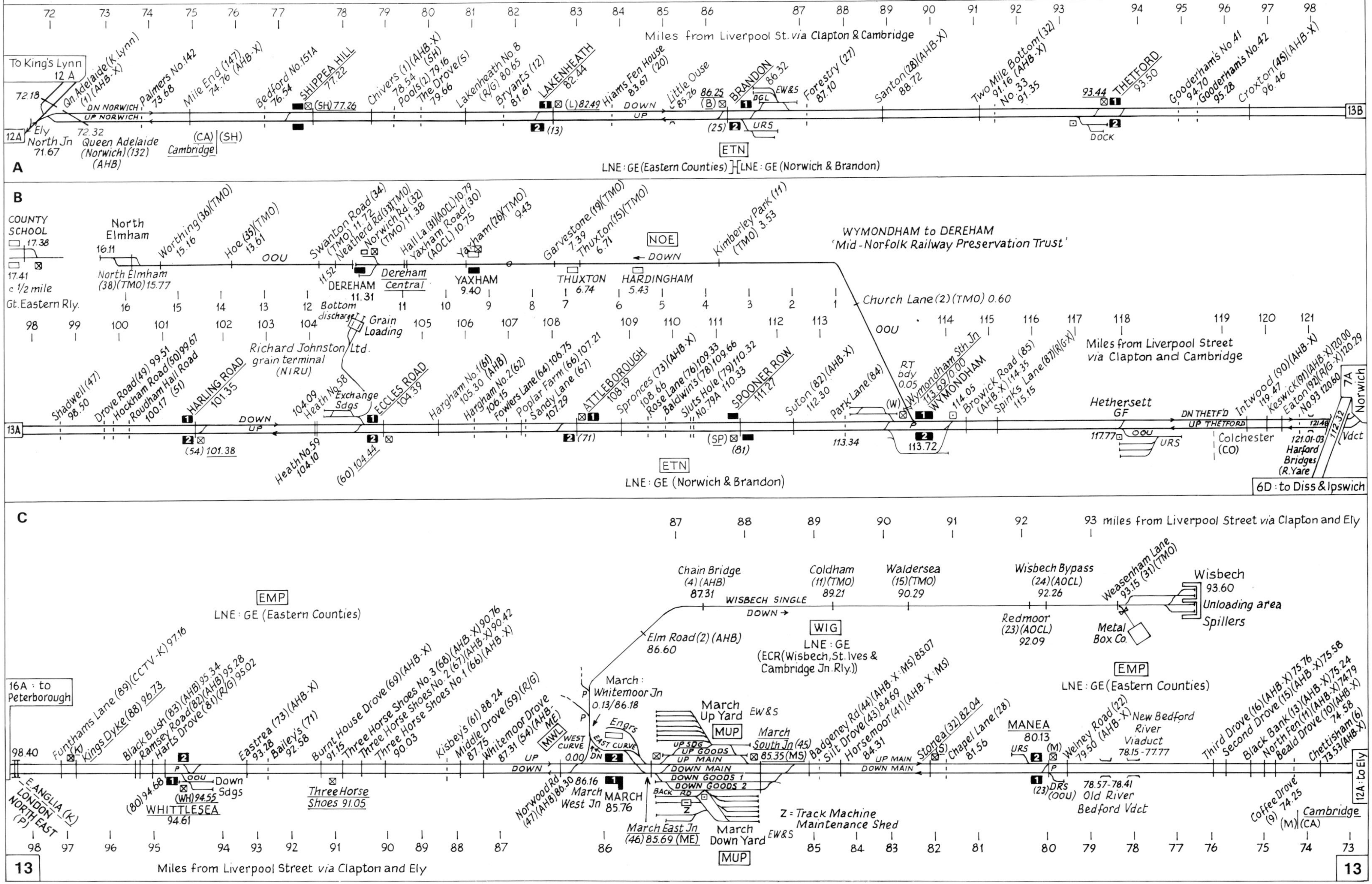

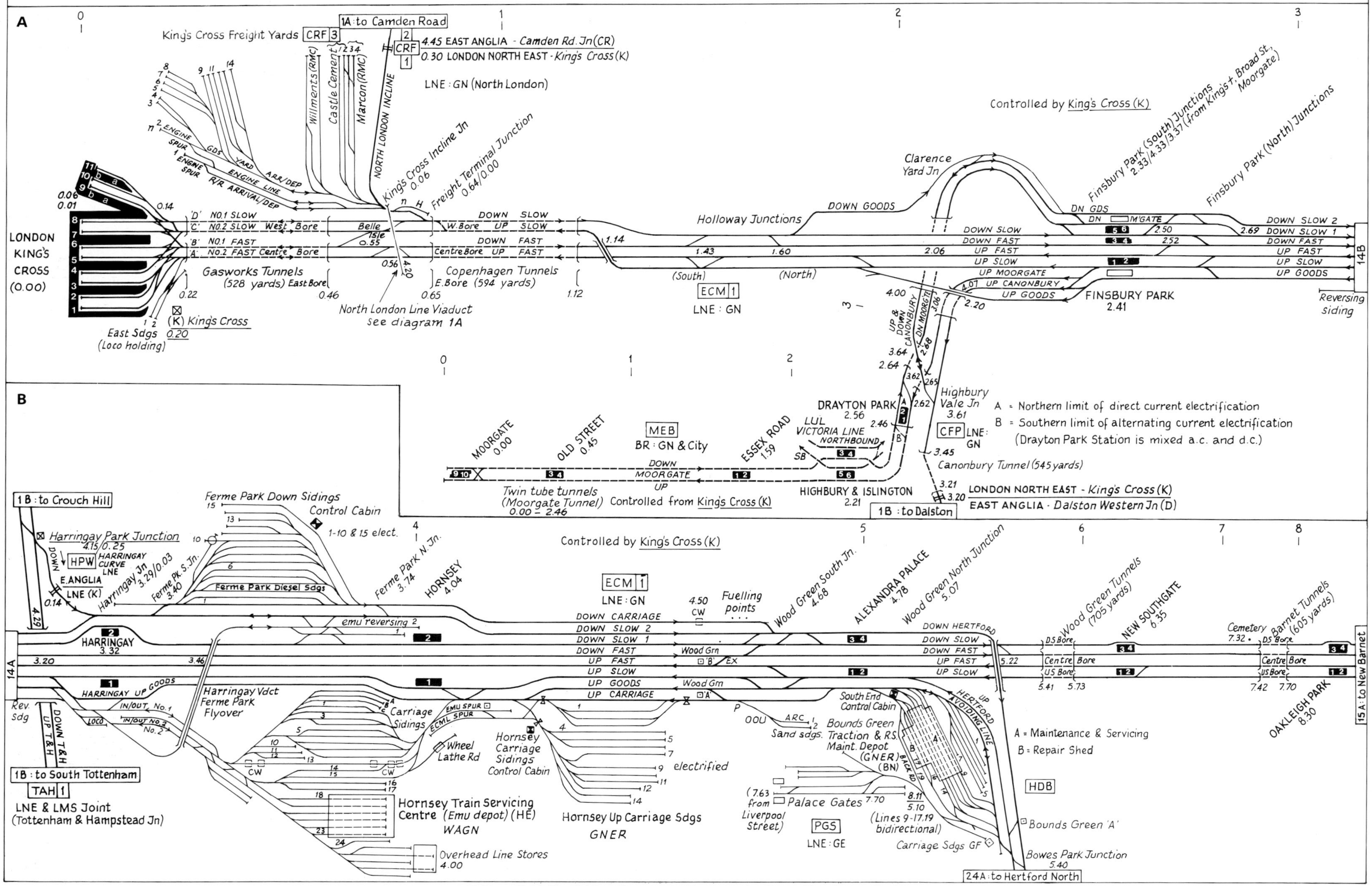
A
King's Cross Freight Yards CRF 3
1A : to Camden Road
4.45 EAST ANGLIA - Camden Rd. Jn (CR)
0.30 LONDON NORTH EAST - King's Cross (K)
LNE : GN (North London)
Willments (RMC)
Castle Cement
Marcon (RMC)
NORTH LONDON INCLINE
King's Cross Incline Jn 0.06
Freight Terminal Junction 0.64/0.00
LONDON KING'S CROSS (0.00)
Gasworks Tunnels (528 yards) East Bore
Belle Isle 0.55
North London Line Viaduct see diagram 1A
Copenhagen Tunnels E. Bore (594 yards)
East Sdgs (Loco holding)
(K) King's Cross 0.20
Holloway Junctions
DOWN GOODS
Clarence Yard Jn
Controlled by King's Cross (K)
Finsbury Park (South) Junctions 2.33/4.33/3.37 (from King's + Broad St. Moorgate)
Finsbury Park (North) Junctions
FINSBURY PARK 2.41
DOWN SLOW 2
DOWN SLOW 1
DOWN FAST
UP FAST
UP SLOW
UP GOODS
UP MOORGATE
UP CANONBURY
Reversing siding
ECM 1
LNE : GN
DRAYTON PARK 2.56
Highbury Vale Jn 3.61
CFP LNE : GN
Canonbury Tunnel (545 yards)
A = Northern limit of direct current electrification
B = Southern limit of alternating current electrification
(Drayton Park Station is mixed a.c. and d.c.)
B
MOORGATE 0.00
OLD STREET 0.45
MEB
BR : GN & City
ESSEX ROAD 1.59
LUL VICTORIA LINE NORTHBOUND
HIGHBURY & ISLINGTON 2.21
Twin tube tunnels (Moorgate Tunnel) 0.00 – 2.46
Controlled from King's Cross (K)
LONDON NORTH EAST - King's Cross (K)
EAST ANGLIA - Dalston Western Jn (D)
1B : to Dalston
1B : to Crouch Hill
Harringay Park Junction 4.15/0.25
HPW HARRINGAY CURVE LNE
E. ANGLIA LNE (K)
Harringay Jn 3.29/0.03
Ferme Pk. S. Jn. 3.40
Ferme Park Down Sidings Control Cabin
1-10 & 15 elect.
Ferme Park Diesel Sdgs
Ferme Park N. Jn. 3.74
HORNSEY 4.04
Controlled by King's Cross (K)
emu reversing
HARRINGAY 3.32
Harringay Vdct Ferme Park Flyover
Carriage Sidings
EMU SPUR
ECML SPUR
Wheel Lathe Rd
Hornsey Carriage Sidings Control Cabin
Hornsey Train Servicing Centre (Emu depot) (HE) WAGN
Overhead Line Stores 4.00
Hornsey Up Carriage Sdgs GNER
electrified
1B : to South Tottenham
TAH 1
LNE & LMS Joint (Tottenham & Hampstead Jn)
DOWN CARRIAGE
UP CARRIAGE
Fuelling points
Wood Green South Jn. 4.68
ALEXANDRA PALACE 4.78
Wood Green North Junction 5.07
DOWN HERTFORD
UP HERTFORD AVOIDING LINE
South End Control Cabin
Bounds Green Traction & RS Maint. Depot (GNER) (BN)
Sand sdgs.
(7.63 from Liverpool Street)
Palace Gates 7.70
(Lines 9-17.19 bidirectional)
PGS
LNE : GE
Carriage Sdgs GF
A = Maintenance & Servicing
B = Repair Shed
HDB
Bounds Green 'A'
Bowes Park Junction 5.40
24A : to Hertford North
Wood Green Tunnels (705 yards)
NEW SOUTHGATE 6.35
Cemetery 7.32
Barnet Tunnels (605 yards)
OAKLEIGH PARK 8.30
15A : to New Barnet

# EAST COAST MAIN LINE : NEW BARNET – HITCHIN – (PETERBOROUGH)



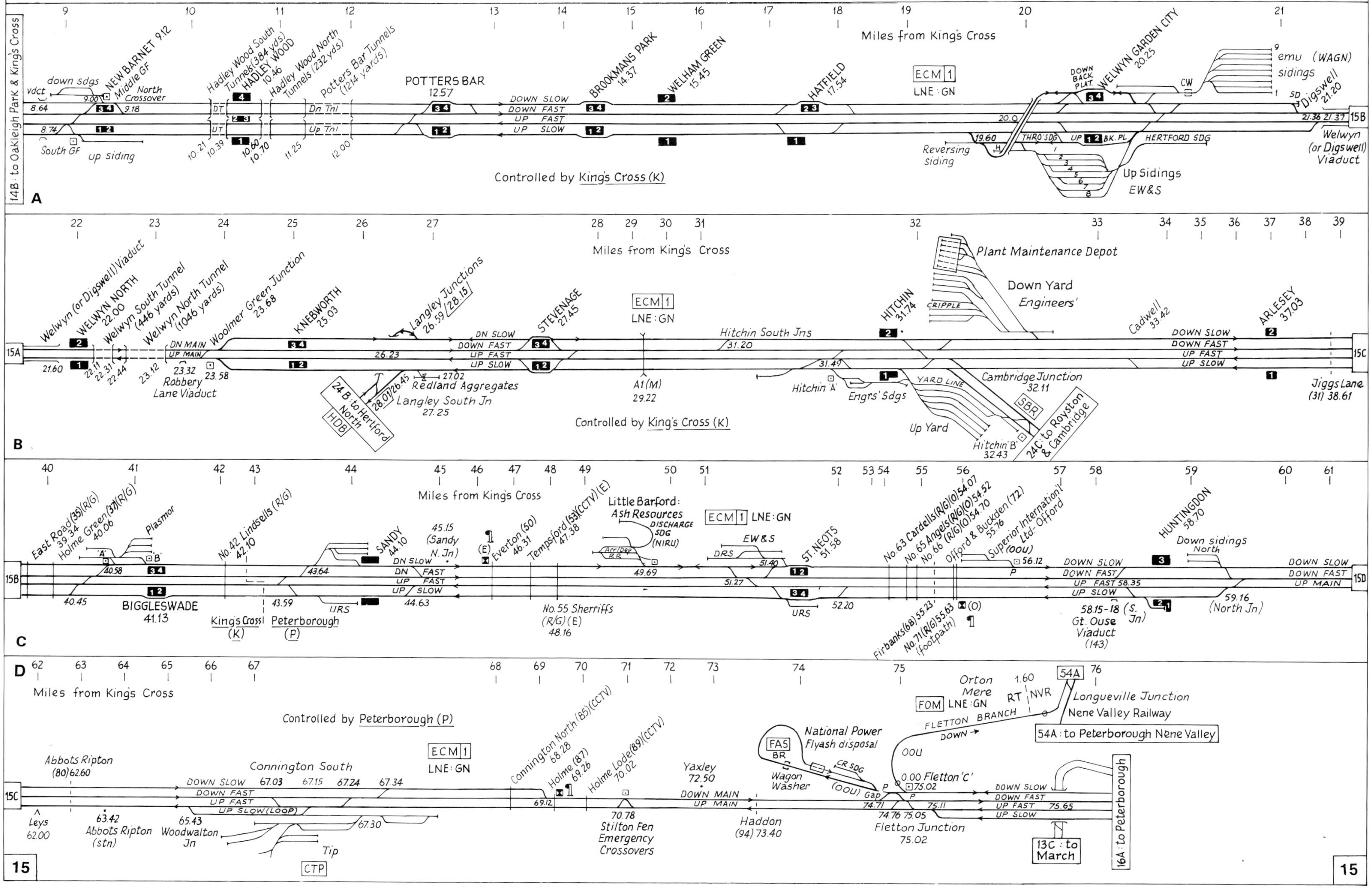

# EAST COAST MAIN LINE : PETERBOROUGH – GRANTHAM – NEWARK



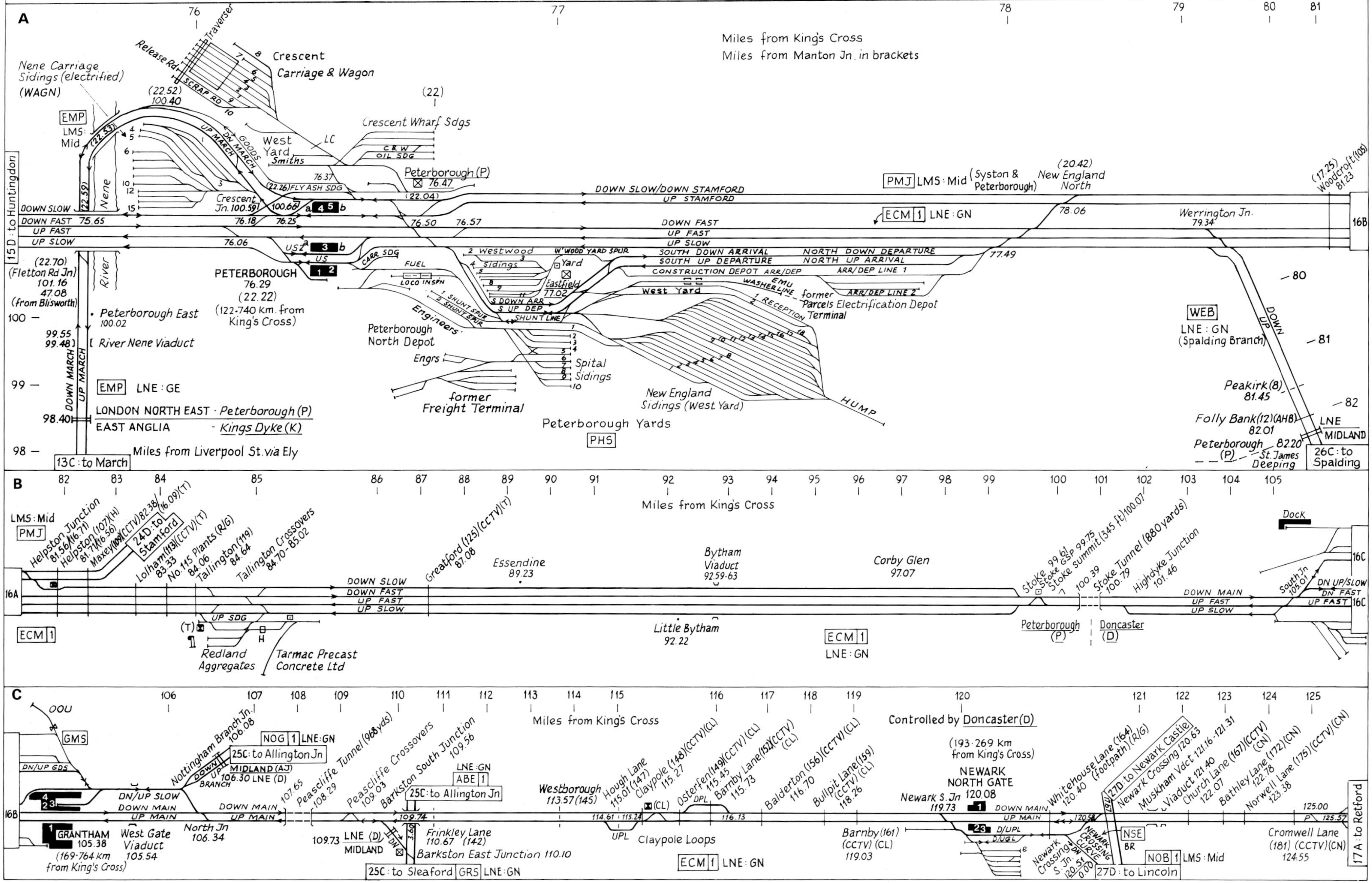

# EAST COAST MAIN LINE : (NEWARK) – RETFORD – DONCASTER



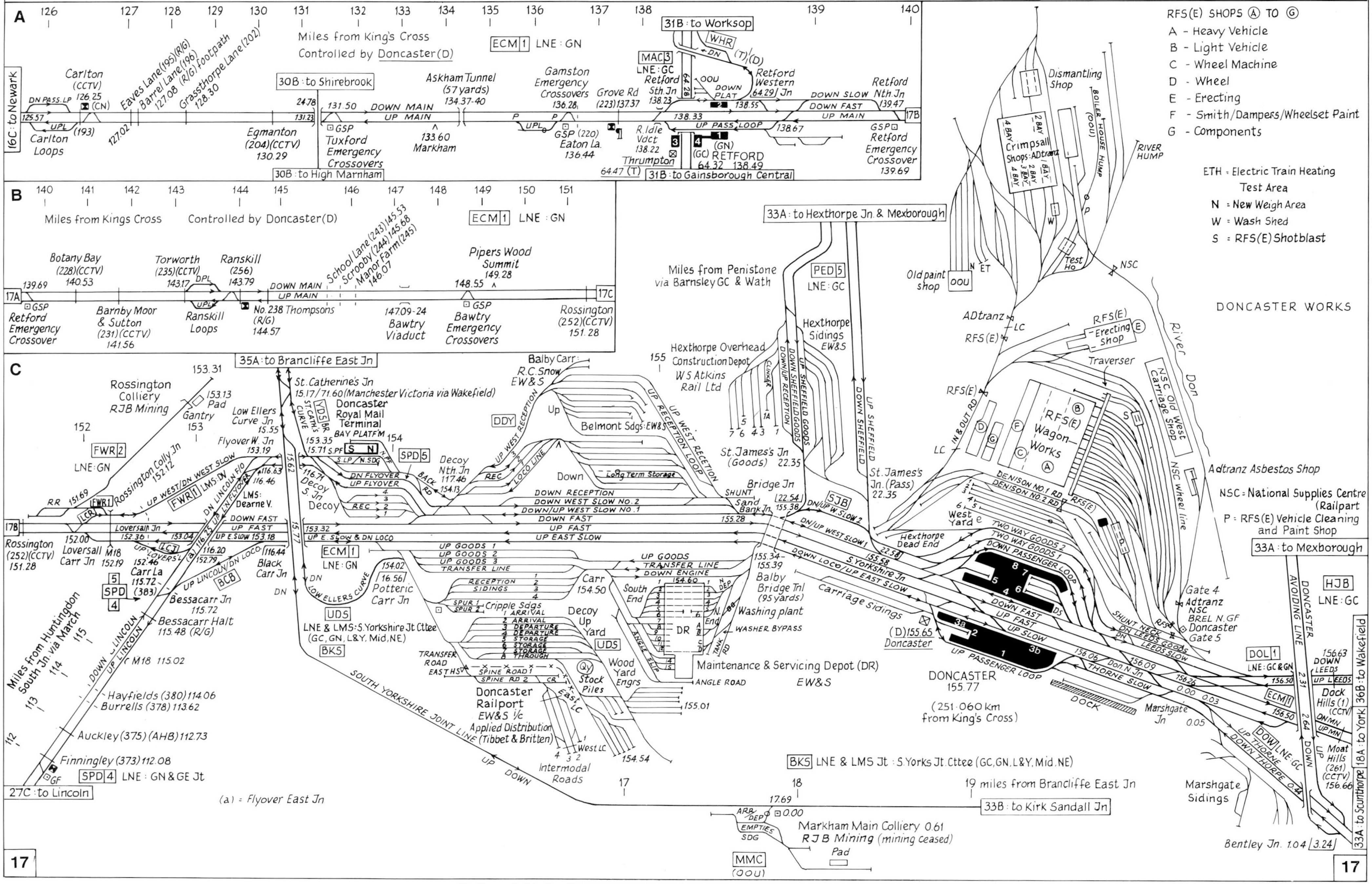

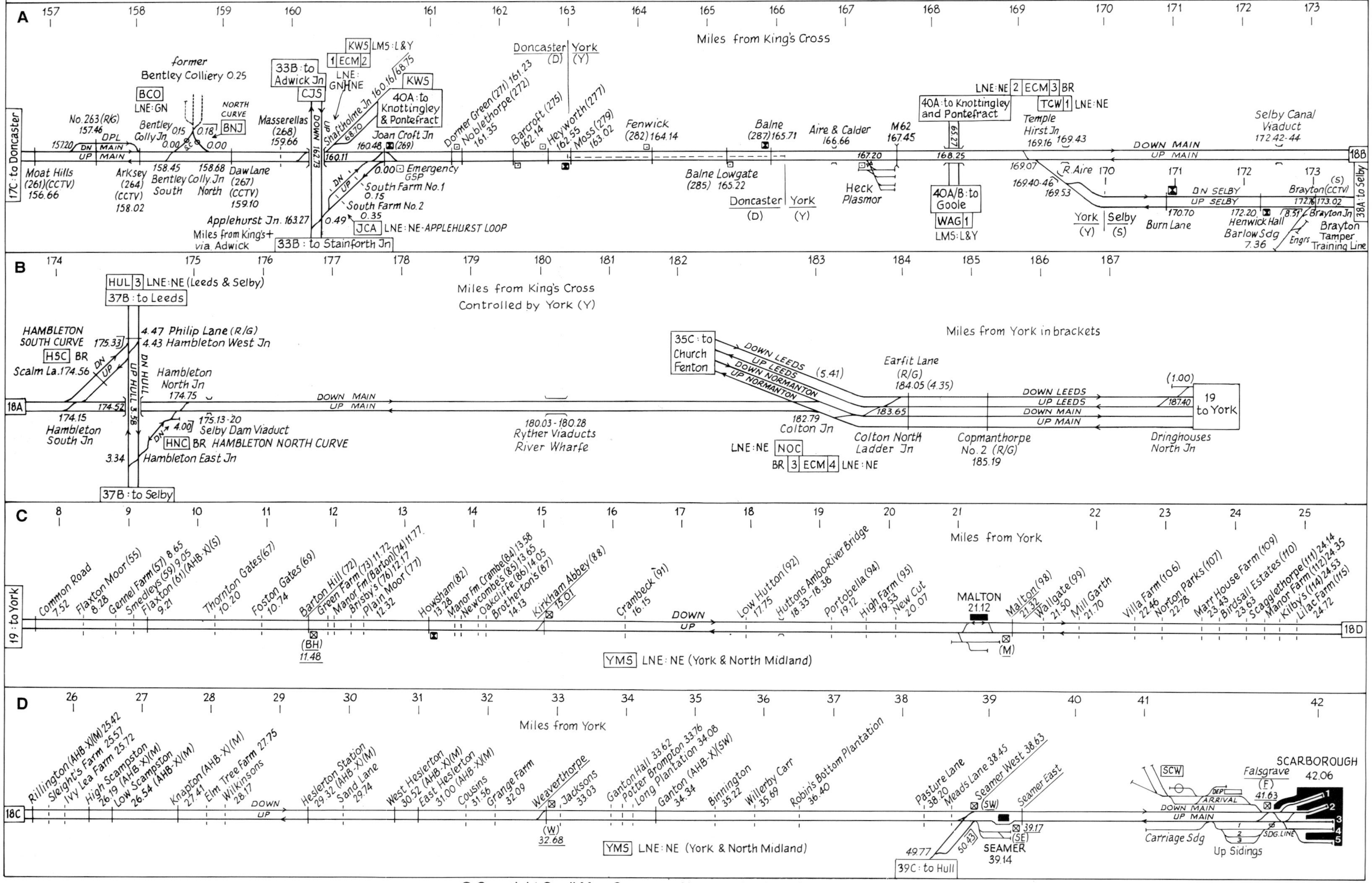
A
Miles from King's Cross
17C: to Doncaster
Moat Hills (261)(CCTV) 156.66
No. 263 (R/G) 157.46
DPL
DN MAIN
UP MAIN
Arksey (264) (CCTV) 158.02
former Bentley Colliery 0.25
BCO LNE:GN
Bentley Colly Jn
158.45 Bentley Colly Jn South
158.68 Bentley Colly Jn North
NORTH CURVE BNJ
Daw Lane (267) (CCTV) 159.10
Masserellas (268) 159.66
33B: to Adwick Jn
CJS
DOWN 162.73
Applehurst Jn. 163.27
Miles from King's+ via Adwick
33B: to Stainforth Jn
KW5 LMS: L&Y
1 ECM 2
LNE: GN NE
Shaftholme Jn 160.16/68.75
KW5
40A: to Knottingley & Pontefract
Joan Croft Jn 160.48 (269)
Emergency GSP 0.00
South Farm No. 1 0.15
South Farm No. 2 0.35
JCA LNE: NE · APPLEHURST LOOP
Dormer Green (271) 161.23
Noblethorpe (272) 161.35
Doncaster (D) | York (Y)
Barcroft (275) 162.14
Heyworth (277) 162.55
Moss (279) 163.02
Fenwick (282) 164.14
Balne (287) 165.71
Balne Lowgate (285) 165.22
Doncaster (D) | York (Y)
Aire & Calder 166.66
Heck Plasmor
M62 167.45
40A: to Knottingley and Pontefract
65.27
168.25
40A/B: to Goole
WAG 1
LMS: L&Y
LNE: NE 2 ECM 3 BR
TCW 1 LNE: NE
Temple Hirst Jn 169.16 169.43
R. Aire
York (Y) | Selby (S)
DOWN MAIN
UP MAIN
DN SELBY
UP SELBY
Burn Lane 170.70
Henwick Hall 172.20
Barlow Sdg 7.36
Selby Canal Viaduct 172.42-44
Brayton (CCTV) (S)
Brayton Jn
Brayton Tamper Training Line
Engrs
38A: to Selby
18B
B
Miles from King's Cross
Controlled by York (Y)
HUL 3 LNE: NE (Leeds & Selby)
37B: to Leeds
HAMBLETON SOUTH CURVE 175.33
HSC BR
Scalm La. 174.56
4.47 Philip Lane (R/G)
4.43 Hambleton West Jn
Hambleton North Jn 174.75
18A
174.15 Hambleton South Jn
UP HULL 3.58
DN HULL
175.13-20 Selby Dam Viaduct
HNC BR HAMBLETON NORTH CURVE
3.34 Hambleton East Jn
37B: to Selby
DOWN MAIN
UP MAIN
180.03-180.28 Ryther Viaducts River Wharfe
Miles from York in brackets
35C: to Church Fenton
DOWN LEEDS
UP LEEDS
DOWN NORMANTON
UP NORMANTON
182.79 Colton Jn
LNE: NE NOC
BR 3 ECM 4 LNE: NE
Earfit Lane (R/G) 184.05 (4.35)
Colton North Ladder Jn
Copmanthorpe No. 2 (R/G) 185.19
Dringhouses North Jn
19 to York
C
Miles from York
19: to York
Common Road 7.52
Flaxton Moor (55) 8.28
Gennel Farm (57) 8.65
Smedleys (59) 9.05
Flaxton (61) (AHB-X) (S) 9.21
Thornton Gates (67) 10.20
Foston Gates (69) 10.74
Barton Hill (72)
(BH) 11.48
Green Farm (73) 11.72
Manor Fm (Barton) (74) 11.77
Brisby's (76) 12.17
Plain Moor (77) 12.32
Howsham (82) 13.28
Manor Fm Crambe (84) 13.58
Newcombes (85) 13.65
Oakcliffe (86) 14.05
Brothertons (87) 14.13
Kirkham Abbey (88) 15.01
Crambeck (91) 16.15
DOWN
UP
Low Hutton (92) 17.75
Huttons Ambo-River Bridge 18.33-18.38
Portobella (94) 19.12
High Farm (95) 19.53
New Cut 20.07
MALTON 21.12
Malton (98) 21.32
(M)
Wallgate (99) 21.50
Mill Garth 21.70
Villa Farm (106) 22.46
Norton Parks (107) 22.78
Marr House Farm (109) 23.43
Birdsall Estates (110) 23.63
Scagglethorpe (111) 24.14
Manor Farm (112) 24.35
Kilby's (114) 24.53
Lilac Farm (115) 24.72
YMS LNE: NE (York & North Midland)
18D
D
Miles from York
18C
Rillington (AHB-X)(M) 25.42
Sleights Farm 25.57
Ivy Lea Farm 25.72
High Scampston 26.19 (AHB-X)(M)
Low Scampston 26.54 (AHB-X)(M)
Knapton (AHB-X)(M) 27.41
Elm Tree Farm 27.75
Wilkinsons 28.17
DOWN
UP
Heslerton Station 29.32 (AHB-X)(M)
Sand Lane 29.74
West Heslerton 30.52 (AHB-X)(M)
East Heslerton 31.00 (AHB-X)(M)
Cousins 31.56
Grange Farm 32.09
Weaverthorpe
(W) 32.68
Jacksons 33.03
Ganton Hall 33.62
Potter Brompton 33.76
Long Plantation 34.08
Ganton (AHB-X)(SW) 34.34
Binnington 35.22
Willerby Carr 35.69
Robins Bottom Plantation 36.40
Pasture Lane 38.20
Meads Lane 38.45
Seamer West 38.63 (SW)
Seamer East 39.17 (SE)
SEAMER 39.14
49.77
50.43
39C: to Hull
YMS LNE: NE (York & North Midland)
SCW
DOWN MAIN
UP MAIN
ARRIVAL
DEP
Carriage Sdg
Up Sidings
SDG. LINE
Falsgrave (F) 41.63
SCARBOROUGH 42.06

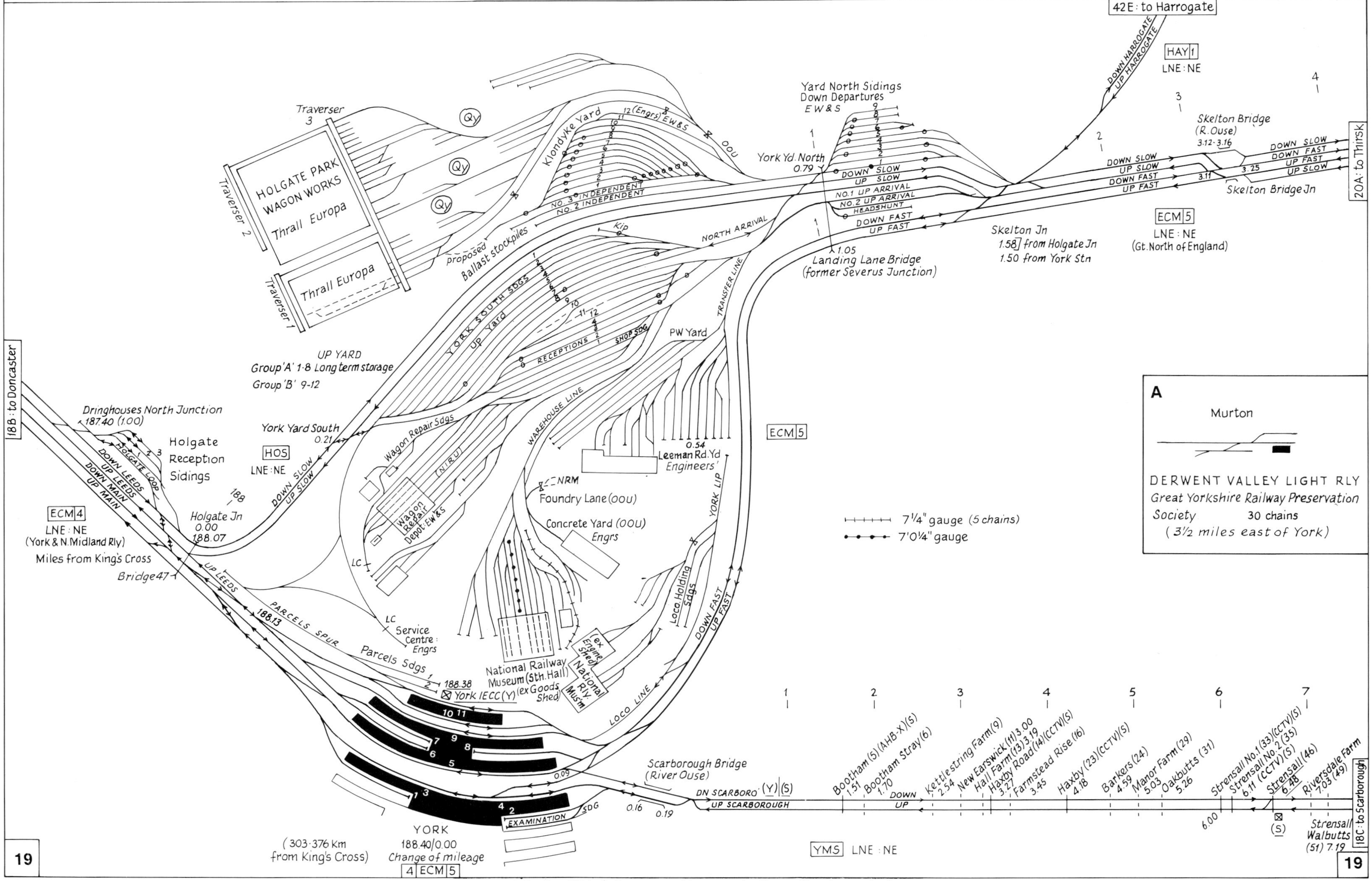
42E: to Harrogate
DOWN HARROGATE
UP HARROGATE
HAY 1
LNE : NE
20A: to Thirsk
Skelton Bridge
(R. Ouse)
3.12-3.16
DOWN SLOW
DOWN FAST
UP FAST
UP SLOW
3.25
3.11
Skelton Bridge Jn
ECM 5
LNE : NE
(Gt. North of England)
Skelton Jn
1.58 from Holgate Jn
1.50 from York Stn
Yard North Sidings
Down Departures
EW & S
York Yd. North
0.79
NO.1 UP ARRIVAL
NO.2 UP ARRIVAL
HEADSHUNT
1.05
Landing Lane Bridge
(former Severus Junction)
NORTH ARRIVAL
TRANSFER LINE
Traverser 3
HOLGATE PARK
WAGON WORKS
Thrall Europa
Traverser 2
Traverser 1
Thrall Europa
Klondyke Yard
12 (Engrs) EW & S
OOU
NO. 3 INDEPENDENT
NO. 2 INDEPENDENT
proposed
Ballast stockpiles
Qy
Kip
YORK SOUTH SDGS
Up Yard
RECEPTIONS
SHOP SDG
PW Yard
UP YARD
Group 'A' 1-8 Long term storage
Group 'B' 9-12
York Yard South
0.21
HOS
LNE : NE
DOWN SLOW
UP SLOW
Wagon Repair Sdgs
(N I R U)
Wagon Repair Depot EW & S
WAREHOUSE LINE
0.54
Leeman Rd. Yd
Engineers'
NRM
Foundry Lane (OOU)
Concrete Yard (OOU)
Engrs
YORK LIP
ECM 5
Loco Holding Sdgs
DOWN FAST
UP FAST
LOCO LINE
(ex Engine Shed)
National Rly. Mus'm
National Railway Museum (Sth. Hall)
(ex Goods Shed)
LC
Service Centre : Engrs
Parcels Sdgs
PARCELS SPUR
188.38
York IECC (Y)
188.13
Dringhouses North Junction
187.40 (1.00)
Holgate Reception Sidings
HOLGATE LOOP
DOWN LEEDS
UP LEEDS
DOWN MAIN
UP MAIN
188
Holgate Jn
0.00
188.07
18B: to Doncaster
ECM 4
LNE : NE
(York & N. Midland Rly)
Miles from King's Cross
Bridge 47
10 11
7 9 8
6 5
1 3
4 2
EXAMINATION
SDG
0.09
YORK
188.40/0.00
Change of mileage
4 ECM 5
(303·376 Km from King's Cross)
Scarborough Bridge
(River Ouse)
0.16
0.19
DN SCARBORO' (Y)|(S)
UP SCARBOROUGH
DOWN
UP
Bootham (S) (AHB-X) (S)
1.51
Bootham Stray (6)
1.70
Kettlestring Farm (9)
2.54
New Earswick (ff) 3.00
Hall Farm (13) 3.19
Haxby Road (14) (CCTV) (S)
3.27
Farmstead Rise (16)
3.45
Haxby (23) (CCTV) (S)
4.18
Barkers (24)
4.59
Manor Farm (29)
5.03
Oakbutts (31)
5.26
6.00
Strensall No.1 (33) (CCTV) (S)
Strensall No.2 (35)
6.11 (CCTV) (S)
Strensall (46)
6.48
Riversdale Farm
7.03 (49)
(S)
Strensall Walbutts
(51) 7.19
18C: to Scarborough
YMS LNE : NE
A
Murton
DERWENT VALLEY LIGHT RLY
Great Yorkshire Railway Preservation Society
30 chains
(3½ miles east of York)
7¼" gauge (5 chains)
7'0¼" gauge

# EAST COAST MAIN LINE : (YORK) – DARLINGTON – DURHAM



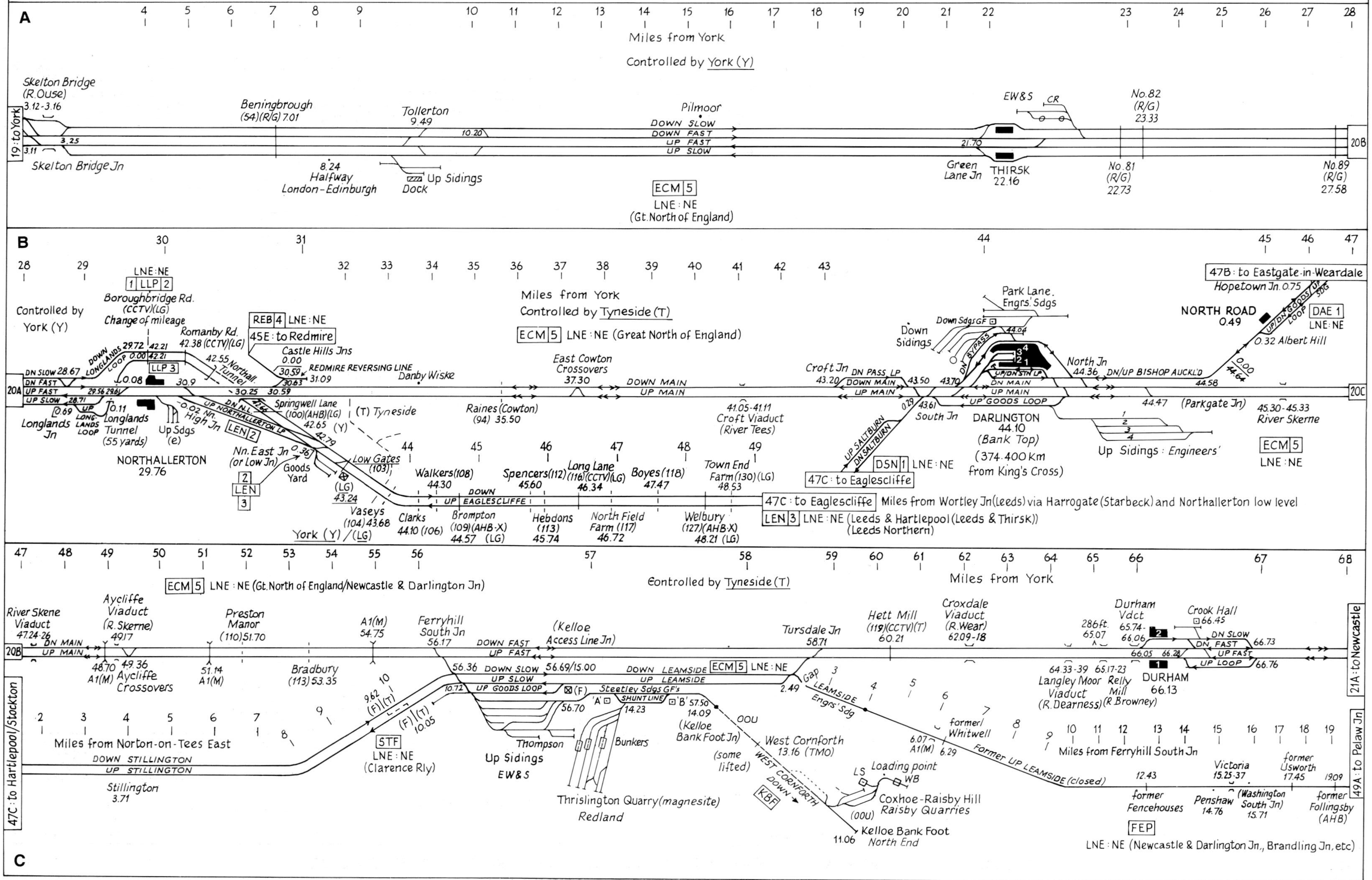

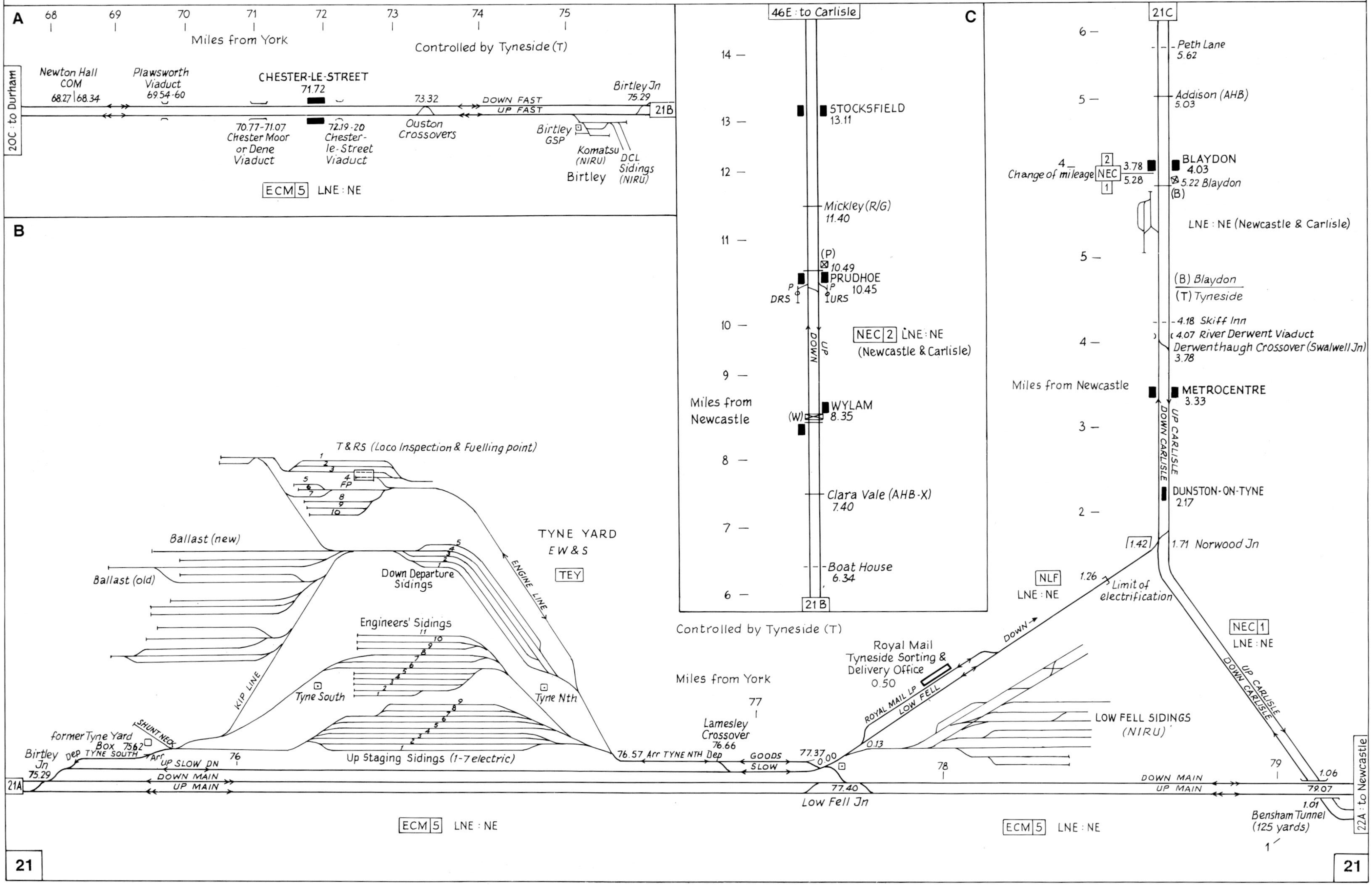
A
Miles from York
Controlled by Tyneside (T)
20C : to Durham
Newton Hall COM 68.27 68.34
Plawsworth Viaduct 69.54-60
CHESTER-LE-STREET 71.72
70.77-71.07 Chester Moor or Dene Viaduct
72.19-20 Chester-le-Street Viaduct
73.32
Ouston Crossovers
DOWN FAST
UP FAST
Birtley Jn 75.29
21B
Birtley GSP
Komatsu (NIRU)
DCL Sidings (NIRU)
Birtley
ECM 5 LNE : NE
B
T & RS (Loco Inspection & Fuelling point)
FP
Ballast (new)
Ballast (old)
Down Departure Sidings
TYNE YARD
EW & S
TEY
ENGINE LINE
Engineers' Sidings
KIP LINE
Tyne South
Tyne Nth
SHUNT NECK
former Tyne Yard Box 75.62
Birtley Jn 75.29
DEP TYNE SOUTH ARR
UP SLOW DN
DOWN MAIN
UP MAIN
21A
Up Staging Sidings (1-7 electric)
76.57 Arr TYNE NTH Dep
Miles from York
Lamesley Crossover 76.66
GOODS
SLOW
77.37 0.00
77.40
Low Fell Jn
Royal Mail Tyneside Sorting & Delivery Office 0.50
ROYAL MAIL LP
LOW FELL
0.13
DOWN
LOW FELL SIDINGS (NIRU)
ECM 5 LNE : NE
ECM 5 LNE : NE
1.06
79.07
1.01
Bensham Tunnel (125 yards)
22A : to Newcastle
C
46E : to Carlisle
STOCKSFIELD 13.11
Mickley (R/G) 11.40
(P) 10.49
PRUDHOE 10.45
DRS
URS
NEC 2 LNE : NE (Newcastle & Carlisle)
DOWN
UP
Miles from Newcastle
WYLAM 8.35
(W)
Clara Vale (AHB-X) 7.40
Boat House 6.34
21B
Controlled by Tyneside (T)
21C
Peth Lane 5.62
Addison (AHB) 5.03
Change of mileage
NEC 2 3.78
NEC 1 5.28
BLAYDON 4.03
5.22 Blaydon (B)
LNE : NE (Newcastle & Carlisle)
(B) Blaydon
(T) Tyneside
4.18 Skiff Inn
4.07 River Derwent Viaduct
Derwenthaugh Crossover (Swalwell Jn) 3.78
Miles from Newcastle
METROCENTRE 3.33
DOWN CARLISLE
UP CARLISLE
DUNSTON-ON-TYNE 2.17
1.42
1.71 Norwood Jn
NLF LNE : NE
1.26 Limit of electrification
NEC 1 LNE : NE
UP CARLISLE
DOWN CARLISLE

A

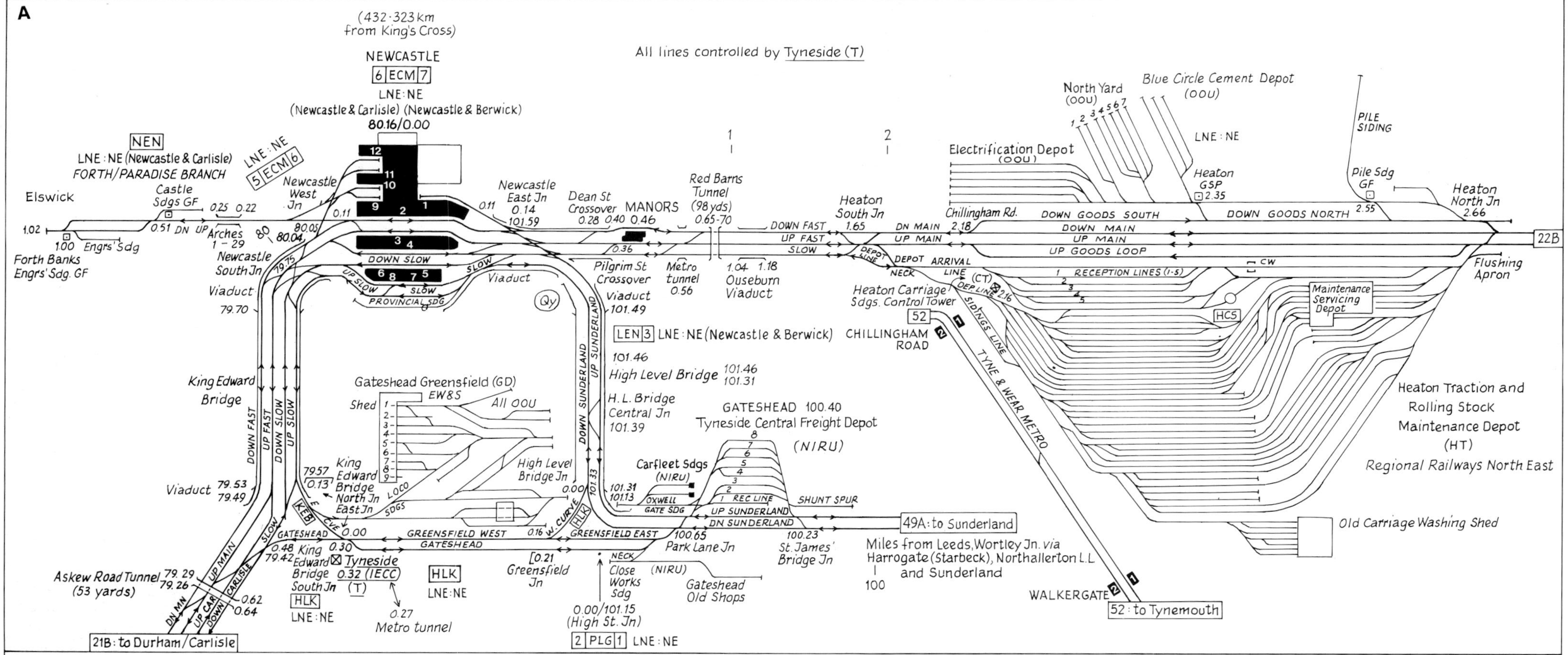


B

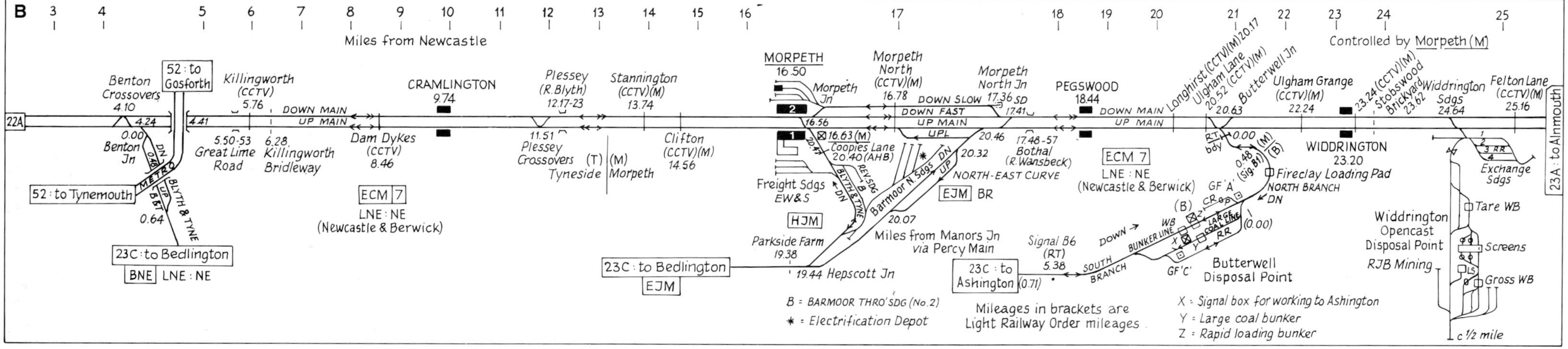


B = BARMOOR THRO' SDG (No. 2)
* = Electrification Depot

Mileages in brackets are Light Railway Order mileages

X = Signal box for working to Ashington
Y = Large coal bunker
Z = Rapid loading bunker

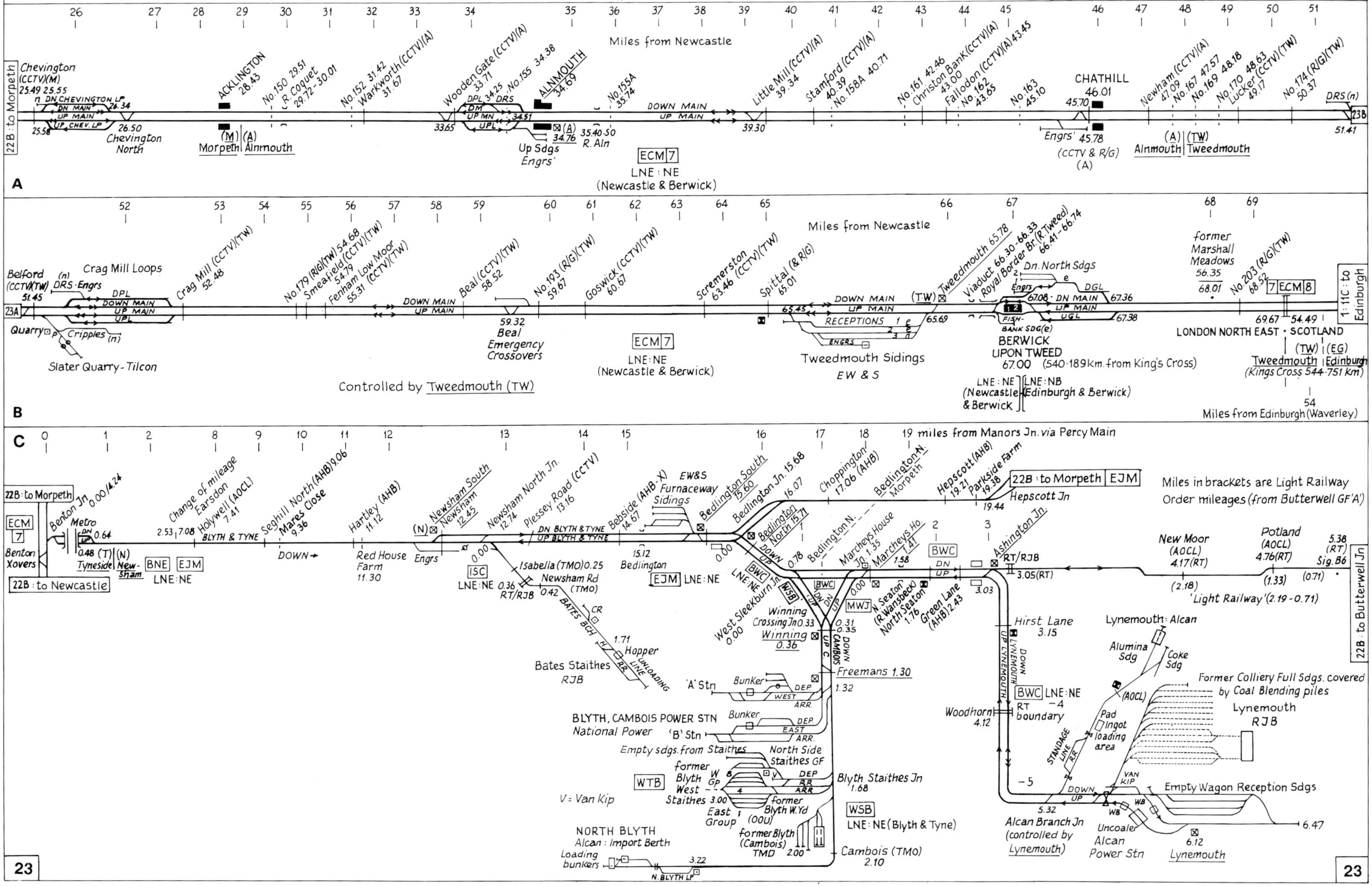
A
Miles from Newcastle
22B : to Morpeth
Chevington (CCTV)(M) 25.49 25.55
DN CHEVINGTON LP 26.34
DN MAIN
UP MAIN
UP CHEV. LP
25.58
26.50 Chevington North
ACKLINGTON 28.43
(M) | (A)
Morpeth | Alnmouth
No.150 29.51
R. Coquet 29.72 - 30.01
No.152 31.42
Warkworth (CCTV)(A) 31.67
Wooden Gate (CCTV)(A) 33.71
DPL 34.25 DRS
No.155 34.38
ALNMOUTH 34.69
33.65
34.51
34.76
Up Sdgs Engrs'
35.40 50 R. Aln
No.155A 35.74
DOWN MAIN
UP MAIN
ECM 7
LNE : NE (Newcastle & Berwick)
Little Mill (CCTV)(A) 39.34
39.30
Stamford (CCTV)(A) 40.39
No.158A 40.71
No.161 42.46
Christon Bank (CCTV)(A) 43.00
Falloden (CCTV)(A) 43.45
No.162 43.65
No.163 45.10
CHATHILL 46.01
45.70
Engrs' 45.78
(CCTV & R/G) (A)
Newham (CCTV)(A) 47.09
No.167 47.57
No.169 48.18
No.170 48.63
Lucker (CCTV)(TW) 49.17
(A) | (TW)
Alnmouth | Tweedmouth
No.174 (R/G)(TW) 50.37
DRS (n)
23B
51.41
B
Miles from Newcastle
Belford (CCTV)(TW) 51.45
(n) DRS · Engrs
Crag Mill Loops
DPL
DOWN MAIN
UP MAIN
UPL
23A
Quarry
Cripples (n)
Slater Quarry - Tilcon
Crag Mill (CCTV)(TW) 52.48
No.179 (R/G)(TW) 54.68
Smeafield (CCTV)(TW) 54.79
Fenham Low Moor (CCTV)(TW) 55.31
Beal (CCTV)(TW) 58.52
59.32 Beal Emergency Crossovers
No.193 (R/G)(TW) 59.67
Goswick (CCTV)(TW) 60.67
ECM 7
LNE : NE (Newcastle & Berwick)
Controlled by Tweedmouth (TW)
Scremerston (CCTV)(TW) 63.46
Spittal (& R/G) 65.01
65.45
DOWN MAIN
UP MAIN
RECEPTIONS
ENGRS
Tweedmouth Sidings
EW & S
(TW)
Tweedmouth 65.78
65.69
Viaduct 66.30 - 66.33
Royal Border Br. (R. Tweed) 66.41 - 66.74
Dn. North Sdgs
DGL
Engrs
67.08 DN MAIN
UP MAIN
UGL
67.36
67.38
FISH-BANK SDG (e)
BERWICK UPON TWEED 67.00 (540·189 km. from King's Cross)
LNE : NE (Newcastle & Berwick)
LNE : NB (Edinburgh & Berwick)
former Marshall Meadows 56.35 68.01
No.203 (R/G)(TW) 68.52
7 ECM 8
69.67 54.49
LONDON NORTH EAST · SCOTLAND
(TW) | (EG)
Tweedmouth | Edinburgh
(Kings Cross 544·751 km)
1 : 11C : to Edinburgh
54
Miles from Edinburgh (Waverley)
C
19 miles from Manors Jn. via Percy Main
22B : to Morpeth
ECM 7
Benton Xovers
22B : to Newcastle
Benton Jn 0.00/4.24
Metro
0.64
0.48 (T) | (N)
Tyneside | New-sham
BNE EJM
LNE : NE
2.53 7.08
Change of mileage Earsdon
Holywell (AOCL) 7.41
BLYTH & TYNE
Seghill North (AHB) 9.06
Mares Close 9.36
DOWN →
Hartley (AHB) 11.12
Red House Farm 11.30
(N)
Newsham South
Newsham 12.45
Engrs
0.00
ISC
LNE : NE 0.36 RT/RJB
Newsham North Jn. 12.74
Plessey Road (CCTV) 13.16
Isabella (TMO) 0.25
Newsham Rd (TMO) 0.42
BATES BCH
CR
1.71 Hopper
UNLOADING LINE
RR
Bates Staithes RJB
DN BLYTH & TYNE
UP BLYTH & TYNE
Bebside (AHB-X) 14.67
EW&S Furnaceway Sidings
15.12 Bedlington
EJM LNE : NE
Bedlington South 15.60
Bedlington Jn. 15.68 16.07
Bedlington North 15.71
Choppington 17.06 (AHB)
Bedlington N. - Morpeth
Hepscott (AHB) 19.21
Parkside Farm 19.38
22B : to Morpeth EJM
19.44
Hepscott Jn
Miles in brackets are Light Railway Order mileages (from Butterwell GF 'A')
BWC LNE:NE
WSB
West Sleekburn Jn 0.00
0.78
Bedlington N.
Marcheys House Jn 1.35
Marcheys Ho. 1.41 1.58
BWC
MWJ
N. Seaton (R. Wansbeck)
North Seaton 1.76
Green Lane (AHB) 2.43
Winning Crossing Jn 0.33
Winning 0.36
0.31 0.35
DOWN CAMBOIS
UP C.
Freemans 1.30
1.32
'A' Stn
Bunker
DEP. WEST ARR.
BLYTH, CAMBOIS POWER STN
National Power
'B' Stn
Bunker
DEP. EAST ARR.
Empty sdgs. from Staithes
North Side Staithes GF
former Blyth West Staithes 3.00
W GP
DEP RR ARR
WTB
V = Van Kip
East Group
former Blyth W. Yd (OOU)
former Blyth (Cambois) TMD 2.00
Blyth Staithes Jn 1.68
WSB
LNE : NE (Blyth & Tyne)
Cambois (TMO) 2.10
NORTH BLYTH
Alcan : Import Berth
Loading bunkers
3.22
N. BLYTH LP
BWC
DN
UP
Ashington Jn.
RT/RJB
3.05 (RT)
3.03
New Moor (AOCL) 4.17 (RT)
(2.18)
Potland (AOCL) 4.76 (RT)
(1.33)
(0.71)
5.38 (RT) Sig. B6
'Light Railway' (2.19 - 0.71)
22B : to Butterwell Jn
Hirst Lane 3.15
UP LYNEMOUTH
DOWN LYNEMOUTH
BWC LNE : NE
RT boundary
-4
Woodhorn 4.12
-5
Lynemouth : Alcan
Alumina Sdg
Coke Sdg
(AOCL)
Pad Ingot loading area
STANDAGE LINE RR
Former Colliery Full Sdgs. covered by Coal Blending piles
Lynemouth RJB
VAN KIP
DOWN
UP
WB
Empty Wagon Reception Sdgs
5.32
Alcan Branch Jn (controlled by Lynemouth)
Uncoaler Alcan Power Stn
6.12 Lynemouth
6.47

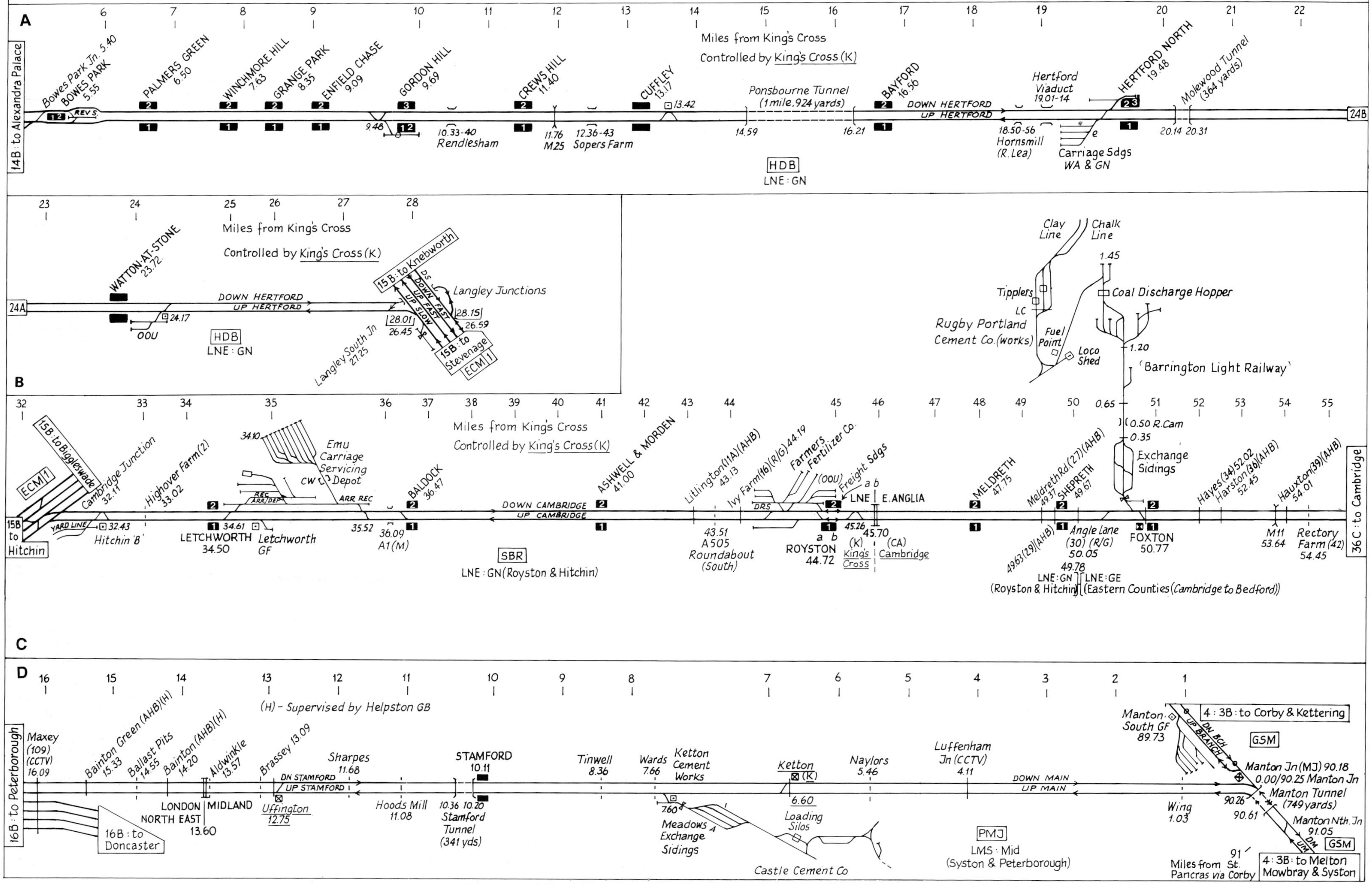
A
14B: to Alexandria Palace
Bowes Park Jn. 5.40
BOWES PARK 5.55
PALMERS GREEN 6.50
WINCHMORE HILL 7.63
GRANGE PARK 8.35
ENFIELD CHASE 9.09
GORDON HILL 9.69
9.48
10.33-40 Rendlesham
CREWS HILL 11.40
11.76 M25
12.36-43 Sopers Farm
CUFFLEY 13.17
13.42
Miles from King's Cross
Controlled by King's Cross (K)
Ponsbourne Tunnel (1 mile, 924 yards)
14.59
16.21
BAYFORD 16.56
DOWN HERTFORD
UP HERTFORD
HDB
LNE: GN
Hertford Viaduct 19.01-14
18.50-56 Hornsmill (R. Lea)
Carriage Sdgs WA & GN
HERTFORD NORTH 19.48
Molewood Tunnel (364 yards)
20.14 20.31
24B
B
24A
WATTON-AT-STONE 23.72
24.17
OOU
HDB
LNE: GN
Miles from King's Cross
Controlled by King's Cross (K)
DOWN HERTFORD
UP HERTFORD
15B: to Knebworth
DOWN FAST
UP FAST
UP SLOW
Langley Junctions
28.15
26.59
28.01
26.45
Langley South Jn 27.25
15B: to Stevenage
ECM1
Clay Line
Chalk Line
1.45
Tipplers
LC
Coal Discharge Hopper
Rugby Portland Cement Co. (works)
Fuel Point
Loco Shed
1.20
'Barrington Light Railway'
0.65
0.50 R. Cam
0.35
Exchange Sidings
15B to Hitchin
15B: to Biggleswade
ECM1
YARD LINE
Cambridge Junction 32.11
32.43 Hitchin 'B'
Highover Farm (2) 33.02
LETCHWORTH 34.50
34.61
Letchworth GF
34.10
Emu Carriage Servicing Depot
CW
ARR REC
ARR DEP
35.52
36.09 A1(M)
BALDOCK 36.47
Miles from King's Cross
Controlled by King's Cross (K)
DOWN CAMBRIDGE
UP CAMBRIDGE
SBR
LNE: GN (Royston & Hitchin)
ASHWELL & MORDEN 41.00
Litlington (11A)(AHB) 43.13
43.51 A505 Roundabout (South)
Ivy Farm (16)(R/G) 44.19
Farmers Fertilizer Co.
(OOU)
DRS
Freight Sdgs
ROYSTON 44.72
a b
45.26
45.70
LNE | E. ANGLIA
(K) King's Cross
(CA) Cambridge
MELDRETH 47.75
Meldreth Rd. (27)(AHB) 49.37
4963 (29)(AHB)
SHEPRETH 49.67
Angle lane (30) (R/G) 50.05
49.78
LNE: GN (Royston & Hitchin)
LNE: GE (Eastern Counties (Cambridge to Bedford))
FOXTON 50.77
Hayes (34) 52.02
Harston (36)(AHB) 52.45
M11 53.64
Hauxton (39)(AHB) 54.01
Rectory Farm (42) 54.45
36C: to Cambridge
C
D
16B: to Peterborough
Maxey (109) (CCTV) 16.09
16B: to Doncaster
Bainton Green (AHB)(H) 15.33
Ballast Pits 14.55
Bainton (AHB)(H) 14.20
LONDON NORTH EAST | MIDLAND 13.60
Aldwinkle 13.57
Brassey 13.09
(H) - Supervised by Helpston GB
Uffington 12.75
DN STAMFORD
UP STAMFORD
Sharpes 11.68
Hoods Mill 11.08
STAMFORD 10.11
10.36 10.20 Stamford Tunnel (341 yds)
Tinwell 8.36
Wards 7.66
Ketton Cement Works
7.60
Meadows 4 Exchange Sidings
Ketton (K)
6.60
Loading Silos
Castle Cement Co
Naylors 5.46
Luffenham Jn (CCTV) 4.11
PMJ
LMS: Mid (Syston & Peterborough)
DOWN MAIN
UP MAIN
Wing 1.03
Manton South GF 89.73
4: 3B: to Corby & Kettering
DN BCH
UP BRANCH
GSM
Manton Jn (MJ) 90.18
0.00/90.25 Manton Jn
Manton Tunnel (749 yards)
90.26
90.61
Manton Nth. Jn 91.05
DM
UM
GSM
91
Miles from St. Pancras via Corby
4: 3B: to Melton Mowbray & Syston

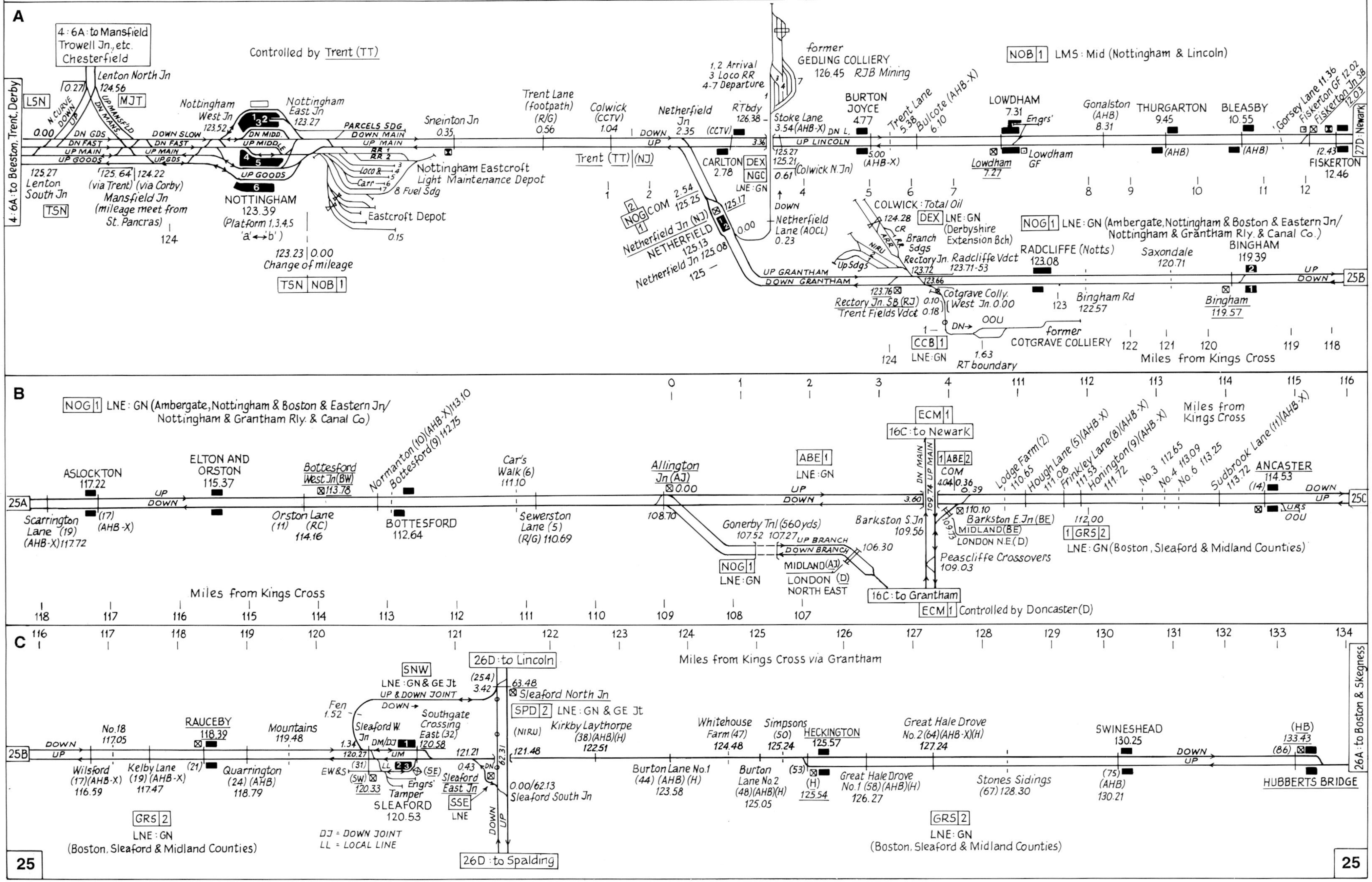
A
4: 6A: to Mansfield
Trowell Jn., etc.
Chesterfield
Controlled by Trent (TT)
4: 6A: to Beeston, Trent, Derby
LSN
MJT
Lenton North Jn
124.56
0.27
0.00
125.27
Lenton
South Jn
TSN
125.64 (via Trent)
124.22 (via Corby)
Mansfield Jn
(mileage meet from St. Pancras)
124
Nottingham
West Jn
123.52
Nottingham
East Jn
123.27
NOTTINGHAM
123.39
(Platform 1,3,4,5 'a' ↔ 'b')
123.23 | 0.00
Change of mileage
TSN NOB 1
PARCELS SDG
DOWN MAIN
UP MAIN
DOWN SLOW
DN FAST
UP MAIN
UP GOODS
Sneinton Jn
0.35
Nottingham Eastcroft
Light Maintenance Depot
8 Fuel Sdg
Eastcroft Depot
0.15
Trent Lane
(footpath)
(R/G)
0.56
Colwick
(CCTV)
1.04
Trent (TT) (NJ)
2 NOG COM 1
Netherfield Jn (NJ)
NETHERFIELD
125.13
Netherfield Jn 125.08
125
Netherfield
Jn
2.35
CARLTON
2.78
DEX
NGC
LNE: GN
1,2 Arrival
3 Loco RR
4-7 Departure
RTbdy
126.38
former
GEDLING COLLIERY
126.45 RJB Mining
Stoke Lane
3.54 (AHB-X)
UP LINCOLN
125.27
125.21 (Colwick N.Jn)
0.61
Netherfield
Lane (AOCL)
0.23
BURTON
JOYCE
4.77
5.00 (AHB-X)
Trent Lane 5.38
Bulcote (AHB-X) 6.10
COLWICK: Total Oil
124.28
DEX LNE: GN
(Derbyshire Extension Bch)
Branch Sdgs
Up Sdgs
Rectory Jn. 123.72
Radcliffe Vdct 123.71-53
UP GRANTHAM
DOWN GRANTHAM
123.76
Rectory Jn. SB (RJ)
Trent Fields Vdct
Cotgrave Colly. West Jn. 0.00
OOU
CCB 1
LNE: GN
1.63
RT boundary
former
COTGRAVE COLLIERY
LOWDHAM
7.31
Engrs'
Lowdham
7.27
Lowdham GF
NOB 1 LMS: Mid (Nottingham & Lincoln)
NOG 1 LNE: GN (Ambergate, Nottingham & Boston & Eastern Jn/ Nottingham & Grantham Rly. & Canal Co.)
RADCLIFFE (Notts)
123.08
Saxondale
120.71
BINGHAM
119.39
Bingham Rd
122.57
Bingham
119.57
Gonalston
(AHB)
8.31
THURGARTON
9.45
BLEASBY
10.55
Gorsey Lane 11.36
Fiskerton GF 12.02
Fiskerton Jn SB 12.03
27D: Newark
FISKERTON
12.46
25B
Miles from Kings Cross
B
NOG 1 LNE: GN (Ambergate, Nottingham & Boston & Eastern Jn/ Nottingham & Grantham Rly. & Canal Co)
25A
ASLOCKTON
117.22
Scarrington Lane (19) (AHB-X) 117.72
(17) (AHB-X)
ELTON AND
ORSTON
115.37
Orston Lane (11) (RC) 114.16
Bottesford West Jn (BW)
113.78
Normanton (10) (AHB-X) 113.10
Bottesford (9) 112.75
BOTTESFORD
112.64
Car's Walk (6) 111.10
Sewerston Lane (5) (R/G) 110.69
Allington Jn (AJ)
0.00
108.70
Gonerby Tnl (560yds)
107.52 107.27
UP BRANCH
DOWN BRANCH
106.30
NOG 1
LNE: GN
MIDLAND (AJ)
LONDON (D)
NORTH EAST
ABE 1
LNE: GN
ECM 1
16C: to Newark
1 ABE 2
COM
Barkston S.Jn
109.56
Barkston E.Jn (BE)
MIDLAND (BE)
LONDON N.E. (D)
Peascliffe Crossovers
109.03
16C: to Grantham
ECM 1 Controlled by Doncaster (D)
Lodge Farm (2) 110.65
Hough Lane (5) (AHB-X) 111.08
Frinkley Lane (8) (AHB-X) 111.53
Honington (9) (AHB-X) 111.72
No.3 112.65
No.4 113.09
No.6 113.25
Sudbrook Lane (11) (AHB-X) 113.72
112.00
1 GRS 2
LNE: GN (Boston, Sleaford & Midland Counties)
ANCASTER
114.53
URS
OOU
25C
Miles from Kings Cross
C
Miles from Kings Cross via Grantham
25B
No.18
117.05
Wilsford (17) (AHB-X) 116.59
Kelby Lane (19) (AHB-X) 117.47
RAUCEBY
118.39
Quarrington (24) (AHB) 118.79
Mountains
119.48
Fen
1.52
SNW
LNE: GN & GE Jt
UP & DOWN JOINT
Sleaford W. Jn
Southgate Crossing East (32) 120.58
SLEAFORD
120.53
Engrs' Tamper
Sleaford East Jn
SSE
LNE
DJ = DOWN JOINT
LL = LOCAL LINE
26D: to Lincoln
63.48
Sleaford North Jn
SPD 2 LNE: GN & GE Jt
Kirkby Laythorpe (38) (AHB) (H) 122.51
0.00/62.13
Sleaford South Jn
26D: to Spalding
GRS 2
LNE: GN
(Boston, Sleaford & Midland Counties)
Whitehouse Farm (47) 124.48
Simpsons (50) 125.24
HECKINGTON
125.57
Burton Lane No.1 (44) (AHB) (H) 123.58
Burton Lane No.2 (48) (AHB) (H) 125.05
Great Hale Drove No.2 (64) (AHB-X) (H) 127.24
Great Hale Drove No.1 (58) (AHB) (H) 126.27
Stones Sidings (67) 128.30
SWINESHEAD
130.25
(75) (AHB) 130.21
(HB)
133.43
HUBBERTS BRIDGE
26A: to Boston & Skegness

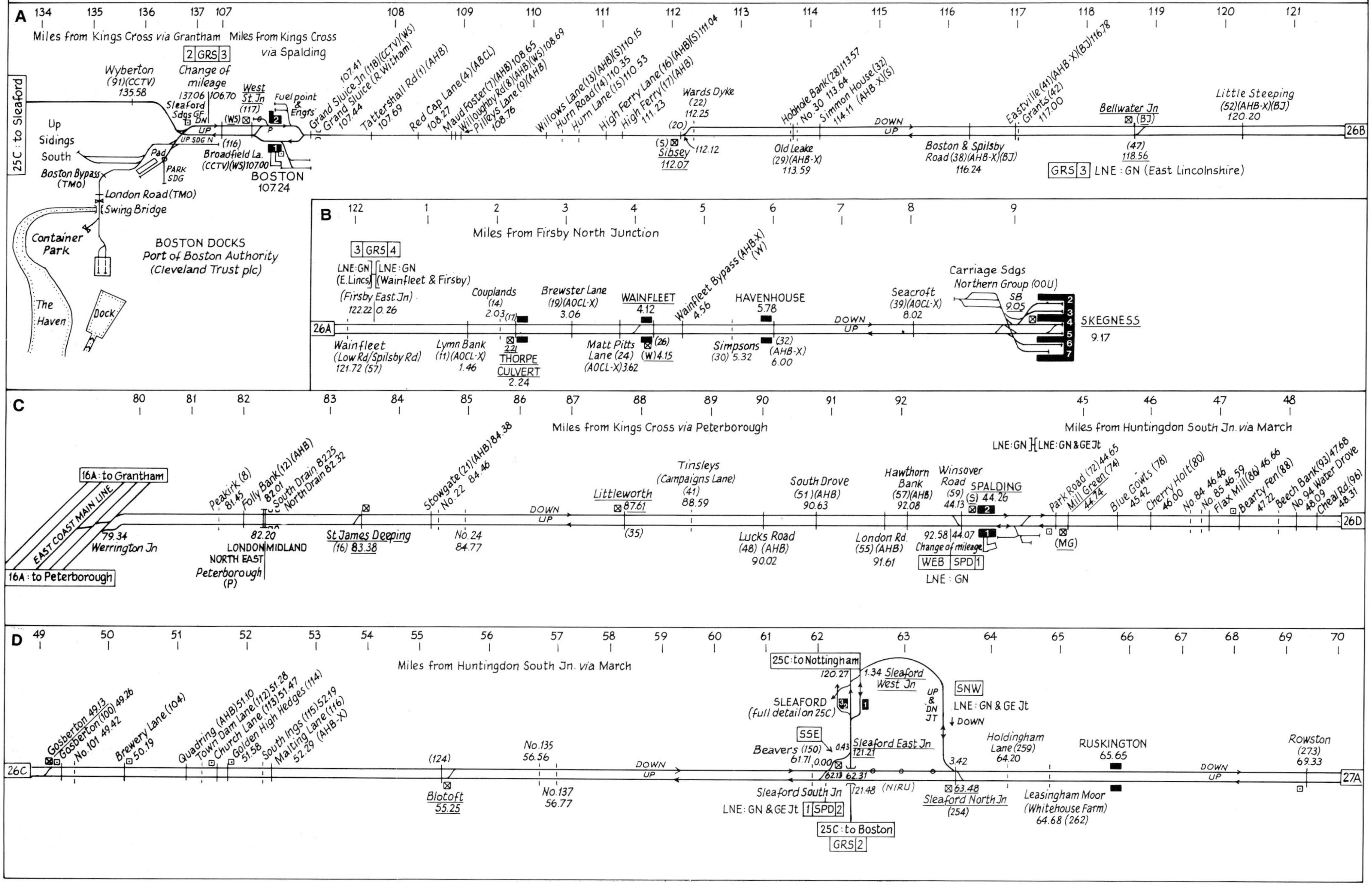
A
134 135 136 137 107 108 109 110 111 112 113 114 115 116 117 118 119 120 121
Miles from Kings Cross via Grantham
Miles from Kings Cross via Spalding
2 GRS 3
25C : to Sleaford
Wyberton (91)(CCTV) 135.58
Change of mileage 137.06 106.70
Sleaford Sdgs GF
West St.Jn (117)
(WS)
Fuel point & Engrs
Up Sidings South
UP SDG N
(116)
Pad
PARK SDG
Broadfield La. (CCTV)(WS)107.00
BOSTON 107.24
Boston Bypass (TMO)
London Road (TMO)
Swing Bridge
Container Park
The Haven
Dock
BOSTON DOCKS
Port of Boston Authority
(Cleveland Trust plc)
Grand Sluice Jn (118)(CCTV)(WS) 107.41
Grand Sluice (R.Witham) 107.44
Tattershall Rd (1)(AHB) 107.69
Red Cap Lane (4)(ABCL) 108.27
Maud Foster (7)(AHB) 108.65
Willoughby Rd (8)(AHB)(WS) 108.69
Pilleys Lane (9)(AHB) 108.76
Willows Lane (13)(AHB)(S) 110.15
Hurn Road (14) 110.35
Hurn Lane (15) 110.53
High Ferry Lane (16)(AHB)(S) 111.04
High Ferry (17)(AHB) 111.23
Wards Dyke (22) 112.25
(20)
(5) Sibsey 112.07
112.12
Hobhole Bank (28) 113.57
No. 30 113.64
Simmon House (32) 114.11 (AHB-X)(S)
Old Leake (29)(AHB-X) 113.59
DOWN
UP
Boston & Spilsby Road (38)(AHB-X)(BJ) 116.24
Eastville (41)(AHB-X)(BJ) 116.78
Grants (42) 117.00
Bellwater Jn (BJ)
(47) 118.56
GRS 3 LNE : GN (East Lincolnshire)
Little Steeping (52)(AHB-X)(BJ) 120.20
26B
B
122 1 2 3 4 5 6 7 8 9
Miles from Firsby North Junction
3 GRS 4
LNE:GN (E.Lincs)
LNE:GN (Wainfleet & Firsby)
(Firsby East Jn) 122.22 0.26
26A
Wainfleet (Low Rd/Spilsby Rd) 121.72 (57)
Couplands (14) 2.03 (17)
Lymn Bank (11)(AOCL-X) 1.46
2.21 THORPE CULVERT 2.24
Brewster Lane (19)(AOCL-X) 3.06
WAINFLEET 4.12
Matt Pitts Lane (24) (AOCL-X) 3.62
(26) (W) 4.15
Wainfleet Bypass (AHB-X) (W) 4.56
HAVENHOUSE 5.78
Simpsons (30) 5.32
(32) (AHB-X) 6.00
DOWN
UP
Seacroft (39)(AOCL-X) 8.02
Carriage Sdgs Northern Group (00U)
SB 9.05
2 3 4 5 6 7
SKEGNESS 9.17
C
80 81 82 83 84 85 86 87 88 89 90 91 92 45 46 47 48
Miles from Kings Cross via Peterborough
Miles from Huntingdon South Jn. via March
16A : to Grantham
EAST COAST MAIN LINE
16A : to Peterborough
79.34 Werrington Jn
Peakirk (8) 81.45
Folly Bank (12)(AHB) 82.01
South Drain 82.25
North Drain 82.32
82.20
LONDON NORTH EAST
MIDLAND
Peterborough (P)
St James Deeping (16) 83.38
Stowgate (21)(AHB) 84.38
No. 22 84.46
No. 24 84.77
DOWN
UP
Littleworth 87.61
(35)
Tinsleys (Campaigns Lane) (41) 88.59
Lucks Road (48) (AHB) 90.02
South Drove (51)(AHB) 90.63
London Rd. (55) (AHB) 91.61
Hawthorn Bank (57)(AHB) 92.08
Winsover Road (59) 44.13
SPALDING (S) 44.26
92.58 44.07
Change of mileage
WEB SPD 1
LNE : GN
LNE:GN LNE:GN & GE Jt
Park Road (72) 44.65
Mill Green (74) 44.74
(MG)
Blue Gowts (78) 45.42
Cherry Holt (80) 46.00
No. 84 46.46
No. 85 46.59
Flax Mill (86) 46.66
Bearty Fen (88) 47.22
Beech Bank (93) 47.68
No. 94 Water Drove 48.09
Cheal Rd (96) 48.31
26D
D
49 50 51 52 53 54 55 56 57 58 59 60 61 62 63 64 65 66 67 68 69 70
Miles from Huntingdon South Jn. via March
26C
Gosberton 49.13
Gosberton (100) 49.26
No. 101 49.42
Brewery Lane (104) 50.19
Quadring (AHB) 51.10
Town Dam Lane (112) 51.28
Church Lane (113) 51.47
Golden High Hedges (114) 51.58
South Ings (115) 52.19
Malting Lane (116) 52.29 (AHB-X)
(124)
Blotoft 55.25
No.135 56.56
No.137 56.77
DOWN
UP
25C : to Nottingham 120.27
1.34 Sleaford West Jn
SLEAFORD (Full detail on 25C)
3 2 1
SSE
Beavers (150) 61.71
0.43
0.00
Sleaford East Jn 121.21
62.13 62.31
Sleaford South Jn
21.48 (NIRU)
LNE : GN & GE Jt 1 SPD 2
25C : to Boston GRS 2
UP & DN JT
SNW
LNE : GN & GE Jt
DOWN
3.42
63.48 Sleaford North Jn (254)
Holdingham Lane (259) 64.20
Leasingham Moor (Whitehouse Farm) 64.68 (262)
RUSKINGTON 65.65
DOWN
UP
Rowston (273) 69.33
27A

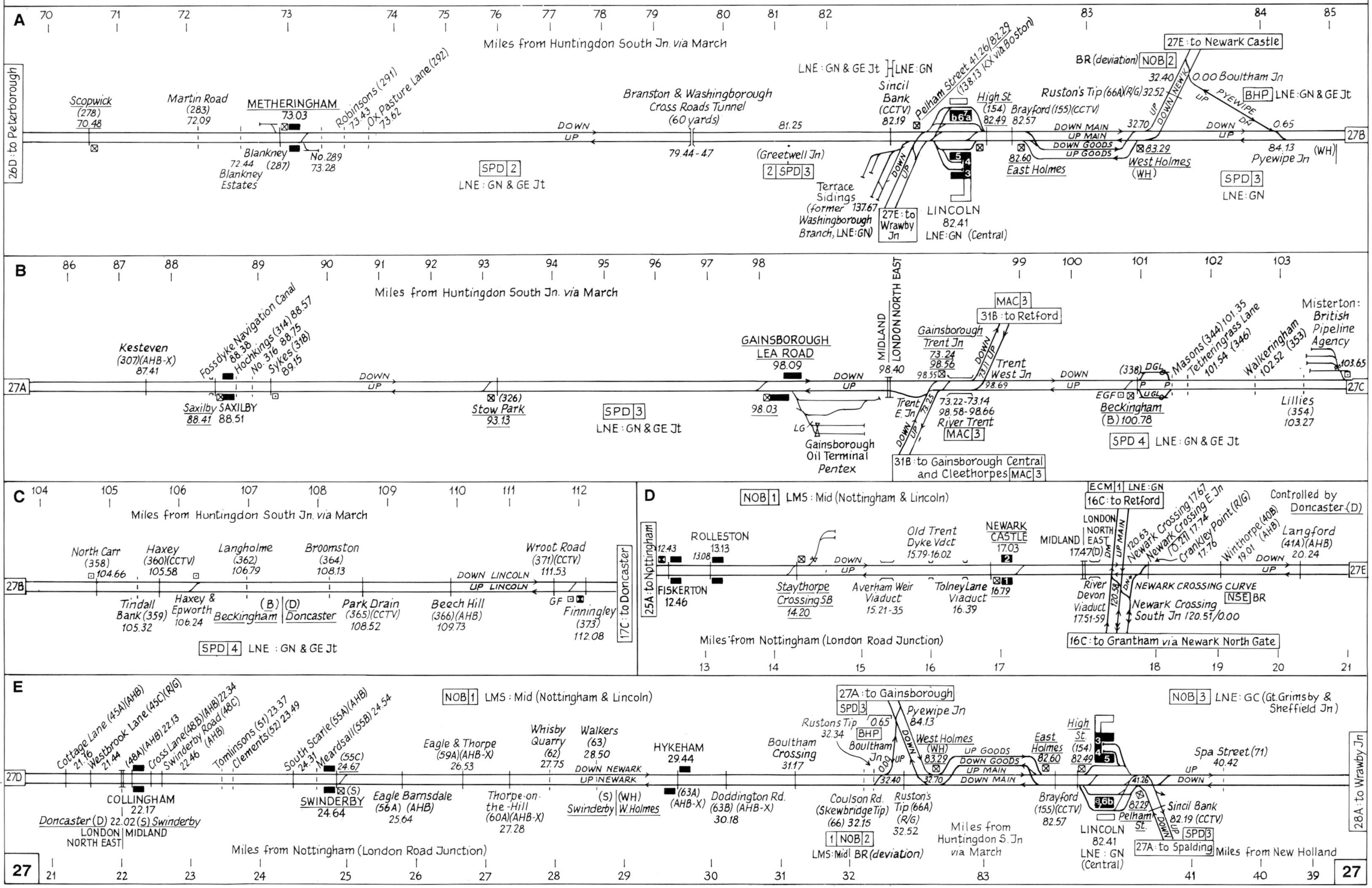
A
Miles from Huntingdon South Jn. via March
26D: to Peterborough
Scopwick (278) 70.48
Martin Road (283) 72.09
METHERINGHAM 73.03
Blankney (287) 72.44
Blankney Estates
No. 289 73.28
Robinsons (291) 73.43
Ox Pasture Lane (292) 73.62
SPD 2
LNE: GN & GE Jt
Branston & Washingborough Cross Roads Tunnel (60 yards)
79.44-47
81.25
(Greetwell Jn)
2 SPD 3
Terrace Sidings (former 137.67 Washingborough Branch, LNE:GN)
27E: to Wrawby Jn
LNE: GN & GE Jt
LNE: GN
Sincil Bank (CCTV) 82.19
Pelham Street 41.26/82.29 (138.13 KX via Boston)
High St (154) 82.49
Brayford (155)(CCTV) 82.57
LINCOLN 82.41 LNE: GN (Central)
82.60 East Holmes
Ruston's Tip (66A)(R/G) 32.52
BR (deviation) NOB 2
32.40
32.70
83.29 West Holmes (WH)
27E: to Newark Castle
0.00 Boultham Jn
BHP LNE: GN & GE Jt
PYEWIPE
0.65
84.13 Pyewipe Jn (WH)
SPD 3
LNE: GN
27B
B
Miles from Huntingdon South Jn. via March
27A
Kesteven (307)(AHB-X) 87.41
Fossdyke Navigation Canal 88.38
Hochkings (314) 88.57
No. 316 88.75
Sykes (318) 89.15
Saxilby 88.41 SAXILBY 88.51
(326) Stow Park 93.13
SPD 3
LNE: GN & GE Jt
GAINSBOROUGH LEA ROAD 98.09
98.03
Gainsborough Oil Terminal Pentex
MIDLAND LONDON NORTH EAST 98.40
Gainsborough Trent Jn 73.24 98.56
98.55
Trent E. Jn
73.22-73.14 98.58-98.66 River Trent MAC 3
Trent West Jn 98.69
MAC 3 31B: to Retford
31B: to Gainsborough Central and Cleethorpes MAC 3
(338)
Beckingham (B) 100.78
SPD 4 LNE: GN & GE Jt
Masons (344) 101.35
Tetheringrass Lane 101.54 (346)
Walkeringham 102.52 (353)
Lillies (354) 103.27
Misterton: British Pipeline Agency
103.65
27C
C
Miles from Huntingdon South Jn. via March
27B
North Carr (358) 104.66
Haxey (360)(CCTV) 105.58
Tindall Bank (359) 105.32
Haxey & Epworth 106.24
Langholme (362) 106.79
(B) Beckingham | (D) Doncaster
Broomston (364) 108.13
Park Drain (365)(CCTV) 108.52
Beech Hill (366)(AHB) 109.73
Wroot Road (371)(CCTV) 111.53
Finningley (373) 112.08
DOWN LINCOLN
UP LINCOLN
SPD 4 LNE: GN & GE Jt
17C: to Doncaster
D
NOB 1 LMS: Mid (Nottingham & Lincoln)
25A: to Nottingham
12.43
FISKERTON 12.46
ROLLESTON 13.13
13.08
Staythorpe Crossing SB 14.20
Averham Weir Viaduct 15.21-35
Old Trent Dyke Vdct 15.79-16.02
Tolney Lane Viaduct 16.39
NEWARK CASTLE 17.03
16.79
MIDLAND | LONDON NORTH EAST 17.47(D)
ECM 1 LNE: GN
16C: to Retford
River Devon Viaduct 17.51-59
120.58
120.63 Newark Crossing 17.67
Newark Crossing E. Jn (0.21) 17.74
Crankley Point (R/G) 17.76
NEWARK CROSSING CURVE
NSE BR
Newark Crossing South Jn 120.51/0.00
Winthorpe (40B) 19.01 (AHB)
Langford (41A)(AHB) 20.24
Controlled by Doncaster (D)
27E
16C: to Grantham via Newark North Gate
Miles from Nottingham (London Road Junction)
E
NOB 1 LMS: Mid (Nottingham & Lincoln)
27D
Cottage Lane (45A)(AHB) 21.16
Westbrook Lane (45C)(R/G) 21.44
(48A)(AHB) 22.13
Cross Lane (48B)(AHB) 22.34
Swinderby Road (48C) 22.46 (AHB)
Tomlinsons (51) 23.37
Clements (52) 23.49
COLLINGHAM 22.17
Doncaster (D) 22.02 (S) Swinderby
LONDON NORTH EAST | MIDLAND
South Scarle (55A)(AHB) 24.31
Meardsall (55B) 24.54
(55C) 24.67
SWINDERBY 24.64
Eagle Barnsdale (56A)(AHB) 25.64
Eagle & Thorpe (59A)(AHB-X) 26.53
Thorpe-on-the-Hill (60A)(AHB-X) 27.28
Whisby Quarry (62) 27.75
Walkers (63) 28.50
(S) Swinderby | (WH) W. Holmes
DOWN NEWARK
UP NEWARK
HYKEHAM 29.44
(63A) (AHB-X)
Doddington Rd. (63B)(AHB-X) 30.18
Boultham Crossing 31.17
Coulson Rd. (Skewbridge Tip) (66) 32.15
1 NOB 2
LMS: Mid BR (deviation)
27A: to Gainsborough
SPD 3
Rustons Tip 32.34
0.65
BHP
Boultham Jn
Pyewipe Jn 84.13
West Holmes (WH) 83.29
32.40
32.70
Ruston's Tip (66A) (R/G) 32.52
Miles from Huntingdon S. Jn via March
East Holmes 82.60
High St (154) 82.49
Brayford (155)(CCTV) 82.57
LINCOLN 82.41 LNE: GN (Central)
41.26
82.29
Pelham St.
Sincil Bank 82.19 (CCTV)
SPD 3
27A: to Spalding
Miles from New Holland
Spa Street (71) 40.42
NOB 3 LNE: GC (Gt. Grimsby & Sheffield Jn)
28A: to Wrawby Jn
Miles from Nottingham (London Road Junction)
27
27

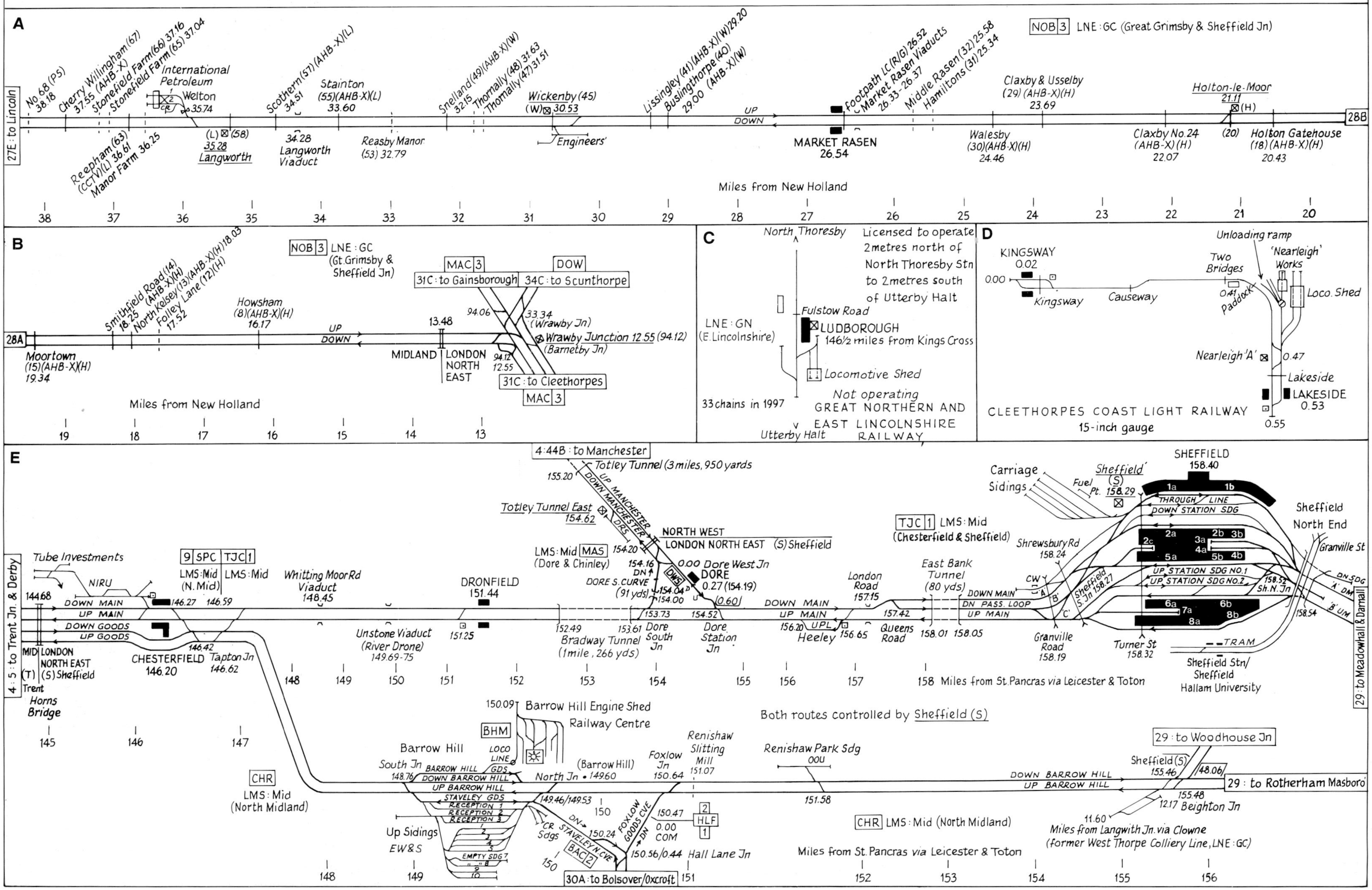
A
NOB 3 LNE : GC (Great Grimsby & Sheffield Jn)
27E : to Lincoln
No 68 (PS) 38.18
Cherry Willingham (67) 37.55 (AHB-X)
Stonefield Farm (66) 37.16
Stonefield Farm (65) 37.04
International Petroleum
Welton 35.74
Reepham (63) (CCTV)(L) 36.61
Manor Farm 36.25
(L) (58) 35.28 Langworth
Scothern (57) (AHB-X)(L) 34.51
34.28 Langworth Viaduct
Stainton (55)(AHB-X)(L) 33.60
Reasby Manor (53) 32.79
Snelland (49)(AHB-X)(W) 32.15
Thornally (48) 31.63
Thornally (47) 31.51
Wickenby (45) (W) 30.53
Engineers'
Lissingley (41)(AHB-X)(W) 29.20
Buslingthorpe (40) 29.00 (AHB-X)(W)
UP
DOWN
Footpath LC (R/G) 26.52
Market Rasen Viaducts 26.33 - 26.37
MARKET RASEN 26.54
Middle Rasen (32) 25.58
Hamiltons (31) 25.34
Walesby (30)(AHB-X)(H) 24.46
Claxby & Usselby (29) (AHB-X)(H) 23.69
Claxby No. 24 (AHB-X) (H) 22.07
Holton-le-Moor 21.11 (H)
(20)
Holton Gatehouse (18) (AHB-X)(H) 20.43
28B
Miles from New Holland
38 37 36 35 34 33 32 31 30 29 28 27 26 25 24 23 22 21 20
B
NOB 3 LNE : GC (Gt.Grimsby & Sheffield Jn)
28A
Moortown (15)(AHB-X)(H) 19.34
Smithfield Road (14) 18.25 (AHB-X)(H)
North Kelsey (13)(AHB-X)(H) 18.03
Folley Lane (12)(H) 17.52
Howsham (8)(AHB-X)(H) 16.17
UP
DOWN
13.48
MIDLAND
LONDON NORTH EAST
MAC 3
31C : to Gainsborough
DOW
34C : to Scunthorpe
94.06
33.34 (Wrawby Jn)
Wrawby Junction 12.55 (94.12)
(Barnetby Jn)
94.12 12.55
31C : to Cleethorpes
MAC 3
Miles from New Holland
19 18 17 16 15 14 13
C
North Thoresby
Licensed to operate 2 metres north of North Thoresby Stn to 2 metres south of Utterby Halt
LNE : GN (E.Lincolnshire)
Fulstow Road
LUDBOROUGH
146½ miles from Kings Cross
Locomotive Shed
33 chains in 1997
Not operating
GREAT NORTHERN AND EAST LINCOLNSHIRE RAILWAY
Utterby Halt
D
KINGSWAY 0.02
0.00
Kingsway
Causeway
Two Bridges
0.41 Paddock
Unloading ramp
'Nearleigh' Works
Loco. Shed
Nearleigh 'A'
0.47
Lakeside
LAKESIDE 0.53
0.55
CLEETHORPES COAST LIGHT RAILWAY
15-inch gauge
E
4 : 44B : to Manchester
Totley Tunnel (3 miles, 950 yards
155.20
UP MANCHESTER
DOWN MANCHESTER
DRS
Totley Tunnel East 154.62
NORTH WEST
LONDON NORTH EAST (S) Sheffield
LMS : Mid MAS (Dore & Chinley)
154.20
154.16 DN
DORE S. CURVE (91 yds)
DWS
154.04
154.00
0.00 Dore West Jn
DORE 0.27 (154.19)
0.60
4 : 5 : to Trent Jn. & Derby
Tube Investments
NIRU
144.68
DOWN MAIN
UP MAIN
DOWN GOODS
UP GOODS
MID
LONDON NORTH EAST
(T)
(S) Sheffield
Trent
Horns Bridge
9 SPC
TJC 1
LMS : Mid (N. Mid)
LMS : Mid
146.27
146.59
146.42
CHESTERFIELD 146.20
Tapton Jn 146.62
Whitting Moor Rd Viaduct 148.45
Unstone Viaduct (River Drone) 149.69 - 75
DRONFIELD 151.44
151.25
152.49
Bradway Tunnel (1 mile, 266 yds)
153.61 Dore South Jn
153.73
154.52
Dore Station Jn
DOWN MAIN
UP MAIN
156.20 UPL
Heeley 156.65
London Road 157.15
157.42
Queens Road
158.01
158.05
TJC 1 LMS : Mid (Chesterfield & Sheffield)
East Bank Tunnel (80 yds)
DOWN MAIN
DN PASS. LOOP
UP MAIN
Shrewsbury Rd 158.24
CW
'A'
'B'
'C'
Sheffield S. Jn 158.27
Granville Road 158.19
Carriage Sidings
Fuel Pt.
Sheffield (S) 158.29
SHEFFIELD 158.40
1a 1b
THROUGH LINE
DOWN STATION SDG
2a 2b 3b 2c 3a 4a 5a 5b 4b
UP STATION SDG NO. 1
UP STATION SDG NO. 2
6a 6b 7a 8a 8b
Turner St 158.32
TRAM
Sheffield Stn/ Sheffield Hallam University
Sheffield North End
Granville St
158.52 Sh. N. Jn
158.54
DN SDG
'A' DM
'B' UM
29 : to Meadowhall & Darnall
145 146 147 148 149 150 151 152 153 154 155 156 157 158 Miles from St. Pancras via Leicester & Toton
Both routes controlled by Sheffield (S)
150.09
Barrow Hill Engine Shed Railway Centre
BHM
LOCO LINE
GDS
Barrow Hill South Jn 148.76
BARROW HILL
DOWN BARROW HILL
UP BARROW HILL
STAVELEY GDS
RECEPTION 1
RECEPTION 2
RECEPTION 3
EMPTY SDG 7
Up Sidings EW & S
CHR LMS : Mid (North Midland)
(Barrow Hill) North Jn • 149.60
149.46/149.53
CR Sdgs
DN STAVELEY N. CVE
150.24
BAC 2
150
Foxlow Jn 150.64
FOXLOW GOODS CVE DN
150.47
0.00 COM
HLF
150.56/0.44 Hall Lane Jn
Renishaw Slitting Mill 151.07
Renishaw Park Sdg OOU
151.58
30A : to Bolsover/Oxcroft
CHR LMS : Mid (North Midland)
DOWN BARROW HILL
UP BARROW HILL
29 : to Woodhouse Jn
Sheffield (S) 155.46
48.06
29 : to Rotherham Masboro'
155.48
12.17 Beighton Jn
11.60
Miles from Langwith Jn. via Clowne (former West Thorpe Colliery Line, LNE : GC)
Miles from St. Pancras via Leicester & Toton
148 149 151 152 153 154 155 156

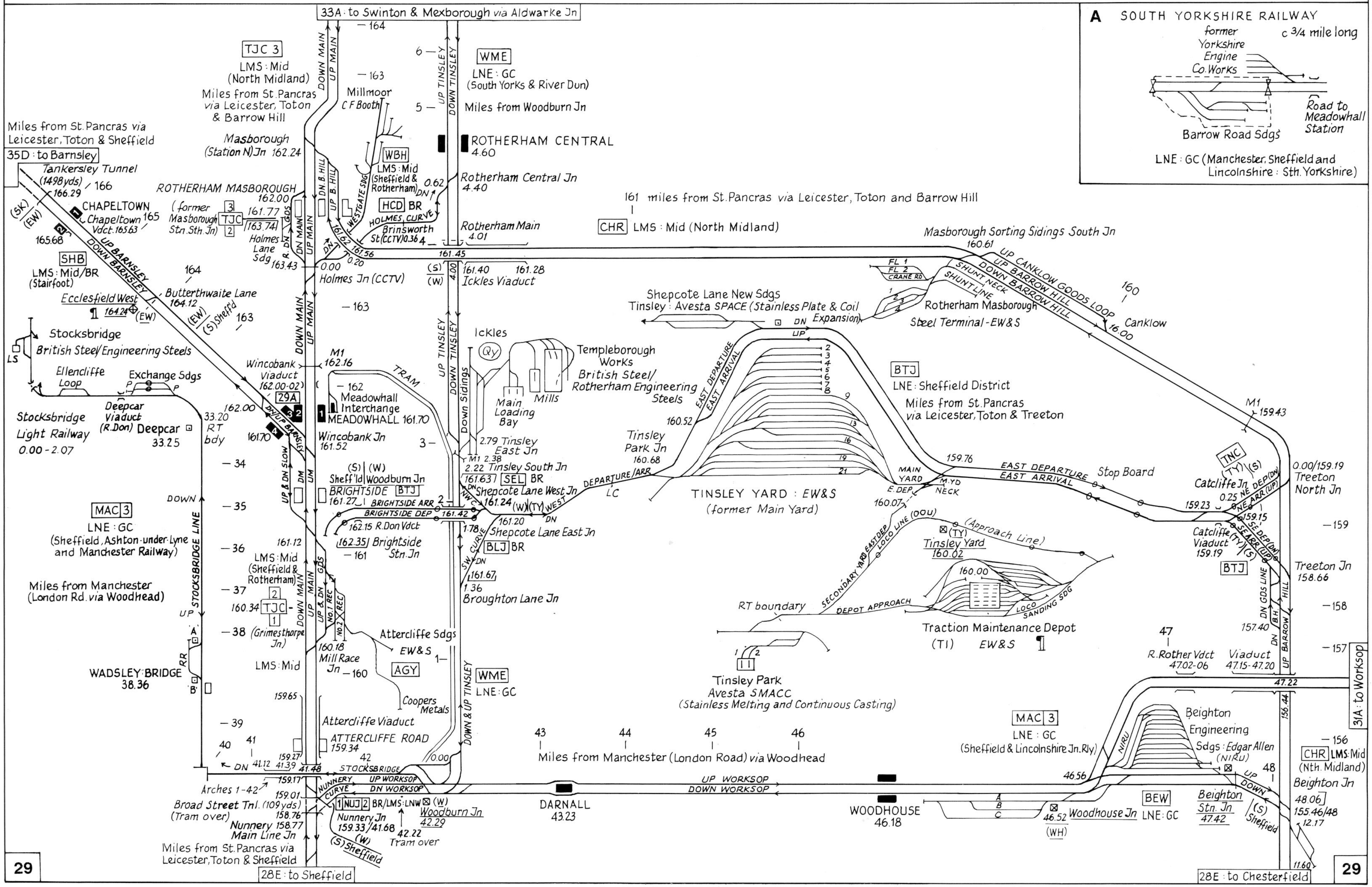

33A: to Swinton & Mexborough via Aldwarke Jn
A SOUTH YORKSHIRE RAILWAY
former Yorkshire Engine Co. Works
c 3/4 mile long
Road to Meadowhall Station
Barrow Road Sdgs
LNE: GC (Manchester, Sheffield and Lincolnshire: Sth. Yorkshire)
TJC 3
LMS: Mid (North Midland)
Miles from St. Pancras via Leicester, Toton & Barrow Hill
Miles from St. Pancras via Leicester, Toton & Sheffield
35D: to Barnsley
Tankersley Tunnel (1498yds) 166.29
CHAPELTOWN
Chapeltown Vdct 165.63
Masborough (Station N) Jn 162.24
ROTHERHAM MASBOROUGH 162.00
(former Masborough Stn. Sth. Jn)
Millmoor C F Booth
WBH
LMS: Mid (Sheffield & Rotherham)
HCD BR
HOLMES CURVE
Brinsworth St (CCTV) 0.36
WME
LNE: GC (South Yorks & River Dun)
Miles from Woodburn Jn
ROTHERHAM CENTRAL 4.60
Rotherham Central Jn 4.40
Rotherham Main 4.01
161 miles from St. Pancras via Leicester, Toton and Barrow Hill
CHR LMS: Mid (North Midland)
Holmes Lane Sdg
Holmes Jn (CCTV)
Ickles Viaduct
SHB
LMS: Mid/BR (Stairfoot)
Ecclesfield West 164.24
Butterthwaite Lane 164.12
UP BARNSLEY
DOWN BARNSLEY
Stocksbridge British Steel/Engineering Steels
Ellencliffe Loop
Exchange Sdgs
Deepcar Viaduct (R. Don)
Deepcar 33.25
RT bdy
Stocksbridge Light Railway 0.00 - 2.07
Wincobank Viaduct 162.00-02
Wincobank Jn 161.52
Meadowhall Interchange
MEADOWHALL 161.70
TRAM
Ickles
Templeborough Works British Steel/ Rotherham Engineering Steels
Mills
Main Loading Bay
Down Sidings
2.79 Tinsley East Jn
2.22 Tinsley South Jn
SEL BR
Shepcote Lane West Jn 161.24
Shepcote Lane East Jn
BLJ BR
Broughton Lane Jn
Sheff'ld Woodburn Jn
BRIGHTSIDE BTJ 161.27
BRIGHTSIDE ARR
BRIGHTSIDE DEP
162.15 R. Don Vdct
162.35 Brightside Stn. Jn
MAC 3
LNE: GC (Sheffield, Ashton-under-Lyne and Manchester Railway)
Miles from Manchester (London Rd. via Woodhead)
STOCKSBRIDGE LINE
WADSLEY BRIDGE 38.36
LMS: Mid (Sheffield & Rotherham)
TJC
(Grimesthorpe Jn)
160.18 Mill Race Jn
Attercliffe Sdgs EW&S
AGY
Coopers Metals
Attercliffe Viaduct
ATTERCLIFFE ROAD 159.34
Arches 1-42
Broad Street Tnl. (109yds) (Tram over)
Nunnery 158.77 Main Line Jn
NUNNERY CURVE
NUJ BR/LMS: LNW
Nunnery Jn 159.33/41.68
Woodburn Jn 42.29
42.22 Tram over
28E: to Sheffield
Shepcote Lane New Sdgs
Tinsley: Avesta SPACE (Stainless Plate & Coil Expansion)
Tinsley Park Jn 160.68
EAST DEPARTURE
EAST ARRIVAL
DEPARTURE/ARR
TINSLEY YARD: EW&S (former Main Yard)
MAIN YARD
M.YD NECK
E.DEP.
SECONDARY YARD EAST DEP
LOCO LINE (OOU)
(Approach Line)
Tinsley Yard 160.02
DEPOT APPROACH
LOCO SANDING SDG
Traction Maintenance Depot (TI) EW&S
RT boundary
Tinsley Park Avesta SMACC (Stainless Melting and Continuous Casting)
Masborough Sorting Sidings South Jn 160.61
UP CANKLOW GOODS LOOP
UP BARROW HILL
DOWN BARROW HILL
SHUNT NECK
SHUNT LINE
Canklow
Rotherham Masborough Steel Terminal - EW&S
BTJ
LNE: Sheffield District
Miles from St. Pancras via Leicester, Toton & Treeton
Stop Board
TNC
Catcliffe Jn
NE DEP(DN)
NE ARR(UP)
SE DEP(DN)
SE ARR(UP)
Catcliffe Viaduct 159.19
0.00/159.19 Treeton North Jn
Treeton Jn 158.66
DN GDS LINE
UP BARROW HILL
R. Rother Vdct 47.02-06
Viaduct 47.15-47.20
31A: to Worksop
Miles from Manchester (London Road) via Woodhead
DARNALL 43.23
WOODHOUSE 46.18
UP WORKSOP
DOWN WORKSOP
MAC 3
LNE: GC (Sheffield & Lincolnshire Jn. Rly)
Beighton Engineering Sdgs: Edgar Allen (NIRU)
Woodhouse Jn 46.52 (WH)
BEW LNE: GC
Beighton Stn. Jn 47.42
CHR LMS: Mid (Nth. Midland)
Beighton Jn 48.06
155.46/48
28E: to Chesterfield

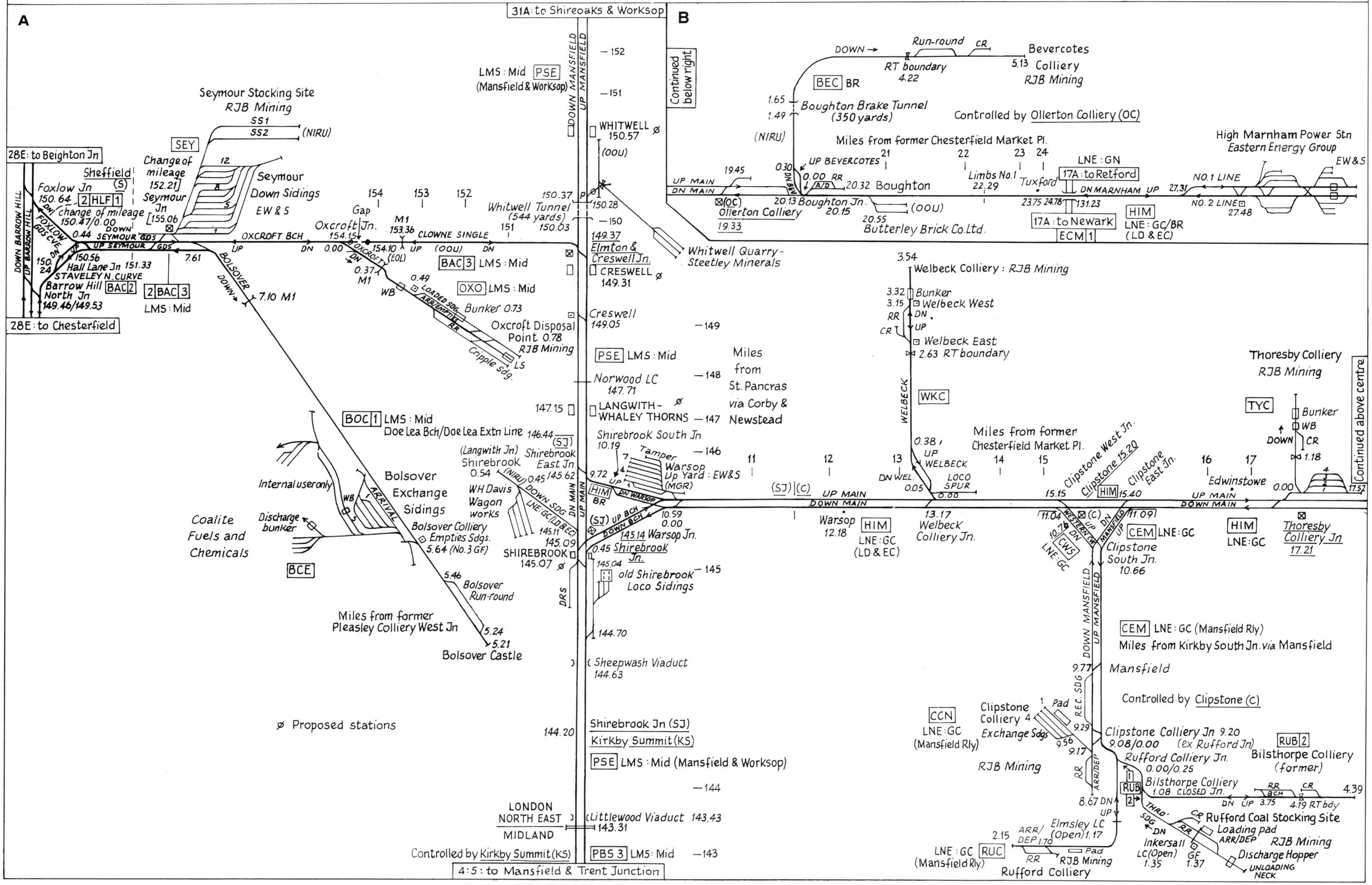
A
B
31A: to Shireoaks & Worksop
28E: to Beighton Jn
28E: to Chesterfield
4:5: to Mansfield & Trent Junction
17A: to Retford
17A: to Newark
ECM 1
Continued below right
Continued above centre
DOWN BARROW HILL
UP BARROW HILL
Sheffield (S)
Foxlow Jn 150.64 2 HLF 1
change of mileage 150.47/0.00
0.44
150.56
150 24
Hall Lane Jn 151.33
STAVELEY N. CURVE
Barrow Hill BAC 2
North Jn 149.46/149.53
2 BAC 3
LMS: Mid
SEY
Change of mileage 152.21
Seymour Jn [155.06
Seymour Stocking Site
RJB Mining
SS1
SS2
(NIRU)
Seymour Down Sidings
EW & S
OXCROFT BCH
UP SEYMOUR GDS
7.61
BOLSOVER
DOWN
7.10 M1
Gap
Oxcroft Jn. 154.15
0.00
154.10 (EOL)
0.37
M1
153.36
CLOWNE SINGLE
(OOU)
BAC 3 LMS: Mid
OXO LMS: Mid
0.49
LOADED SDG
ARR/EMPTIES
Bunker 0.73
Oxcroft Disposal Point 0.78
RJB Mining
Cripple Sdg.
LS
154
153
152
151
Whitwell Tunnel (544 yards)
150.37
150.03
LMS: Mid PSE
(Mansfield & Worksop)
DOWN MANSFIELD
UP MANSFIELD
WHITWELL 150.57
(OOU)
150.28
149.37
Elmton & Creswell Jn.
CRESWELL 149.31
Creswell 149.05
Whitwell Quarry - Steetley Minerals
PSE LMS: Mid
Norwood LC 147.71
147.15
LANGWITH - WHALEY THORNS
Miles from St. Pancras via Corby & Newstead
Shirebrook South Jn 10.19
Tamper
Warsop Up Yard: EW&S (MGR)
BOC 1 LMS: Mid
Doe Lea Bch/Doe Lea Extn Line
146.44 (SJ)
(Langwith Jn) Shirebrook 0.54
Shirebrook East Jn 145.62
0.45
(NIRU)
DOWN SDG
LNE: GC (LD & EC)
145.11
145.09
WH Davis Wagon works
SHIREBROOK 145.07
9.72
HIM BR
DN WARSOP
UP BCH
DOWN BCH
10.59 0.00
145.14 Warsop Jn.
0.45 Shirebrook Jn.
145.04
old Shirebrook Loco Sidings
144.70
DRS
Sheepwash Viaduct 144.63
Bolsover Exchange Sidings
ARRIVAL
Internal user only
WB
Discharge bunker
Coalite Fuels and Chemicals
BCE
Bolsover Colliery Empties Sdgs. 5.64 (No.3 GF)
5.46
Bolsover Run-round
Miles from former Pleasley Colliery West Jn
5.24
5.21
Bolsover Castle
ø Proposed stations
144.20
Shirebrook Jn (SJ)
Kirkby Summit (KS)
PSE LMS: Mid (Mansfield & Worksop)
LONDON NORTH EAST
MIDLAND
Littlewood Viaduct 143.43
143.31
PBS 3 LMS: Mid
Controlled by Kirkby Summit (KS)
DOWN
Run-round
CR
RT boundary 4.22
5.13
Bevercotes Colliery
RJB Mining
BEC BR
1.65
1.49
Boughton Brake Tunnel (350 yards)
Controlled by Ollerton Colliery (OC)
(NIRU)
Miles from former Chesterfield Market Pl.
UP BEVERCOTES
0.30
0.00 RR
A/D
20.32 Boughton
UP MAIN
DN MAIN
19.45
(OC) Ollerton Colliery 19.33
20.13 Boughton Jn. 20.15
(OOU)
20.55 Butterley Brick Co. Ltd.
Limbs No.1 22.29
Tuxford
23.75 24.78
131.23
LNE: GN
DN MARNHAM UP
HIM LNE: GC/BR (LD & EC)
27.31
NO.1 LINE
NO.2 LINE 27.48
High Marnham Power Stn
Eastern Energy Group
EW&S
3.54
Welbeck Colliery: RJB Mining
3.32 Bunker
3.15 Welbeck West
RR
CR
DN
UP
Welbeck East
2.63 RT boundary
WELBECK
WKC
0.38
UP WELBECK
DN WEL.
0.05
LOCO SPUR
0.00
Miles from former Chesterfield Market Pl.
(SJ) (C)
UP MAIN
DOWN MAIN
Warsop 12.18
HIM LNE: GC (LD & EC)
13.17 Welbeck Colliery Jn.
Clipstone West Jn.
Clipstone 15.20
Clipstone East Jn.
15.15
HIM 15.40
11.04
(C)
11.09
WESTERN CR
CWS
LNE: GC
CEM LNE: GC
Clipstone South Jn. 10.66
Edwinstowe
0.00
17.52
Thoresby Colliery
RJB Mining
TYC
Bunker
WB
DOWN
CR
1.18
HIM LNE: GC
Thoresby Colliery Jn 17.21
CEM LNE: GC (Mansfield Rly)
Miles from Kirkby South Jn. via Mansfield
DOWN MANSFIELD
UP MANSFIELD
9.77
Mansfield
REC. SDG
Controlled by Clipstone (C)
CCN LNE: GC (Mansfield Rly)
Clipstone Colliery Exchange Sdgs
Pad
9.29
9.56
9.17
RJB Mining
Clipstone Colliery Jn 9.20
9.08/0.00 (ex Rufford Jn)
Rufford Colliery Jn. 0.00/0.25
Bilsthorpe Colliery 1.08 CLOSED Jn.
RUB 2
Bilsthorpe Colliery (former)
RR
BCH
CR
4.39
DN UP 3.75
4.19 RT bdy
RUB
ARR/DEP
8.67 DN
UP
THRO' SDG
DN
Rufford Coal Stocking Site
Loading pad
ARR/DEP
RJB Mining
Discharge Hopper
UNLOADING NECK
Inkersall LC (Open) 1.35
GF 1.37
Elmsley LC (Open) 1.17
2.15
ARR/DEP 1.70
Pad
RJB Mining
LNE: GC RUC
(Mansfield Rly)
Rufford Colliery

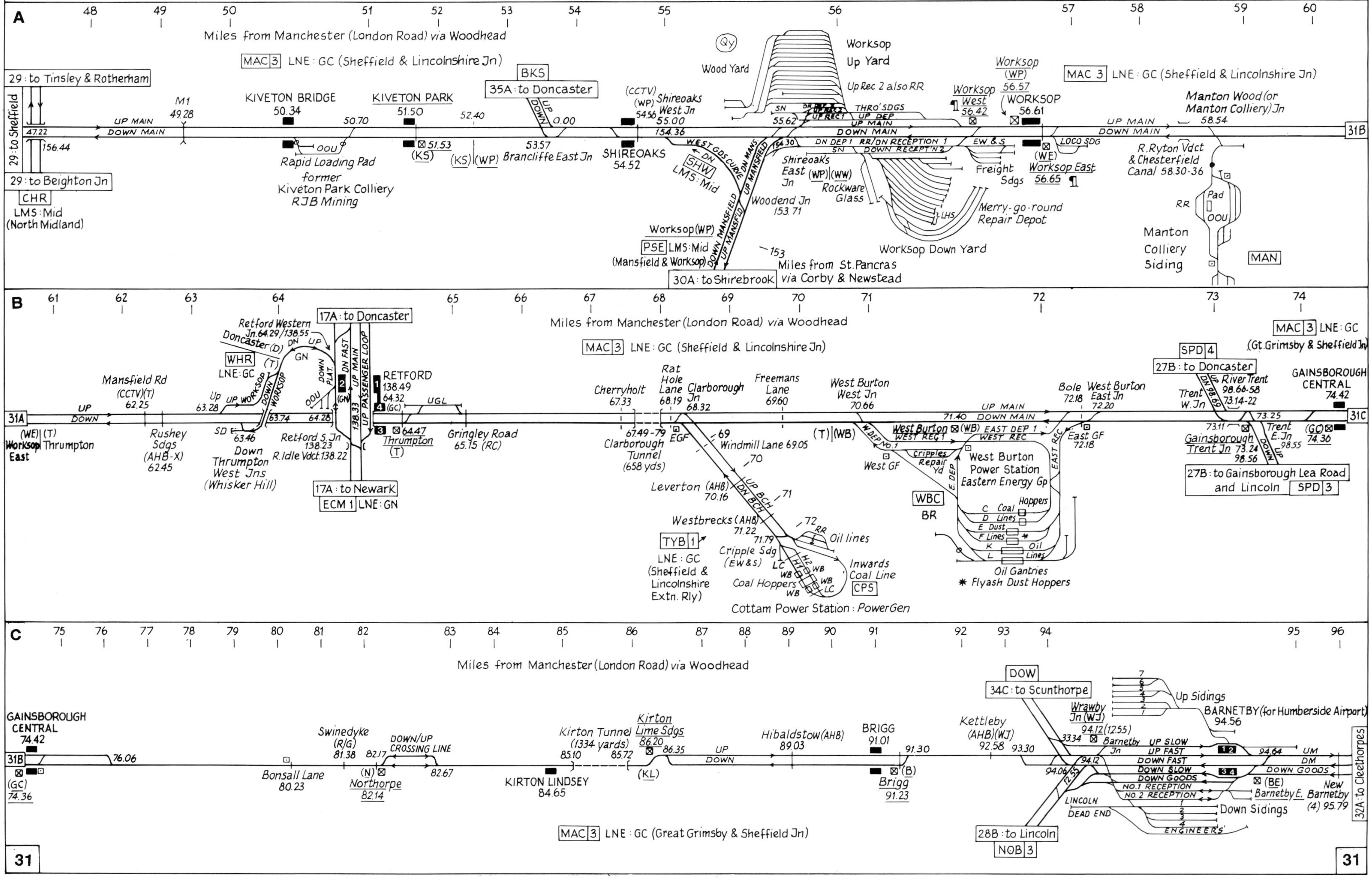
A
Miles from Manchester (London Road) via Woodhead
MAC 3 LNE : GC (Sheffield & Lincolnshire Jn)
29 : to Tinsley & Rotherham
29 : to Sheffield
29 : to Beighton Jn
CHR
LMS : Mid (North Midland)
M1 49.28
UP MAIN
DOWN MAIN
KIVETON BRIDGE 50.34
Rapid Loading Pad
former Kiveton Park Colliery
RJB Mining
KIVETON PARK 51.50
51.53 (KS)
(KS) (WP)
BKS
35A : to Doncaster
53.57 Brancliffe East Jn
(CCTV) (WP) Shireoaks West Jn 55.00
SHIREOAKS 54.52
SHW LMS : Mid
Worksop (WP)
PSE LMS : Mid (Mansfield & Worksop)
30A : to Shirebrook
Miles from St. Pancras via Corby & Newstead
Wood Yard
Worksop Up Yard
Up Rec 2 also RR
Shireoaks East (WP) (WW) Jn
Woodend Jn 153.71
Rockware Glass
Worksop Down Yard
Worksop West 56.42
Worksop (WP) 56.57
WORKSOP 56.61
(WE) Worksop East 56.65
Freight Sdgs
Merry-go-round Repair Depot
MAC 3 LNE : GC (Sheffield & Lincolnshire Jn)
Manton Wood (or Manton Colliery) Jn 58.54
R. Ryton Vdct & Chesterfield Canal 58.30-36
Manton Colliery Siding
MAN
31B
B
Miles from Manchester (London Road) via Woodhead
MAC 3 LNE : GC (Sheffield & Lincolnshire Jn)
31A
(WE) (T) Worksop East Thrumpton
Mansfield Rd (CCTV) (T) 62.25
Rushey Sdgs (AHB-X) 62.45
Retford Western Jn 64.29/138.55
Doncaster (D)
WHR LNE : GC
Down Thrumpton West Jns (Whisker Hill)
Retford S. Jn 138.23
R. Idle Vdct 138.22
17A : to Doncaster
RETFORD 138.49 64.32
17A : to Newark
ECM 1 LNE : GN
64.47 Thrumpton (T)
Gringley Road 65.15 (RC)
Cherryholt 67.33
Rat Hole Lane 68.19
Clarborough Jn 68.32
Clarborough Tunnel (658 yds)
Freemans Lane 69.60
Windmill Lane 69.05
Leverton (AHB) 70.16
Westbrecks (AHB) 71.22
TYB 1 LNE : GC (Sheffield & Lincolnshire Extn. Rly)
Cripple Sdg (EW&S)
Coal Hoppers
Oil lines
Inwards Coal Line
CPS
Cottam Power Station : PowerGen
West Burton West Jn 70.66
West GF
West Burton
West Burton Power Station Eastern Energy Gp
WBC BR
Oil Gantries
* Flyash Dust Hoppers
Bole 72.18
West Burton East Jn 72.20
East GF 72.18
SPD 4
27B : to Doncaster
Trent W. Jn
River Trent 98.66-58
Gainsborough Trent Jn 73.24 98.56
Trent E. Jn 98.55
27B : to Gainsborough Lea Road and Lincoln SPD 3
MAC 3 LNE : GC (Gt. Grimsby & Sheffield Jn)
GAINSBOROUGH CENTRAL 74.42
(GC) 74.36
31C
C
Miles from Manchester (London Road) via Woodhead
GAINSBOROUGH CENTRAL 74.42
(GC) 74.36
31B
76.06
Bonsall Lane 80.23
Swinedyke (R/G) 81.38
DOWN/UP CROSSING LINE
(N) Northorpe 82.14
82.67
KIRTON LINDSEY 84.65
Kirton Tunnel (1334 yards)
Kirton Lime Sdgs 86.20
(KL)
Hibaldstow (AHB) 89.03
BRIGG 91.01
(B) Brigg 91.23
Kettleby (AHB) (WJ) 92.58
DOW
34C : to Scunthorpe
Wrawby Jn (WJ) 94.12 (12.55)
Barnetby Jn
UP SLOW
UP FAST
DOWN FAST
DOWN SLOW
DOWN GOODS
NO.1 RECEPTION
NO.2 RECEPTION
LINCOLN DEAD END
28B : to Lincoln
NOB 3
Up Sidings
BARNETBY (for Humberside Airport) 94.56
(BE) Barnetby E.
New Barnetby (4) 95.79
Down Sidings
ENGINEERS'
32A : to Cleethorpes
MAC 3 LNE : GC (Great Grimsby & Sheffield Jn)

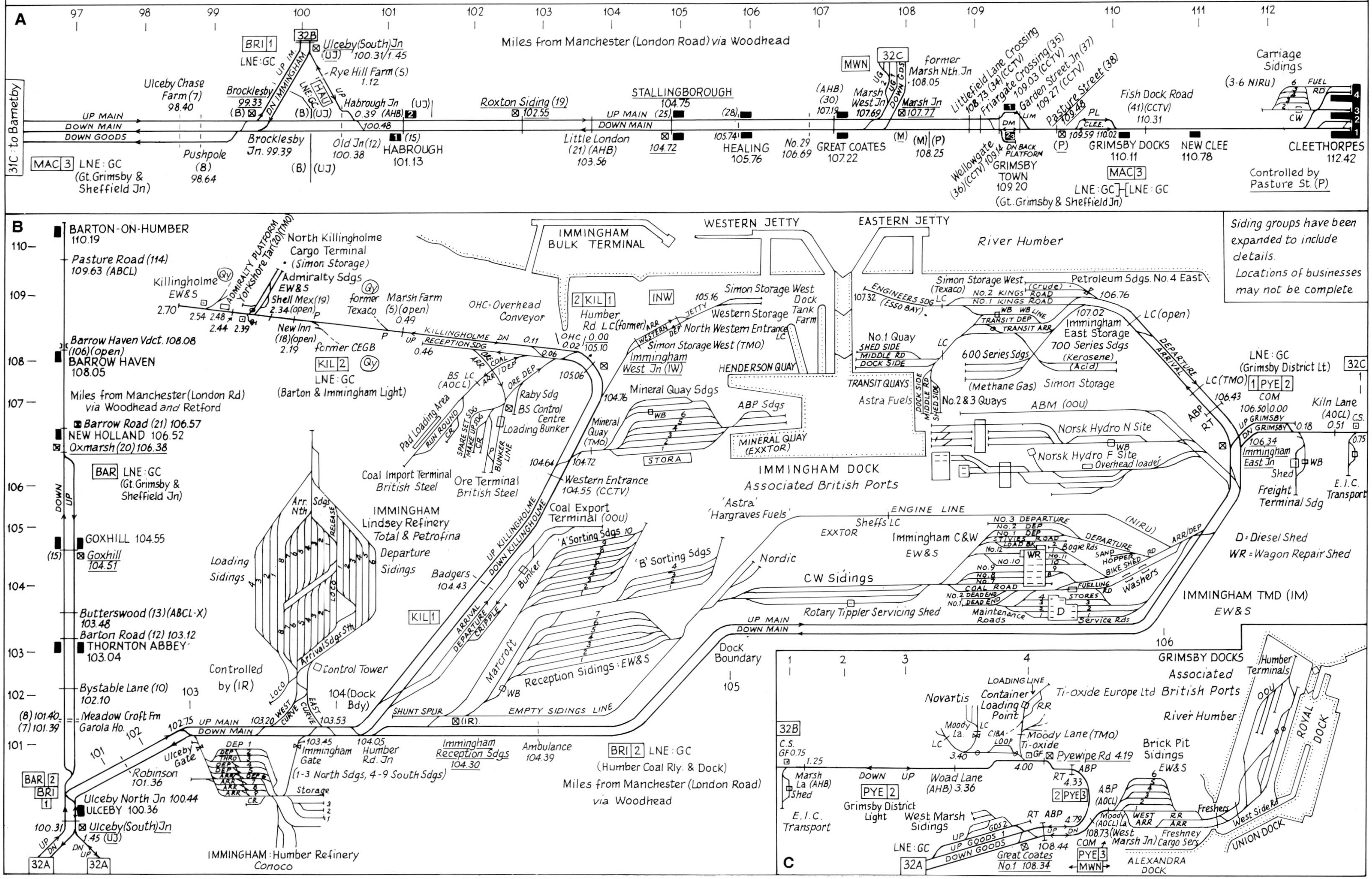
A
Miles from Manchester (London Road) via Woodhead
31C to Barnetby
UP MAIN
DOWN MAIN
DOWN GOODS
MAC 3 LNE:GC (Gt.Grimsby & Sheffield Jn)
Ulceby Chase Farm (7) 98.40
Pushpole (8) 98.64
Brocklesby 99.33
Brocklesby Jn. 99.39
BRI 1 LNE:GC
32B
Ulceby (South) Jn (UJ) 100.31/1.45
Rye Hill Farm (5) 1.12
Habrough Jn 0.39 (AHB)
Old Jn (12) 100.38
HABROUGH 101.13
Roxton Siding (19) 102.55
Little London (21) (AHB) 103.56
STALLINGBOROUGH 104.75
104.72
HEALING 105.76
No. 29 106.69
GREAT COATES 107.22
MWN
32C
Marsh West Jn 107.69
Marsh Jn 107.77
former Marsh Nth. Jn 108.05
(M) (P) 108.25
Littlefield Lane Crossing 108.73 (34) (CCTV)
Friargate Crossing (35) 109.03 (CCTV)
Garden Street Jn (37) 109.27 (CCTV)
Pasture Street (38) 109.48
Wellowgate (36) (CCTV) 109.14
DN BACK PLATFORM
GRIMSBY TOWN 109.20 (Gt. Grimsby & Sheffield Jn)
GRIMSBY DOCKS 110.11
MAC 3
LNE:GC LNE:GC
Fish Dock Road (41) (CCTV) 110.31
NEW CLEE 110.78
Carriage Sidings (3-6 NIRU)
CLEETHORPES 112.42
Controlled by Pasture St. (P)
B
BARTON-ON-HUMBER 110.19
Pasture Road (114) 109.63 (ABCL)
Barrow Haven Vdct. 108.08 (106) (open)
BARROW HAVEN 108.05
Miles from Manchester (London Rd) via Woodhead and Retford
Barrow Road (21) 106.57
NEW HOLLAND 106.52
Oxmarsh (20) 106.38
BAR LNE:GC (Gt.Grimsby & Sheffield Jn)
GOXHILL 104.55
Goxhill 104.51
Butterswood (13) (ABCL-X) 103.48
Barton Road (12) 103.12
THORNTON ABBEY 103.04
Bystable Lane (10) 102.10
(8) 101.40 (7) 101.39 Meadow Croft Fm Garola Ho.
Ulceby North Jn 100.44
ULCEBY 100.36
Ulceby (South) Jn 1.45 (UJ)
Robinson 101.36
Ulceby Gate
Killingholme EW&S
ADMIRALTY PLATFORM
Yorkshore Tar (20) (TMO)
North Killingholme Cargo Terminal (Simon Storage)
Admiralty Sdgs EW&S
Shell Mex (19) 2.34 (open)
New Inn (18) (open) 2.19
former Texaco
Marsh Farm (5) (open) 0.49
former CEGB
KIL 2 LNE:GC (Barton & Immingham Light)
OHC: Overhead Conveyor
KILLINGHOLME RECEPTION SDG
IMMINGHAM BULK TERMINAL
2 KIL 1
Humber Rd. LC (former)
INW
WESTERN JETTY
EASTERN JETTY
River Humber
Simon Storage West Dock Tank Farm
Western Storage
North Western Entrance
Simon Storage West (TMO)
Immingham West Jn (IW)
HENDERSON QUAY
Mineral Quay Sdgs
ABP Sdgs
MINERAL QUAY (EXXTOR)
STORA
Raby Sdg
BS Control Centre
Loading Bunker
Pad Loading Area
Coal Import Terminal British Steel
Ore Terminal British Steel
Western Entrance 104.55 (CCTV)
IMMINGHAM Lindsey Refinery Total & Petrofina
Departure Sidings
Loading Sidings
Badgers 104.43
Coal Export Terminal (OOU)
'A' Sorting Sdgs
'B' Sorting Sdgs
Reception Sidings: EW&S
Marcroft
KIL 1
Control Tower
Controlled by (IR)
104 (Dock Bdy)
Immingham Gate (1-3 North Sdgs, 4-9 South Sdgs)
Humber Rd. Jn
Immingham Reception Sdgs 104.30
Ambulance 104.39
SHUNT SPUR
EMPTY SIDINGS LINE
IMMINGHAM: Humber Refinery Conoco
BRI 2 LNE:GC (Humber Coal Rly. & Dock)
Miles from Manchester (London Road) via Woodhead
Dock Boundary
IMMINGHAM DOCK Associated British Ports
'Astra' 'Hargraves Fuels'
Nordic
CW Sidings
Rotary Tippler Servicing Shed
Immingham C&W EW&S
Sheffs LC
EXXTOR
ENGINE LINE
IMMINGHAM TMD (IM) EW&S
Simon Storage West (Texaco)
Petroleum Sdgs. No. 4 East
ENGINEERS SDG (ESSO BAY)
Immingham East Storage
700 Series Sdgs (Kerosene) (Acid)
600 Series Sdgs (Methane Gas)
Simon Storage
ABM (OOU)
No. 1 Quay
TRANSIT QUAYS
Astra Fuels
No. 2 & 3 Quays
Norsk Hydro N Site
Norsk Hydro F Site
Overhead loader
LC (open)
DEPARTURE ARRIVAL
LNE:GC (Grimsby District Lt)
1 PYE 2
COM 106.50 0.00
Immingham East Jn 106.34
Freight Terminal Sdg
Kiln Lane (AOCL) 0.51
E.I.C. Transport
Siding groups have been expanded to include details.
Locations of businesses may not be complete
D: Diesel Shed
WR: Wagon Repair Shed
C
32B
C.S. GF0.75
Marsh La (AHB) Shed
E.I.C. Transport
PYE 2 Grimsby District Light
Wood Lane (AHB) 3.36
West Marsh Sidings
Novartis
Container Loading Point
Ti-oxide Europe Ltd
Moody Lane (TMO)
Pyewipe Rd 4.19
2 PYE 3
Great Coates No. 1 108.34
LNE:GC 32A
Brick Pit Sidings EW&S
GRIMSBY DOCKS Associated British Ports
River Humber
Humber Terminals
ROYAL DOCK
UNION DOCK
ALEXANDRA DOCK
Freshney Cargo Serv
PYE 3 MWN

A

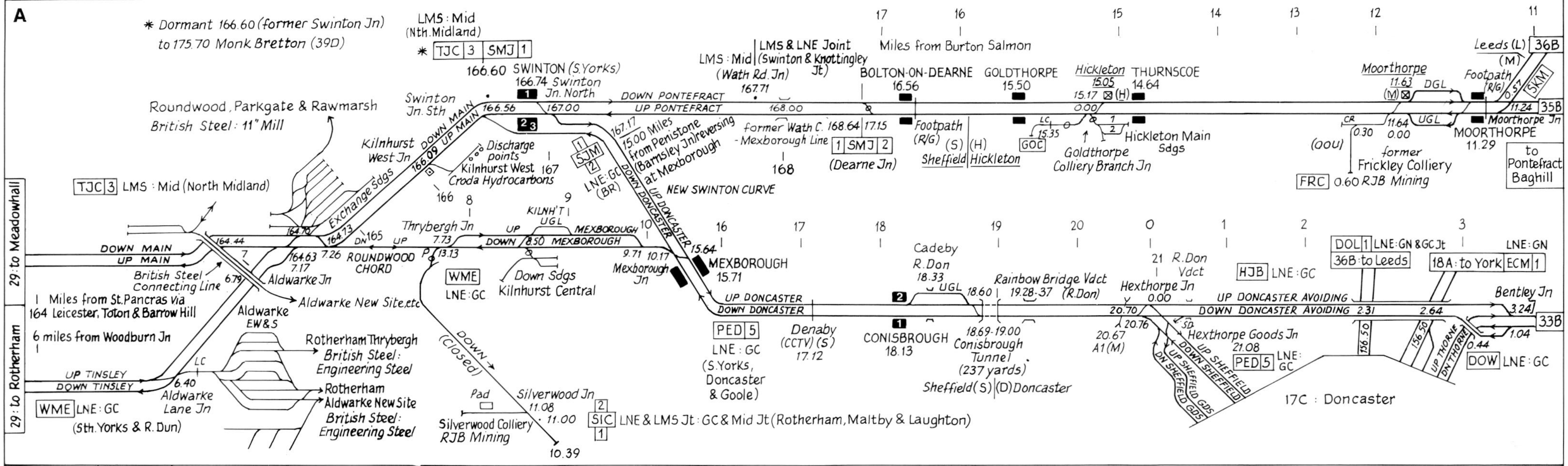
* Dormant 166.60 (former Swinton Jn) to 175.70 Monk Bretton (39D)
LMS : Mid (Nth. Midland)
TJC 3 SMJ 1
166.60 SWINTON (S.Yorks)
166.74 Swinton Jn. North
Roundwood, Parkgate & Rawmarsh
British Steel : 11" Mill
Swinton Jn. Sth
Kilnhurst West Jn
Exchange Sdgs
Discharge points
Kilnhurst West 167
Croda Hydrocarbons
TJC 3 LMS : Mid (North Midland)
DOWN MAIN
UP MAIN
British Steel Connecting Line
Aldwarke Jn
Aldwarke New Site, etc
1 Miles from St. Pancras via
164 Leicester, Toton & Barrow Hill
6 miles from Woodburn Jn
Aldwarke EW&S
Rotherham Thrybergh British Steel : Engineering Steel
Rotherham Aldwarke New Site British Steel : Engineering Steel
UP TINSLEY
DOWN TINSLEY
Aldwarke Lane Jn
WME LNE : GC (Sth. Yorks & R. Dun)
ROUNDWOOD CHORD
Thrybergh Jn 7.73
WME LNE : GC
KILNH'T UGL
MEXBOROUGH
Down Sdgs Kilnhurst Central
DOWN (Closed)
Pad
Silverwood Jn 11.08
11.00
Silverwood Colliery RJB Mining
10.39
SIC LNE & LMS Jt : GC & Mid Jt (Rotherham, Maltby & Laughton)
DOWN PONTEFRACT
UP PONTEFRACT
15.00 Miles from Penistone (Barnsley Jn) reversing at Mexborough
SJM LNE : GC (BR)
UP DONCASTER
DOWN DONCASTER
NEW SWINTON CURVE
MEXBOROUGH 15.64 15.71
Mexborough Jn
LMS : Mid (Wath Rd. Jn) 167.71
LMS & LNE Joint (Swinton & Knottingley Jt)
former Wath C. 168.64 - Mexborough Line
1 SMJ 2 (Dearne Jn)
168
Miles from Burton Salmon
BOLTON-ON-DEARNE 16.56
GOLDTHORPE 15.50
Hickleton 15.05
THURNSCOE 14.64
Footpath (R/G)
(S) (H) Sheffield Hickleton
GOC
Goldthorpe Colliery Branch Jn
Hickleton Main Sdgs
PED 5 LNE : GC (S.Yorks, Doncaster & Goole)
Denaby (CCTV) (S) 17.12
CONISBROUGH 18.13
Cadeby R. Don 18.33
18.69-19.00 Conisbrough Tunnel (237 yards)
Sheffield (S) (D) Doncaster
Rainbow Bridge Vdct 19.28-37 (R. Don)
Hexthorpe Jn 0.00
R. Don Vdct
20.67 A1(M)
Hexthorpe Goods Jn 21.08
PED 5 LNE : GC
UP SHEFFIELD
DOWN SHEFFIELD
UP SHEFFIELD GDS
DN SHEFFIELD GDS
HJB LNE : GC
UP DONCASTER AVOIDING
DOWN DONCASTER AVOIDING
DOL 1 LNE : GN & GC Jt 36B : to Leeds
18A : to York ECM 1 LNE : GN
Bentley Jn 3.24
33B
DOW LNE : GC
UP THORNE
DN THORNE
17C : Doncaster
Moorthorpe 11.63
DGL
UGL
(OOU)
former Frickley Colliery
FRC 0.60 RJB Mining
Leeds (L) (M) 36B
Footpath (R/G)
SKM
35B
Moorthorpe Jn
MOORTHORPE 11.29
to Pontefract Baghill
29 : to Meadowhall
29 : to Rotherham

B

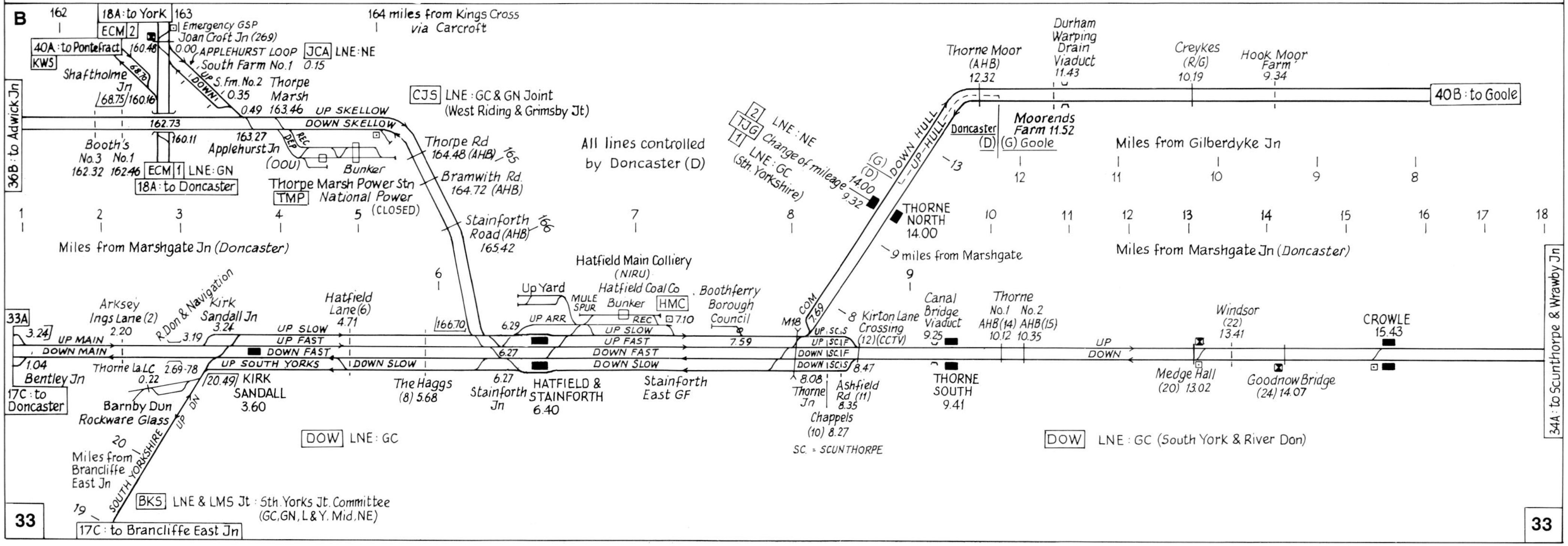
18A : to York
ECM 2
40A : to Pontefract
KWS
Shaftholme Jn
Emergency GSP
Joan Croft Jn (269)
0.00 APPLEHURST LOOP
South Farm No.1
JCA LNE : NE
S. Fm. No.2 0.35
Thorpe Marsh
UP SKELLOW
DOWN SKELLOW
Booth's No.3 No.1 162.32 162.46
ECM 1 LNE : GN
18A : to Doncaster
Applehurst Jn
(OOU)
Bunker
Thorpe Marsh Power Stn National Power (CLOSED)
TMP
164 miles from Kings Cross via Carcroft
CJS LNE : GC & GN Joint (West Riding & Grimsby Jt)
Thorpe Rd 164.48 (AHB)
Bramwith Rd. 164.72 (AHB)
Stainforth Road (AHB) 165.42
All lines controlled by Doncaster (D)
Miles from Marshgate Jn (Doncaster)
36B : to Adwick Jn
33A
Arksey Ings Lane (2) 2.20
R. Don & Navigation
Kirk Sandall Jn 3.24
UP MAIN
DOWN MAIN
Bentley Jn
17C : to Doncaster
Thorne La. LC 0.22
Barnby Dun Rockware Glass
UP SOUTH YORKS
KIRK SANDALL 3.60
UP SLOW
UP FAST
DOWN FAST
DOWN SLOW
Hatfield Lane (6) 4.71
The Haggs (8) 5.68
Miles from Brancliffe East Jn
SOUTH YORKSHIRE
BKS LNE & LMS Jt : Sth. Yorks Jt. Committee (GC, GN, L&Y, Mid, NE)
17C : to Brancliffe East Jn
DOW LNE : GC
Hatfield Main Colliery (NIRU)
Up Yard
MULE SPUR
Hatfield Coal Co Bunker
HMC
UP ARR
REC
Boothferry Borough Council
6.27 Stainforth Jn
HATFIELD & STAINFORTH 6.40
Stainforth East GF
LNE : NE
TJG
Change of mileage
LNE : GC (Sth. Yorkshire)
(G) (D) 14.00 9.32
DOWN HULL
UP HULL
THORNE NORTH 14.00
9 miles from Marshgate
COM
M18
8 Kirton Lane Crossing (12) (CCTV)
UP SC.S
8.08 Thorne Jn
Ashfield Rd (11) 8.35
Chappels (10) 8.27
SC. = SCUNTHORPE
Canal Bridge Viaduct 9.25
THORNE SOUTH 9.41
Thorne No.1 No.2 AHB (14) AHB (15) 10.12 10.35
Thorne Moor (AHB) 12.32
Durham Warping Drain Viaduct 11.43
Moorends Farm 11.52
Doncaster (D) (G) Goole
Creykes (R/G) 10.19
Hook Moor Farm 9.34
40B : to Goole
Miles from Gilberdyke Jn
Miles from Marshgate Jn (Doncaster)
UP
DOWN
Windsor (22) 13.41
Medge Hall (20) 13.02
Goodnow Bridge (24) 14.07
CROWLE 15.43
DOW LNE : GC (South York & River Don)
34A : to Scunthorpe & Wrawby Jn

# ALTHORPE – SCUNTHORPE – WRAWBY JUNCTION



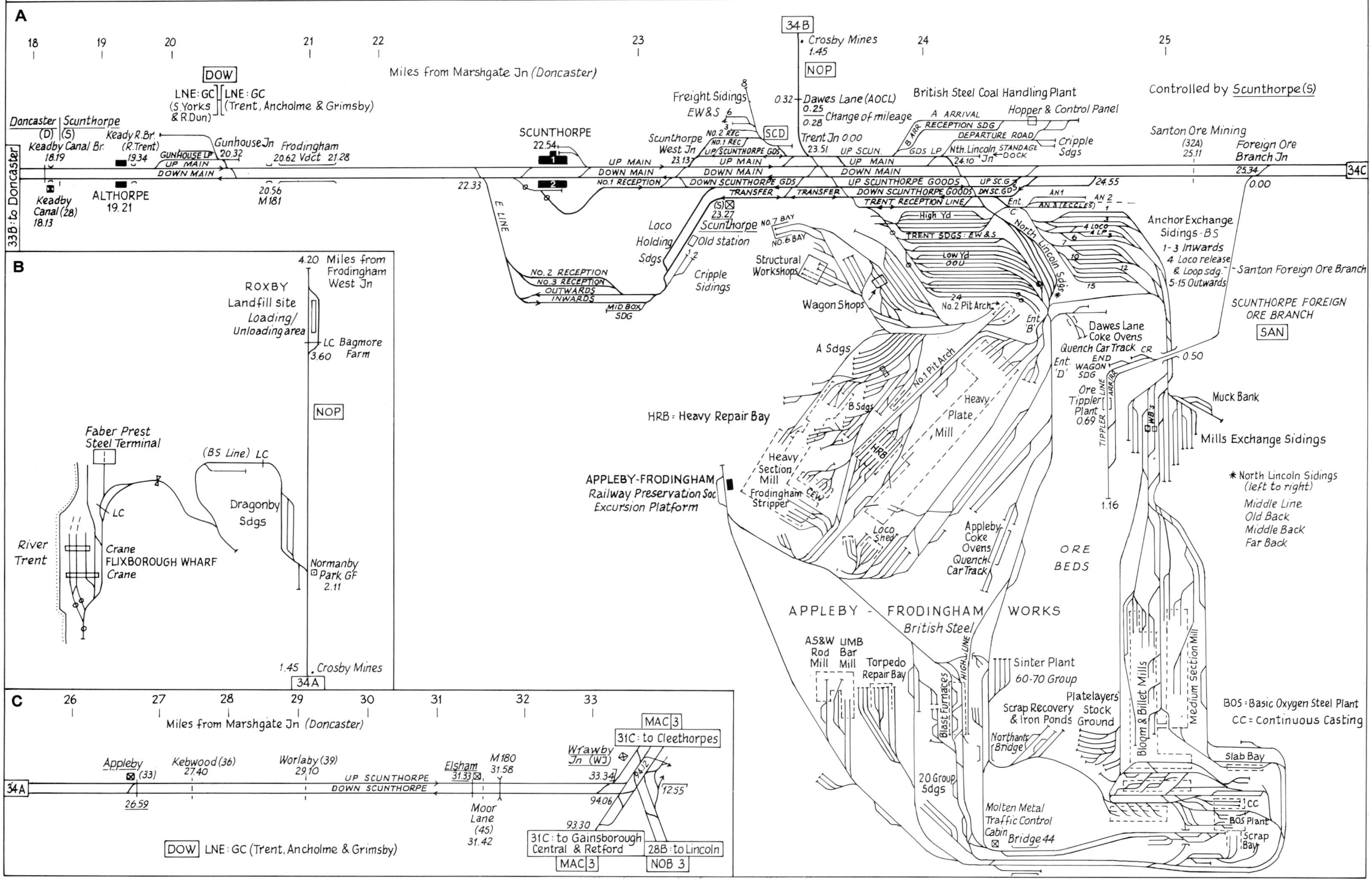

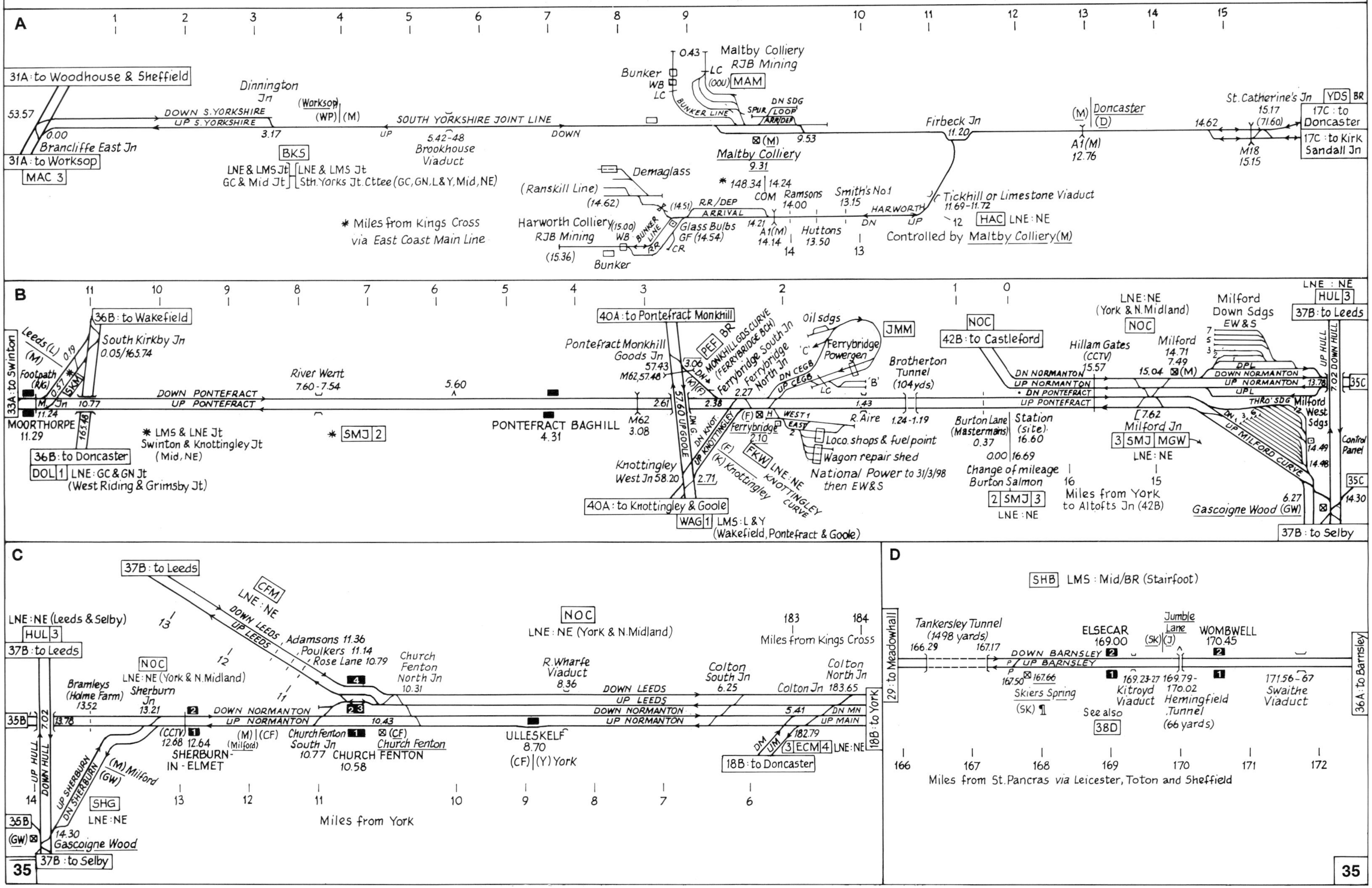
A
31A: to Woodhouse & Sheffield
53.57
0.00
Brancliffe East Jn
31A: to Worksop
MAC 3
DOWN S.YORKSHIRE
UP S.YORKSHIRE
Dinnington Jn
3.17
(Worksop) (WP) (M)
BKS
LNE & LMS Jt
GC & Mid Jt
LNE & LMS Jt
Sth.Yorks Jt.Cttee (GC, GN, L&Y, Mid, NE)
SOUTH YORKSHIRE JOINT LINE
UP
DOWN
5.42-48
Brookhouse Viaduct
* Miles from Kings Cross via East Coast Main Line
Bunker
WB
LC
0.43
Maltby Colliery
RJB Mining
MAM
(OOU)
BUNKER LINE
SPUR
DN SDG
LOOP
ARR/DEP
(M)
9.53
Maltby Colliery
9.31
Demaglass
(Ranskill Line)
(14.62)
* 148.34
14.24
COM
Ramsons
14.00
Smith's No1
13.15
(14.51)
RR/DEP
ARRIVAL
Harworth Colliery
RJB Mining
(15.00)
WB
BUNKER LINE
Glass Bulbs
GF (14.54)
CR
(15.36)
Bunker
14.21
A1(M)
14.14
Huttons
13.50
HARWORTH
DN
UP
Firbeck Jn
11.20
Tickhill or Limestone Viaduct
11.69-11.72
12
HAC
LNE: NE
Controlled by Maltby Colliery (M)
(M)
Doncaster
(D)
A1(M)
12.76
14.62
St. Catherine's Jn
15.17
(71.60)
M18
15.15
YDS
BR
17C: to Doncaster
17C: to Kirk Sandall Jn
B
33A: to Swinton
Leeds (L)
(M)
0.19
Footpath
(NG)
0.51
SKM
36B: to Wakefield
South Kirkby Jn
0.05/165.74
M Jn
10.77
11.24
MOORTHORPE
11.29
163.48
36B: to Doncaster
DOL 1
LNE: GC & GN Jt
(West Riding & Grimsby Jt)
* LMS & LNE Jt
Swinton & Knottingley Jt
(Mid, NE)
DOWN PONTEFRACT
UP PONTEFRACT
River Went
7.60-7.54
* SMJ 2
5.60
PONTEFRACT BAGHILL
4.31
M62
3.08
40A: to Pontefract Monkhill
Pontefract Monkhill Goods Jn
57.43
M62, 57.48
2.61
57.60 UP GOOLE
DN G.
DN KNOT
UP KNOTTINGLEY
Knottingley West Jn 58.20
2.71
40A: to Knottingley & Goole
WAG 1
LMS: L&Y
(Wakefield, Pontefract & Goole)
3.06
PEF
BR
MONKHILL GDS CURVE
(FERRYBRIDGE BCH)
Ferrybridge South Jn
Ferrybridge North Jn
2.38
2.27
DN CEGB
UP CEGB
Oil sdgs
'C'
Ferrybridge Powergen
'B'
LC
JMM
(F)
H
Ferrybridge
2.10
WEST 1
EAST 2
(F)
(K) Knottingley
FKW
LNE: NE
KNOTTINGLEY CURVE
1.43
R. Aire
Loco. shops & fuel point
Wagon repair shed
National Power to 31/3/98 then EW&S
Brotherton Tunnel
(104yds)
1.24-1.19
Burton Lane
(Mastermans)
0.37
Station (site)
16.60
0.00
16.69
Change of mileage Burton Salmon
2 SMJ 3
LNE: NE
NOC
42B: to Castleford
DN NORMANTON
UP NORMANTON
DN PONTEFRACT
UP PONTEFRACT
Hillam Gates
(CCTV)
15.57
LNE: NE
(York & N.Midland)
NOC
16
Miles from York to Altofts Jn (42B)
15
Milford
14.71
7.49
15.04
(M)
7.62
Milford Jn
3 SMJ MGW
LNE: NE
Milford Down Sdgs
EW&S
DPL
DOWN NORMANTON
UP NORMANTON
UPL
THRO' SDG
Milford West Sdgs
DN
UP MILFORD CURVE
14.49
14.48
Control Panel
6.27
Gascoigne Wood (GW)
LNE: NE
HUL 3
37B: to Leeds
UP HULL
DOWN HULL
7.02
13.78
35C
14.30
37B: to Selby
C
LNE: NE (Leeds & Selby)
HUL 3
37B: to Leeds
37B: to Leeds
CFM
LNE: NE
DOWN LEEDS
UP LEEDS
Adamsons 11.36
Poulkers 11.14
Rose Lane 10.79
NOC
LNE: NE (York & N.Midland)
Bramleys (Holme Farm)
13.52
Sherburn Jn
13.21
DOWN NORMANTON
UP NORMANTON
35B
7.02
13.78
(CCTV)
12.68
12.64
SHERBURN-IN-ELMET
(M) (CF)
(Milford)
Church Fenton South Jn
10.77
CHURCH FENTON
10.58
(CF)
Church Fenton
10.43
Church Fenton North Jn
10.31
UP HULL
DOWN HULL
UP SHERBURN
DN SHERBURN
(M) Milford
(GW)
SHG
LNE: NE
35B
(GW)
14.30
Gascoigne Wood
37B: to Selby
Miles from York
NOC
LNE: NE (York & N.Midland)
R. Wharfe Viaduct
8.36
ULLESKELF
8.70
(CF) (Y) York
DOWN LEEDS
UP LEEDS
DOWN NORMANTON
UP NORMANTON
Colton South Jn
6.25
Colton Jn 183.65
Colton North Jn
5.41
183
184
Miles from Kings Cross
DN MN
UP MAIN
DM
UM
182.79
3 ECM 4
LNE: NE
18B: to Doncaster
18B: to York
D
SHB
LMS: Mid/BR (Stairfoot)
29: to Meadowhall
Tankersley Tunnel
(1498 yards)
166.29
167.17
DOWN BARNSLEY
UP BARNSLEY
167.50
167.66
Skiers Spring
(SK)
ELSECAR
169.00
169.23-27
Kitroyd Viaduct
See also 38D
(SK) (J)
Jumble Lane
169.79-170.02
Hemingfield Tunnel
(66 yards)
WOMBWELL
170.45
171.56-67
Swaithe Viaduct
36A: to Barnsley
Miles from St.Pancras via Leicester, Toton and Sheffield

# BARNSLEY – (HUDDERSFIELD) ● BARNSLEY – HORBURY JN ● (DONCASTER) – WAKEFIELD – (LEEDS)



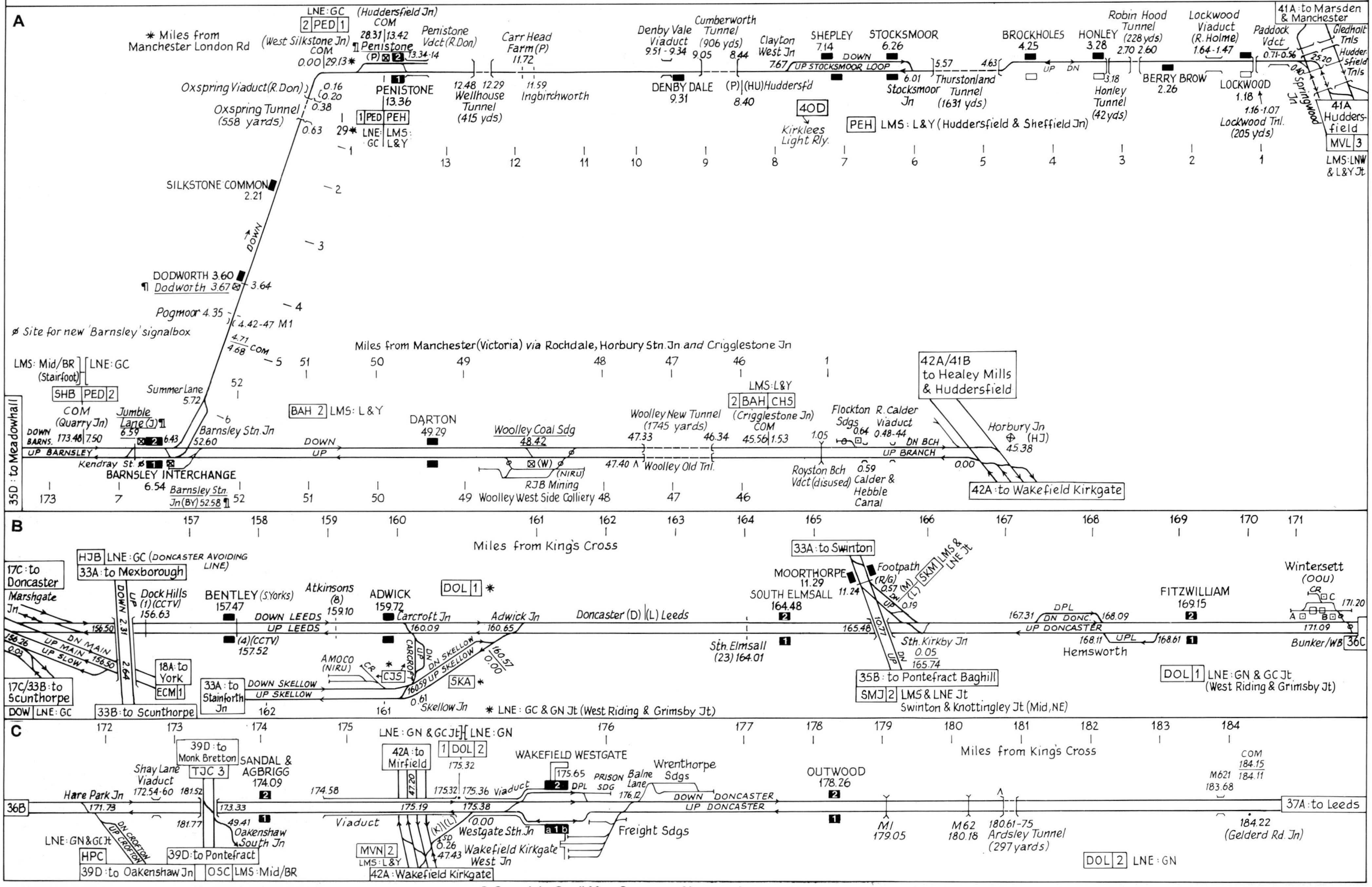

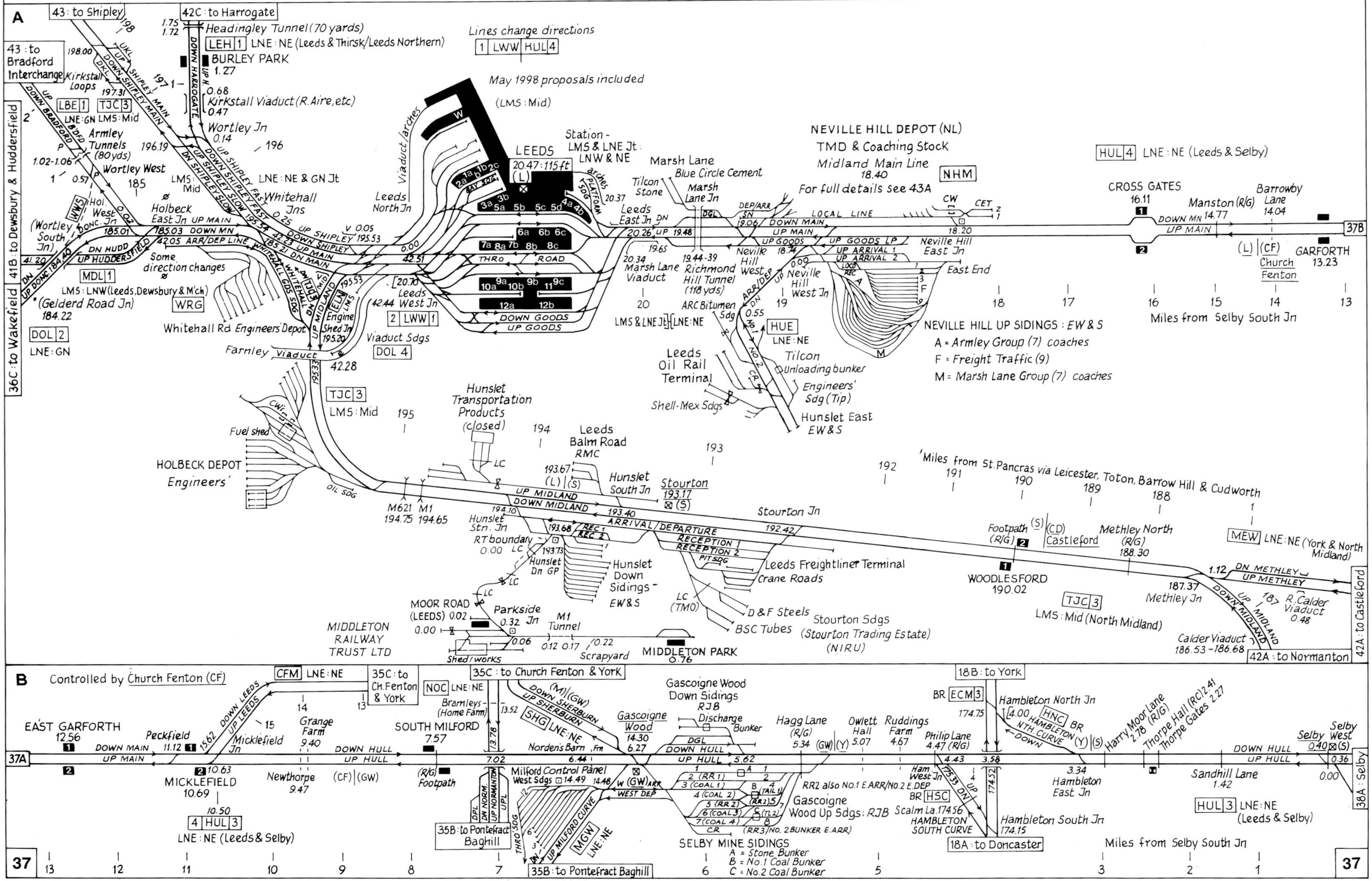
A
43 : to Shipley
42C : to Harrogate
43 : to Bradford Interchange
Headingley Tunnel (70 yards)
LEH 1 LNE : NE (Leeds & Thirsk/Leeds Northern)
BURLEY PARK 1.27
Kirkstall Viaduct (R. Aire, etc)
Kirkstall Loops
Wortley Jn 0.14
LBE 1 TJC 3
LNE : GN LMS : Mid
Armley Tunnels (80 yds)
Wortley West
LNE : NE & GN Jt
Whitehall Jns
Holbeck East Jn
Some direction changes
MDL 1
LMS : LNW (Leeds, Dewsbury & M'ch)
(Gelderd Road Jn) 184.22
WRG
DOL 2
LNE : GN
Whitehall Rd Engineers' Depot
Farnley Viaduct
Viaduct Sdgs
DOL 4
Lines change directions
1 LWW HUL 4
May 1998 proposals included
(LMS : Mid)
LEEDS 20.47 : 115 ft (L)
Station - LMS & LNE Jt : LNW & NE
Leeds North Jn
Leeds West Jn
Leeds East Jn
2 LWW 1
Marsh Lane
Blue Circle Cement
Tilcon Stone
Marsh Lane Jn
Marsh Lane Viaduct
Richmond Hill Tunnel (118 yds)
Neville Hill West Jn
Neville Hill East Jn
East End
NEVILLE HILL DEPOT (NL)
TMD & Coaching Stock
Midland Main Line 18.40
For full details see 43A
NHM
NEVILLE HILL UP SIDINGS : EW & S
A = Armley Group (7) coaches
F = Freight Traffic (9)
M = Marsh Lane Group (7) coaches
HUL 4 LNE : NE (Leeds & Selby)
CROSS GATES 16.11
Manston (R/G) 14.77
Barrowby Lane 14.04
(L) (CF) Church Fenton
GARFORTH 13.23
37B
Miles from Selby South Jn
LMS & LNE Jt LNE : NE
ARC Bitumen Sdg
HUE LNE : NE
Leeds Oil Rail Terminal
Tilcon Unloading bunker
Engineers' Sdg (Tip)
Shell-Mex Sdgs
Hunslet East EW & S
TJC 3 LMS : Mid
Fuel shed
HOLBECK DEPOT Engineers'
Hunslet Transportation Products (closed)
Leeds Balm Road RMC
Hunslet South Jn
Stourton 193.17
Stourton Jn
Miles from St. Pancras via Leicester, Toton, Barrow Hill & Cudworth
M621 194.75
M1 194.65
Hunslet Stn. Jn
RT boundary 0.00
Hunslet Dn GP
Hunslet Down Sidings - EW & S
Leeds Freightliner Terminal
Crane Roads
D & F Steels
BSC Tubes
Stourton Sdgs (Stourton Trading Estate) (NIRU)
MOOR ROAD (LEEDS) 0.02
Parkside Jn 0.32
M1 Tunnel
Scrapyard
MIDDLETON PARK 0.76
MIDDLETON RAILWAY TRUST LTD
Shed/works
Footpath (S) (R/G)
(CD) Castleford
WOODLESFORD 190.02
Methley North (R/G) 188.30
TJC 3 LMS : Mid (North Midland)
MEW LNE : NE (York & North Midland)
Methley Jn
R. Calder Viaduct 0.48
Calder Viaduct 186.53 – 186.68
42A : to Normanton
42A : to Castleford
41B : to Dewsbury & Huddersfield
36C : to Wakefield
B
Controlled by Church Fenton (CF)
CFM LNE : NE
35C : to Ch. Fenton & York
NOC LNE : NE
35C : to Church Fenton & York
EAST GARFORTH 12.56
Peckfield 11.12
MICKLEFIELD 10.69
Micklefield Jn
4 HUL 3
LNE : NE (Leeds & Selby)
Grange Farm 9.40
Newthorpe 9.47
SOUTH MILFORD 7.57
Bramleys (Home Farm)
SHG LNE : NE
Nordens Barn
Milford Control Panel
West Sdgs 14.49
MGW LNE : NE
35B : to Pontefract Baghill
Gascoigne Wood 14.30 6.27
Gascoigne Wood Down Sidings RJB
Discharge Bunker
SELBY MINE SIDINGS
A = Stone Bunker
B = No. 1 Coal Bunker
C = No. 2 Coal Bunker
Gascoigne Wood Up Sdgs : RJB
RR2 also No. 1 E.ARR/No. 2 E.DEP
Hagg Lane (R/G) 5.34
Owlett Hall 5.07
Ruddings Farm 4.67
Philip Lane 4.47 (R/G)
18B : to York
BR ECM 3
Hambleton North Jn
HNC BR HAMBLETON NTH. CURVE
Ham West Jn
BR HSC
Scalm La. 174.56
HAMBLETON SOUTH CURVE
Hambleton East Jn 3.34
Hambleton South Jn 174.15
18A : to Doncaster
Harry Moor Lane 2.78 (R/G)
Thorpe Hall (RC) 2.41
Thorpe Gates 2.27
Sandhill Lane 1.42
HUL 3 LNE : NE (Leeds & Selby)
Selby West 0.40 (S)
38A : Selby
Miles from Selby South Jn
37A

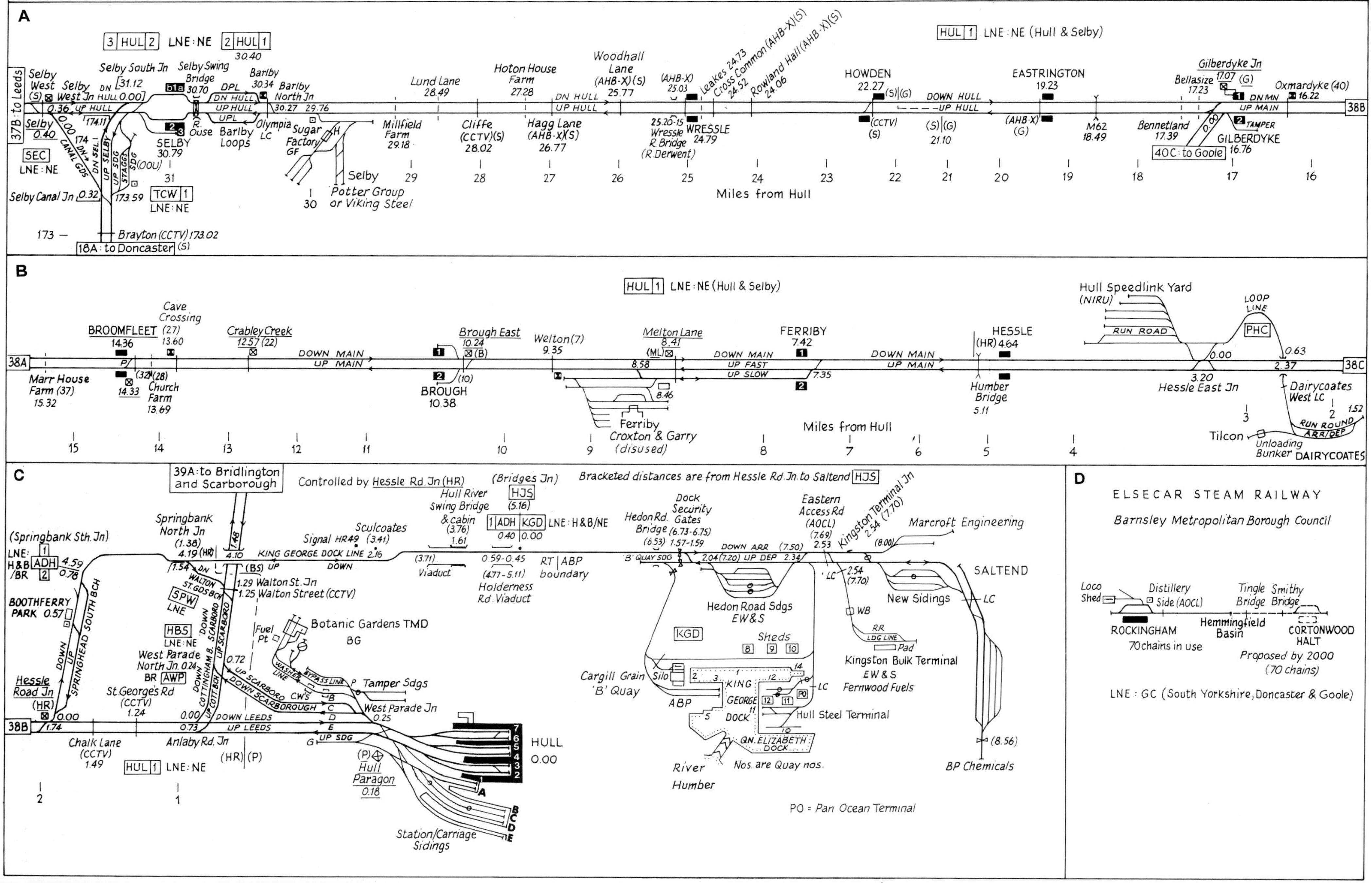
A
3 HUL 2 LNE : NE 2 HUL 1
HUL 1 LNE : NE (Hull & Selby)
37B : to Leeds
Selby West (S)
Selby West Jn
Selby 0.40
SEC LNE : NE
Selby Canal Jn 0.32
Selby South Jn 31.12
Selby Swing Bridge 30.70
SELBY 30.79
R. Ouse
Barlby Loops
Barlby North Jn
Olympia LC
Sugar Factory GF
Selby Potter Group or Viking Steel
TCW 1 LNE : NE
Brayton (CCTV) 173.02
18A : to Doncaster (S)
Millfield Farm 29.18
Lund Lane 28.49
Cliffe (CCTV)(S) 28.02
Hoton House Farm 27.28
Hagg Lane (AHB-X)(S) 26.77
Woodhall Lane (AHB-X)(S) 25.77
Wressle R. Bridge (R. Derwent)
WRESSLE 24.79
Leakes 24.73
Cross Common (AHB-X)(S) 24.52
Rowland Hall (AHB-X)(S) 24.06
HOWDEN 22.27
EASTRINGTON 19.23
M62 18.49
Bennetland 17.39
Bellasize 17.23
Gilberdyke Jn 17.07 (G)
GILBERDYKE 16.76
40C : to Goole
Oxmardyke (40) 16.22
38B
Miles from Hull
B
HUL 1 LNE : NE (Hull & Selby)
38A
Marr House Farm (37) 15.32
BROOMFLEET 14.36
Cave Crossing (27) 13.60
Church Farm 13.69
Crabley Creek 12.57 (22)
BROUGH 10.38
Brough East 10.24
Welton (7) 9.35
Melton Lane 8.41
Ferriby Croxton & Garry (disused)
FERRIBY 7.42
HESSLE (HR) 4.64
Humber Bridge 5.11
Hull Speedlink Yard (NIRU)
RUN ROAD
LOOP LINE
PHC
Hessle East Jn 3.20
Dairycoates West LC
Tilcon
Unloading Bunker
DAIRYCOATES
38C
Miles from Hull
C
39A : to Bridlington and Scarborough
Controlled by Hessle Rd. Jn (HR)
Bracketed distances are from Hessle Rd. Jn. to Saltend HJS
(Springbank Sth. Jn)
Springbank North Jn (1.38)
Sculcoates (3.41)
Signal HR49
KING GEORGE DOCK LINE
Hull River Swing Bridge & cabin (3.76)
(Bridges Jn) HJS (5.16)
1 ADH KGD LNE : H&B/NE
Holderness Rd. Viaduct
RT | ABP boundary
BOOTHFERRY PARK 0.57
SPRINGHEAD SOUTH BCH
Hessle Road Jn (HR)
38B
Chalk Lane (CCTV) 1.49
HUL 1 LNE : NE
Anlaby Rd. Jn
St. George's Rd (CCTV) 1.24
West Parade North Jn. 0.24
1.29 Walton St. Jn
1.25 Walton Street (CCTV)
Botanic Gardens TMD BG
Tamper Sdgs
West Parade Jn 0.25
Hull Paragon 0.18
HULL 0.00
Station/Carriage Sidings
Hedon Rd. Bridge
Dock Security Gates
Eastern Access Rd (AOCL)
Kingston Terminal Jn
Marcroft Engineering
SALTEND
Hedon Road Sdgs EW&S
New Sidings
KGD
Sheds
Cargill Grain Silo 'B' Quay
ABP
KING GEORGE DOCK
QN. ELIZABETH DOCK
Hull Steel Terminal
Kingston Bulk Terminal EW&S
Fernwood Fuels
River Humber
Nos. are Quay nos.
BP Chemicals (8.56)
PO = Pan Ocean Terminal
D
ELSECAR STEAM RAILWAY
Barnsley Metropolitan Borough Council
Loco Shed
Distillery Side (AOCL)
ROCKINGHAM
70chains in use
Hemmingfield Basin
Tingle Bridge
Smithy Bridge
CORTONWOOD HALT
Proposed by 2000 (70 chains)
LNE : GC (South Yorkshire, Doncaster & Goole)

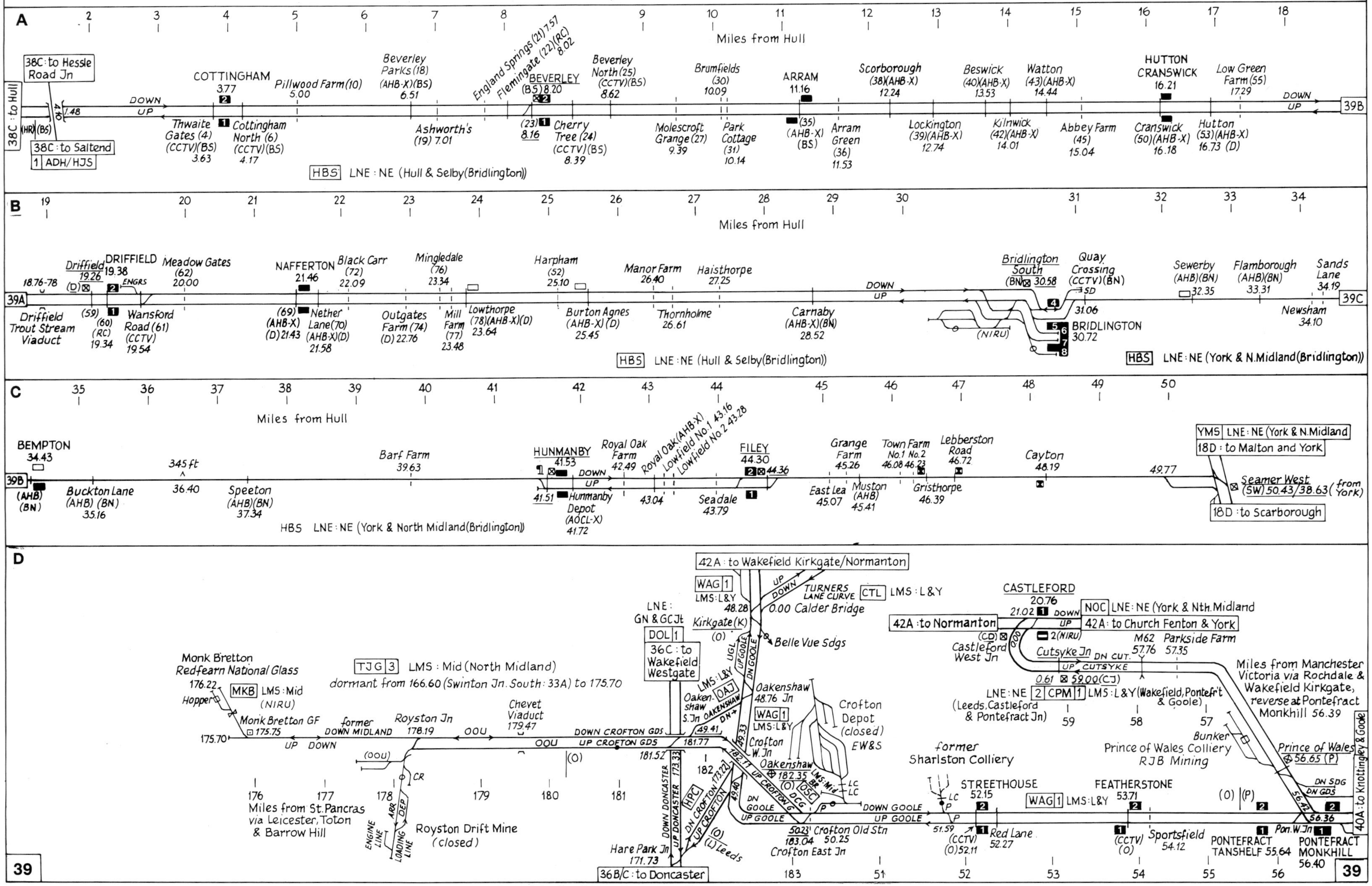
A
Miles from Hull
38C: to Hull
38C: to Hessle Road Jn
38C: to Saltend
1 ADH/HJS
COTTINGHAM 3.77
Thwaite Gates (4) (CCTV)(BS) 3.63
Cottingham North (6) (CCTV)(BS) 4.17
Pillwood Farm (10) 5.00
Beverley Parks (18) (AHB-X)(BS) 6.51
Ashworth's (19) 7.01
England Springs (21) 7.57
Flemingate (22)(RC) 8.02
BEVERLEY (BS) 8.20
(23) 8.16
Cherry Tree (24) (CCTV)(BS) 8.39
Beverley North (25) (CCTV)(BS) 8.62
Molescroft Grange (27) 9.39
Brumfields (30) 10.09
Park Cottage (31) 10.14
ARRAM 11.16
(35) (AHB-X) (BS)
Arram Green (36) 11.53
Scorborough (38)(AHB-X) 12.24
Lockington (39)(AHB-X) 12.74
Beswick (40)(AHB-X) 13.53
Kilnwick (42)(AHB-X) 14.01
Watton (43)(AHB-X) 14.44
Abbey Farm (45) 15.04
HUTTON CRANSWICK 16.21
Cranswick (50)(AHB-X) 16.18
Hutton (53)(AHB-X) 16.73 (D)
Low Green Farm (55) 17.29
DOWN UP
39B
HBS LNE: NE (Hull & Selby (Bridlington))
B
Miles from Hull
39A
18.76-78
Driffield 19.26 (D)
DRIFFIELD 19.38
ENGRS
Driffield Trout Stream Viaduct
(59)
(60) (RC) 19.34
Wansford Road (61) (CCTV) 19.54
Meadow Gates (62) 20.00
NAFFERTON 21.46
(69) (AHB-X) (D) 21.43
Nether Lane (70) (AHB-X)(D) 21.58
Black Carr (72) 22.09
Outgates Farm (74) (D) 22.76
Mingledale (76) 23.34
Mill Farm (77) 23.48
Lowthorpe (78)(AHB-X)(D) 23.64
Harpham (52) 25.10
Burton Agnes (AHB-X) (D) 25.45
Manor Farm 26.40
Thornholme 26.61
Haisthorpe 27.25
HBS LNE: NE (Hull & Selby (Bridlington))
Carnaby (AHB-X)(BN) 28.52
(NIRU)
Bridlington South (BN) 30.58
Quay Crossing (CCTV)(BN)
SD
31.06
BRIDLINGTON 30.72
Sewerby (AHB)(BN) 32.35
Flamborough (AHB)(BN) 33.31
Sands Lane 34.19
Newsham 34.10
39C
HBS LNE: NE (York & N. Midland (Bridlington))
C
Miles from Hull
BEMPTON 34.43
39B
(AHB) (BN)
Buckton Lane (AHB) (BN) 35.16
345 ft
36.40
Speeton (AHB)(BN) 37.34
Barf Farm 39.63
HBS LNE: NE (York & North Midland (Bridlington))
HUNMANBY 41.53
41.51
Hunmanby Depot (AOCL-X) 41.72
Royal Oak Farm 42.49
Royal Oak (AHB-X)
Lowfield No.1 43.16
Lowfield No.2 43.28
43.04
Seadale 43.79
FILEY 44.30
44.36
East Lea 45.07
Grange Farm 45.26
Muston (AHB) 45.41
Town Farm No.1 No.2 46.08 46.23
Gristhorpe 46.39
Lebberston Road 46.72
Cayton 48.19
49.77
YMS LNE: NE (York & N. Midland
18D: to Malton and York
Seamer West (SW) 50.43/38.63 (from York)
18D: to Scarborough
D
Monk Bretton Redfearn National Glass 176.22
Hopper
MKB LMS: Mid (NIRU)
Monk Bretton GF 175.75
175.70
UP DOWN
TJG 3 LMS: Mid (North Midland)
dormant from 166.60 (Swinton Jn. South: 33A) to 175.70
former DOWN MIDLAND
Royston Jn 178.19
OOU
(OOU)
CR
ARR DEP
ENGINE LINE
LOADING LINE
Royston Drift Mine (closed)
Miles from St. Pancras via Leicester, Toton & Barrow Hill
Chevet Viaduct 179.47
DOWN CROFTON GDS
UP CROFTON GDS
(O)
181.52
181.77
LNE: GN & GCJt
DOL 1
36C: to Wakefield Westgate
42A: to Wakefield Kirkgate/Normanton
WAG 1 LMS: L&Y 48.28
Kirkgate (K) (O)
UGL
UP GOOLE
DN GOOLE
TURNERS LANE CURVE
CTL LMS: L&Y
0.00 Calder Bridge
Belle Vue Sdgs
LMS: L&Y
Oakenshaw S.Jn
OAJ
49.41
49.33
Oakenshaw 48.76 Jn
WAG 1 LMS: L&Y
Crofton W. Jn
Oakenshaw 182.35
(O)
OSC
DCG
LMS: Mid
Crofton Depot (closed) EW&S
182
182.11 UP CROFTON G
DOWN DONCASTER 173.33
UP DONCASTER
HPC
DN CROFTON 173.22
UP CROFTON
49.40
(O) (L) Leeds
Hare Park Jn 171.73
36B/C: to Doncaster
DN GOOLE UP GOOLE
50.23 Crofton Old Stn 183.04 50.25
Crofton East Jn
DOWN GOOLE UP GOOLE
CASTLEFORD 20.76
21.02 DOWN UP
42A: to Normanton
(CD)
Castleford West Jn
OOO
2 (NIRU)
NOC LNE: NE (York & Nth. Midland
42A: to Church Fenton & York
Cutsyke Jn DN CUT.
UP CUTSYKE
M62 57.76
Parkside Farm 57.35
0.61 59.00 (CJ)
LNE: NE (Leeds, Castleford & Pontefract Jn)
2 CPM 1 LMS: L&Y (Wakefield, Pontefr't & Goole)
Miles from Manchester Victoria via Rochdale & Wakefield Kirkgate, reverse at Pontefract Monkhill 56.39
former Sharlston Colliery
LC P
51.59
STREETHOUSE 52.15
(CCTV) (O) 52.11
Red Lane 52.27
WAG 1 LMS: L&Y
FEATHERSTONE 53.71
(CCTV) (O)
Sportsfield 54.12
Bunker
Prince of Wales Colliery RJB Mining
Prince of Wales 56.65 (P)
(O) (P)
DN SDG
DN GDS
56.42
56.36
Pon. W. Jn
PONTEFRACT TANSHELF 55.64
PONTEFRACT MONKHILL 56.40
40A: to Knottingley & Goole
176 177 178 179 180 181 183 51 52 53 54 55 56 57 58 59
39

# PONTEFRACT – GOOLE – GILBERDYKE ● KIRKLEES LIGHT RAILWAY



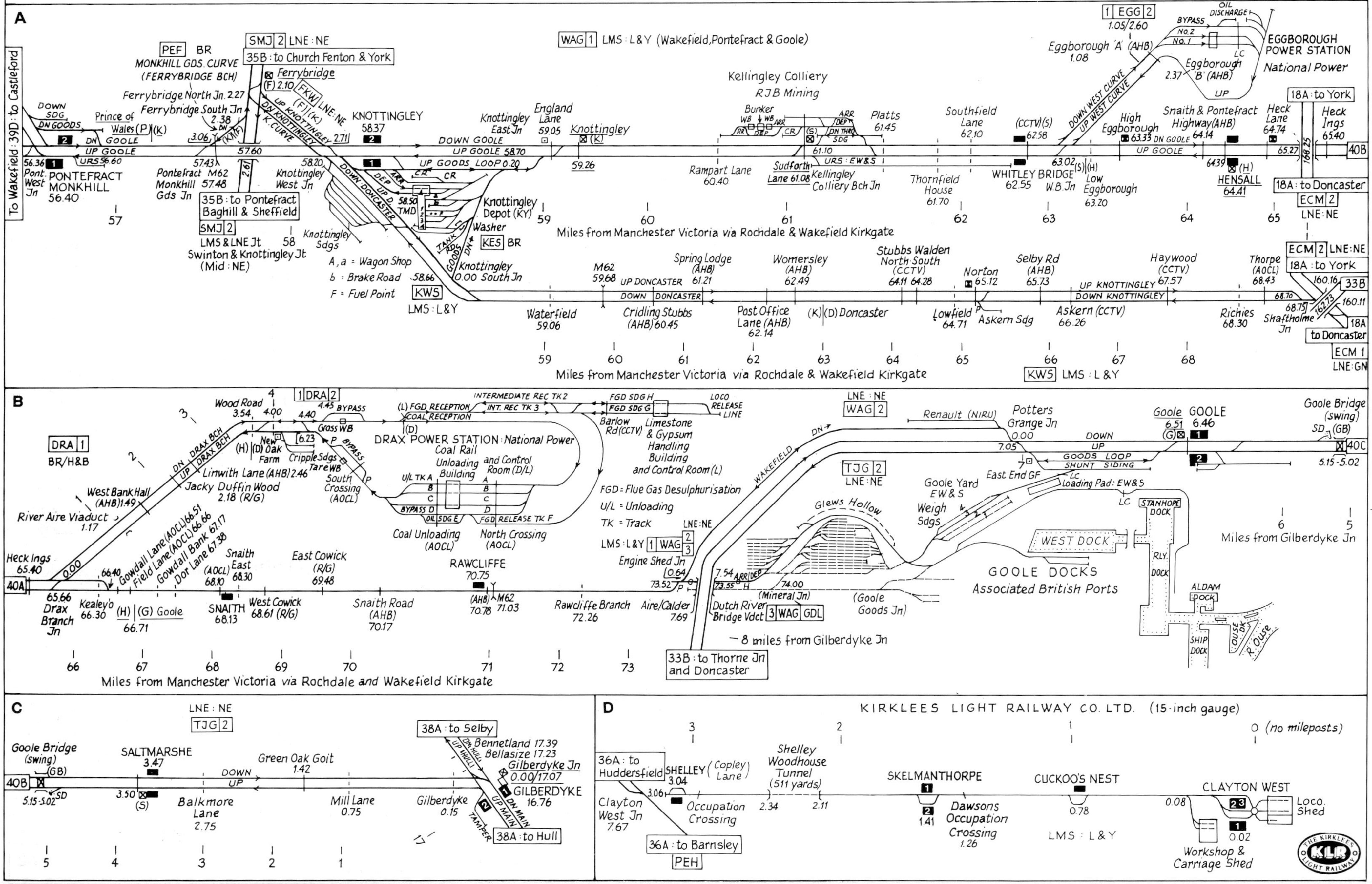

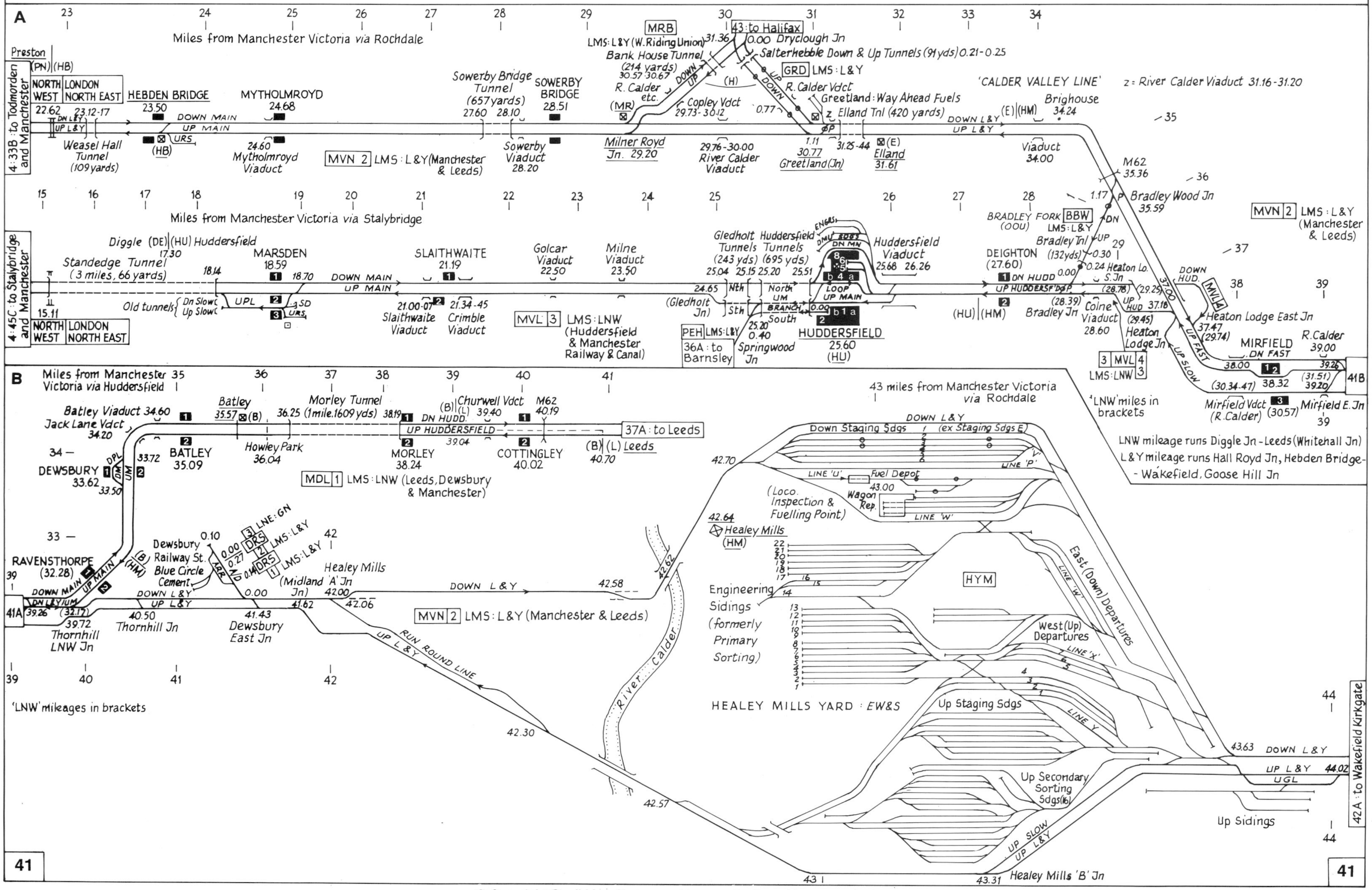
A
Miles from Manchester Victoria via Rochdale
4:33B: to Todmorden and Manchester
Preston
(PN)(HB)
NORTH WEST | LONDON NORTH EAST
HEBDEN BRIDGE 23.50
MYTHOLMROYD 24.68
DOWN MAIN
UP MAIN
Weasel Hall Tunnel (109 yards)
24.60 Mytholmroyd Viaduct
MVN 2 LMS: L&Y (Manchester & Leeds)
Sowerby Bridge Tunnel (657 yards) 27.60 28.10
SOWERBY BRIDGE 28.51
Sowerby Viaduct 28.20
MRB
LMS: L&Y (W. Riding Union) 31.36
Bank House Tunnel (214 yards) 30.57 30.67
R. Calder etc.
Milner Royd Jn. 29.20
Copley Vdct 29.73-30.12
29.76-30.00 River Calder Viaduct
43: to Halifax
0.00 Dryclough Jn
Salterhebble Down & Up Tunnels (91 yds) 0.21-0.25
GRD LMS: L&Y
R. Calder Vdct
Greetland: Way Ahead Fuels
Elland Tnl (420 yards)
1.11 30.77 Greetland (Jn)
31.25-44
Elland 31.61
'CALDER VALLEY LINE'
z: River Calder Viaduct 31.16-31.20
Brighouse 34.24
DOWN L&Y
UP L&Y
Viaduct 34.00
M62 35.36
Bradley Wood Jn 35.59
MVN 2 LMS: L&Y (Manchester & Leeds)
Miles from Manchester Victoria via Stalybridge
4:45C: to Stalybridge and Manchester
Diggle (DE) (HU) Huddersfield 17.30
Standedge Tunnel (3 miles, 66 yards)
Old tunnels Dn Slow Up Slow
15.11
NORTH WEST | LONDON NORTH EAST
MARSDEN 18.59
SLAITHWAITE 21.19
21.00-07 Slaithwaite Viaduct
21.34-45 Crimble Viaduct
Golcar Viaduct 22.50
Milne Viaduct 23.50
MVL 3 LMS: LNW (Huddersfield & Manchester Railway & Canal)
Gledholt Tunnels (243 yds) 25.04 25.15
Huddersfield Tunnels (695 yds) 25.20 25.51
(Gledholt Jn)
PEH LMS: L&Y
36A: to Barnsley
25.20 0.40 Springwood Jn
HUDDERSFIELD 25.60 (HU)
Huddersfield Viaduct 25.68 26.26
BRADLEY FORK (OOU) BBW LMS: L&Y
Bradley Tnl (132 yds)
DEIGHTON (27.60)
DN HUDD
UP HUDDERSFIELD
Bradley Jn
Heaton Lo. S. Jn
Colne Viaduct 28.60
Heaton Lodge Jn
3 MVL 4 LMS: LNW 3
Heaton Lodge East Jn 37.47 (29.74)
MIRFIELD DN FAST
R. Calder 39.00
UP FAST
UP SLOW
Mirfield Vdct (R. Calder) (30.57)
Mirfield E. Jn
41B
B
Miles from Manchester Victoria via Huddersfield
Batley Viaduct 34.60
Jack Lane Vdct 34.20
DEWSBURY 33.62
Batley 35.57 (B)
BATLEY 35.09
Morley Tunnel (1 mile 1609 yds) 36.25 38.19
Howley Park 36.04
MORLEY 38.24
Churwell Vdct 39.40
M62 40.19
COTTINGLEY 40.02
37A: to Leeds
(B) (L) Leeds 40.70
MDL 1 LMS: LNW (Leeds, Dewsbury & Manchester)
RAVENSTHORPE (32.28)
41A
Thornhill LNW Jn
40.50 Thornhill Jn
Dewsbury Railway St. Blue Circle Cement
LINE: GN
DRS LMS: L&Y
41.43 Dewsbury East Jn
Healey Mills (Midland 'A' Jn) 42.00
MVN 2 LMS: L&Y (Manchester & Leeds)
RUN ROUND LINE
River Calder
'LNW' mileages in brackets
43 miles from Manchester Victoria via Rochdale
'LNW' miles in brackets
LNW mileage runs Diggle Jn - Leeds (Whitehall Jn)
L&Y mileage runs Hall Royd Jn, Hebden Bridge - Wakefield, Goose Hill Jn
Down Staging Sdgs
(ex Staging Sdgs E)
Fuel Depot
Wagon Rep.
(Loco. Inspection & Fuelling Point)
Healey Mills (HM)
Engineering Sidings (formerly Primary Sorting)
HYM
East (Down) Departures
West (Up) Departures
HEALEY MILLS YARD: EW&S
Up Staging Sdgs
Up Secondary Sorting Sdgs (16)
Up Sidings
UGL
Healey Mills 'B' Jn
42A: to Wakefield Kirkgate
41

# WAKEFIELD KIRKGATE – CASTLEFORD – MILFORD ● (LEEDS) – HARROGATE – (YORK)



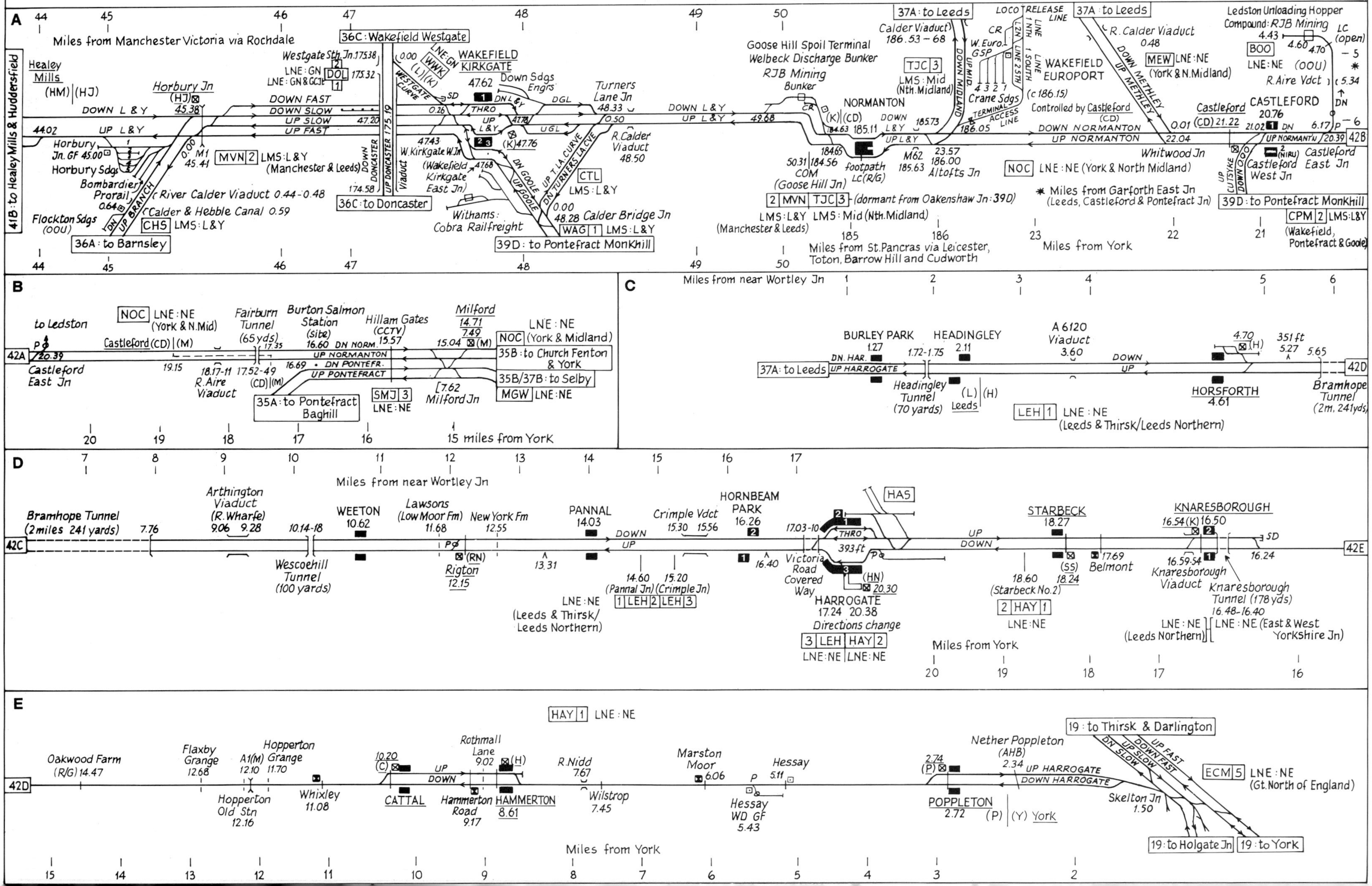

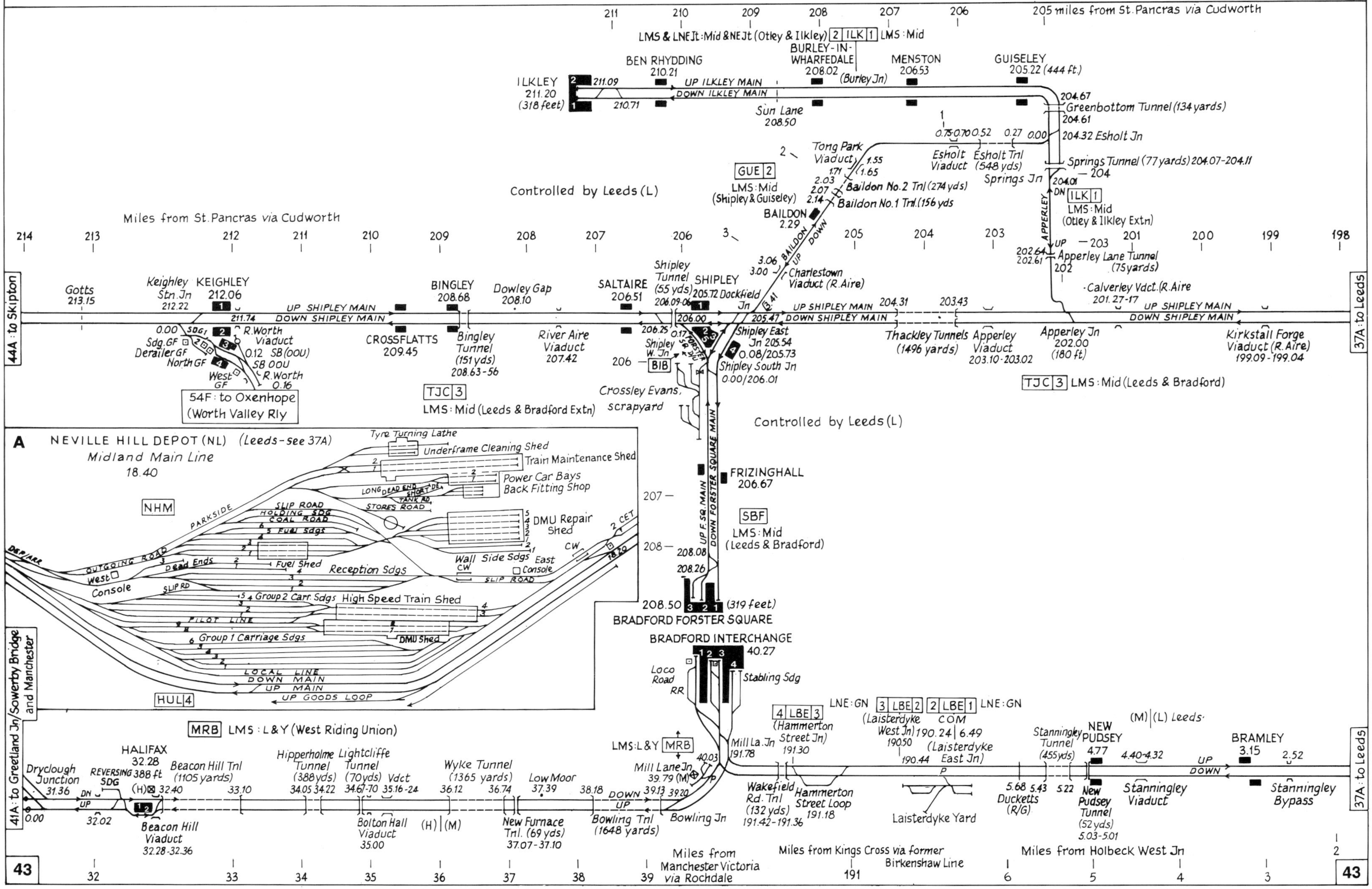
205 miles from St. Pancras via Cudworth
LMS & LNEJt: Mid & NEJt (Otley & Ilkley) 2 ILK 1 LMS: Mid
ILKLEY 211.20 (318 feet)
BEN RHYDDING 210.21
BURLEY-IN-WHARFEDALE 208.02
(Burley Jn)
MENSTON 206.53
GUISELEY 205.22 (444 ft.)
UP ILKLEY MAIN
DOWN ILKLEY MAIN
Sun Lane 208.50
Greenbottom Tunnel (134 yards)
204.32 Esholt Jn
Esholt Viaduct
Esholt Tnl (548 yds)
Springs Tunnel (77 yards) 204.07-204.11
Springs Jn
Tong Park Viaduct
Baildon No.2 Tnl (274 yds)
Baildon No.1 Tnl (156 yds
GUE 2
LMS: Mid (Shipley & Guiseley)
BAILDON 2.29
ILK 1
LMS: Mid (Otley & Ilkley Extn)
Controlled by Leeds (L)
Miles from St. Pancras via Cudworth
44A: to Skipton
Gotts 213.15
Keighley Stn. Jn 212.22
KEIGHLEY 212.06
UP SHIPLEY MAIN
DOWN SHIPLEY MAIN
R. Worth Viaduct
54F: to Oxenhope (Worth Valley Rly)
CROSSFLATTS 209.45
BINGLEY 208.68
Bingley Tunnel (151 yds) 208.63-56
Dowley Gap 208.10
River Aire Viaduct 207.42
TJC 3
LMS: Mid (Leeds & Bradford Extn)
SALTAIRE 206.51
Shipley Tunnel (55 yds)
SHIPLEY
205.72 Dockfield Jn
Charlestown Viaduct (R. Aire)
Shipley East Jn 205.54
Shipley South Jn
Shipley W. Jn
BIB
Crossley Evans, scrapyard
Apperley Lane Tunnel (75 yards)
Calverley Vdct. (R. Aire 201.27-17
Thackley Tunnels (1496 yards)
Apperley Viaduct 203.10-203.02
Apperley Jn 202.00 (180 ft)
Kirkstall Forge Viaduct (R. Aire) 199.09-199.04
TJC 3 LMS: Mid (Leeds & Bradford)
37A: to Leeds
Controlled by Leeds (L)
FRIZINGHALL 206.67
SBF
LMS: Mid (Leeds & Bradford)
UP F.SQ. MAIN
DOWN FORSTER SQUARE MAIN
208.50 (319 feet)
BRADFORD FORSTER SQUARE
A NEVILLE HILL DEPOT (NL) (Leeds - see 37A)
Midland Main Line 18.40
NHM
Tyre Turning Lathe
Underframe Cleaning Shed
Train Maintenance Shed
Power Car Bays
Back Fitting Shop
DMU Repair Shed
Wall Side Sdgs
Reception Sdgs
Fuel Shed
Group 2 Carr. Sdgs
High Speed Train Shed
Group 1 Carriage Sdgs
DMU Shed
LOCAL LINE
DOWN MAIN
UP MAIN
UP GOODS LOOP
HUL 4
BRADFORD INTERCHANGE 40.27
Loco Road
Stabling Sdg
4 LBE 3 (Hammerton Street Jn) 191.30
LNE: GN
3 LBE 2 (Laisterdyke West Jn)
2 LBE 1 LNE: GN
COM 190.24 | 6.49 (Laisterdyke East Jn)
Laisterdyke Yard
Mill La. Jn 191.78
Wakefield Rd. Tnl (132 yds) 191.42-191.36
Hammerton Street Loop 191.18
Duckets (R/G)
Stanningley Tunnel (455 yds)
NEW PUDSEY 4.77
New Pudsey Tunnel (52 yds) 5.03-5.01
Stanningley Viaduct
(M) | (L) Leeds
BRAMLEY 3.15
Stanningley Bypass
MRB LMS: L&Y (West Riding Union)
41A: to Greetland Jn/Sowerby Bridge and Manchester
Dryclough Junction 31.36
HALIFAX 32.28
REVERSING SDG
Beacon Hill Tnl (1105 yards)
Beacon Hill Viaduct 32.28-32.36
Hipperholme Tunnel (388 yds)
Lightcliffe Tunnel (70 yds)
Vdct
Bolton Hall Viaduct 35.00
(H) | (M)
Wyke Tunnel (1365 yards)
New Furnace Tnl. (69 yds) 37.07-37.10
Low Moor 37.39
Bowling Tnl (1648 yards)
Bowling Jn
LMS: L&Y MRB
Mill Lane Jn 39.79 (M)
Miles from Manchester Victoria via Rochdale
Miles from Kings Cross via former Birkenshaw Line
Miles from Holbeck West Jn

## (KEIGHLEY) – SKIPTON – SETTLE JN. – CARNFORTH ● RYLSTONE BRANCH ● EMBSAY & BOLTON ABBEY STEAM RLY.



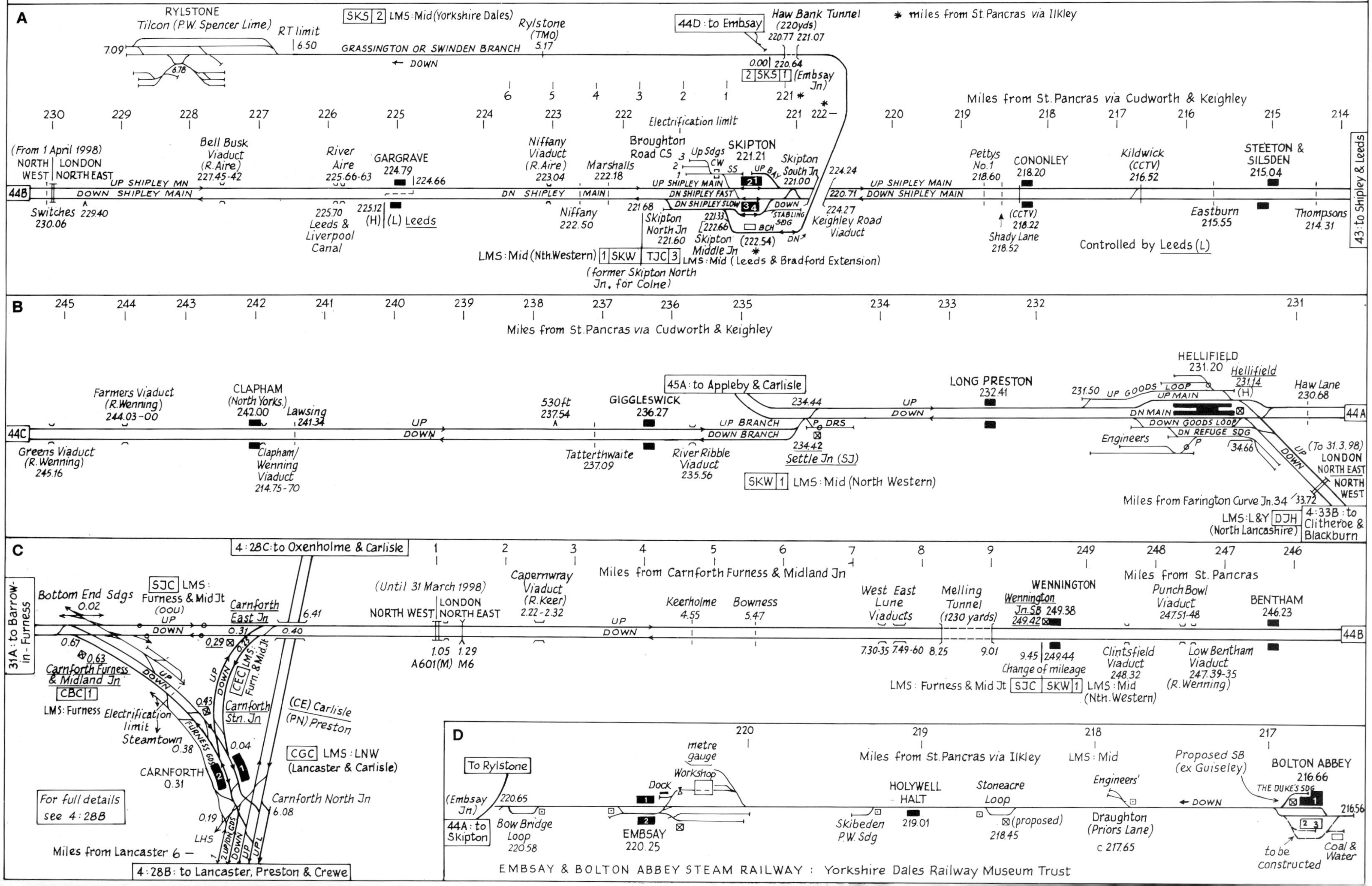

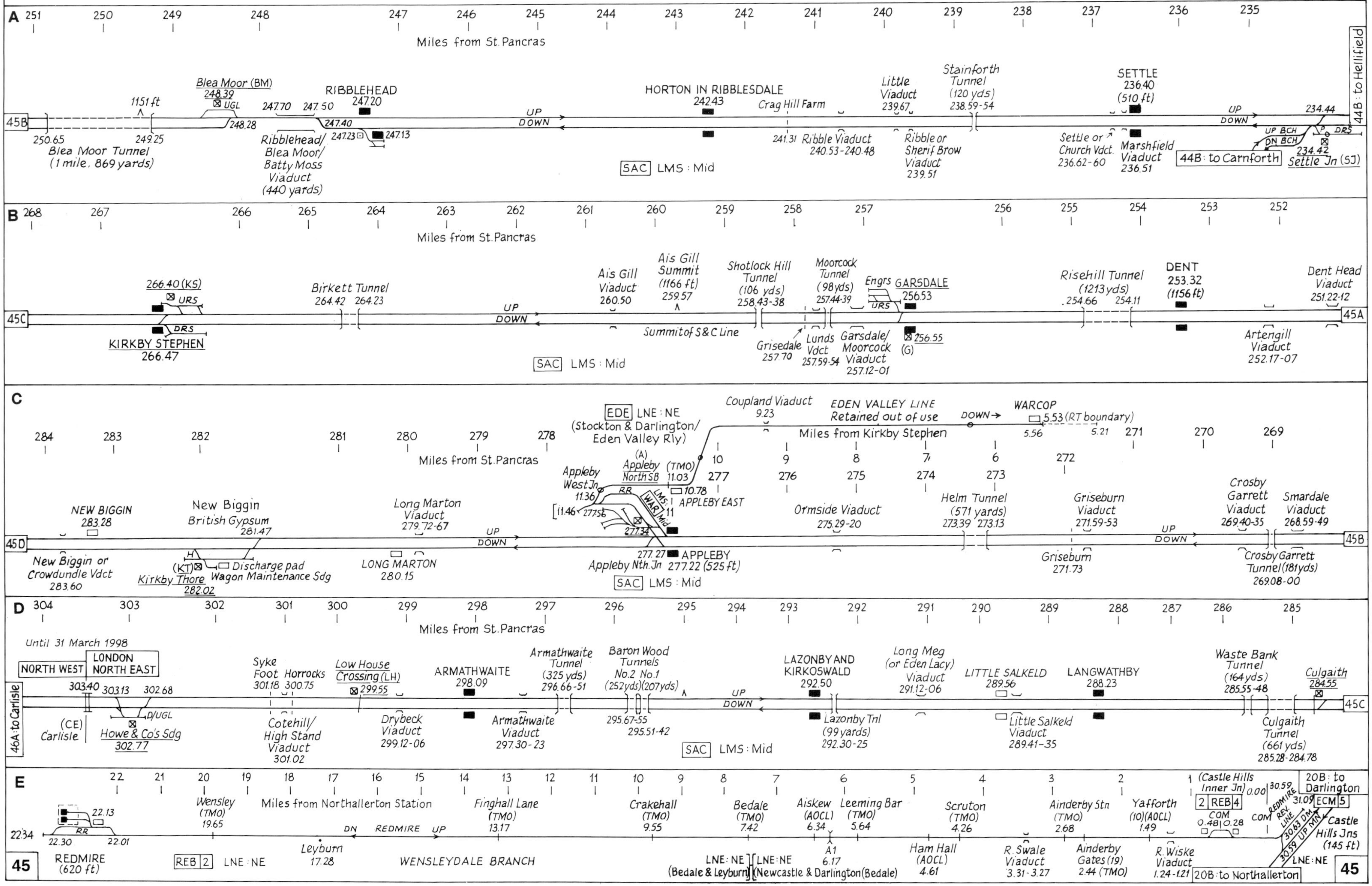
A
Miles from St. Pancras
45B
Blea Moor (BM) 248.39 UGL
1151 ft
250.65 Blea Moor Tunnel (1 mile, 869 yards)
249.25
248.28
RIBBLEHEAD 247.20
247.70 247.50 247.40
247.23 247.13
Ribblehead/ Blea Moor/ Batty Moss Viaduct (440 yards)
UP DOWN
HORTON IN RIBBLESDALE 242.43
Crag Hill Farm
241.31 Ribble Viaduct 240.53-240.48
Little Viaduct 239.67
Stainforth Tunnel (120 yds) 238.59-54
Ribble or Sherif Brow Viaduct 239.51
SAC LMS : Mid
SETTLE 236.40 (510 ft)
Settle or Church Vdct. 236.62-60
Marshfield Viaduct 236.51
234.44
UP BCH DN BCH DRS
234.42 Settle Jn (SJ)
44B: to Carnforth
44B: to Hellifield
B
Miles from St. Pancras
45C
266.40 (KS) URS DRS
KIRKBY STEPHEN 266.47
Birkett Tunnel 264.42 264.23
UP DOWN
Ais Gill Viaduct 260.50
Ais Gill Summit (1166 ft) 259.57
Summit of S&C Line
Shotlock Hill Tunnel (106 yds) 258.43-38
Moorcock Tunnel (98 yds) 257.44-39
Grisedale 257.70
Lunds Vdct 257.59-54
Engrs URS GARSDALE 256.53
Garsdale/ Moorcock Viaduct 257.12-01
256.55 (G)
SAC LMS : Mid
Risehill Tunnel (1213 yds) 254.66 254.11
DENT 253.32 (1156 ft)
Dent Head Viaduct 251.22-12
Artengill Viaduct 252.17-07
45A
C
Miles from St. Pancras
45D
NEW BIGGIN 283.28
New Biggin or Crowdundle Vdct 283.60
New Biggin British Gypsum 281.47
H (KT) Discharge pad Wagon Maintenance Sdg
Kirkby Thore 282.02
Long Marton Viaduct 279.72-67
LONG MARTON 280.15
UP DOWN
EDE LNE : NE (Stockton & Darlington/ Eden Valley Rly)
Appleby West Jn 11.36
11.46 277.56
(A) Appleby North SB (TMO) 11.03
RR LMS:1 WAR Mid
10.78 APPLEBY EAST
277.34
277.27 APPLEBY 277.22 (525 ft)
Appleby Nth. Jn
SAC LMS : Mid
Coupland Viaduct 9.23
EDEN VALLEY LINE Retained out of use
Miles from Kirkby Stephen
DOWN →
WARCOP 5.53 (RT boundary) 5.56 5.21
Ormside Viaduct 275.29-20
Helm Tunnel (571 yards) 273.39 273.13
Griseburn Viaduct 271.59-53
Griseburn 271.73
Crosby Garrett Viaduct 269.40-35
Smardale Viaduct 268.59-49
Crosby Garrett Tunnel (181 yds) 269.08-00
45B
D
Miles from St. Pancras
Until 31 March 1998
NORTH WEST LONDON NORTH EAST
46A: to Carlisle
303.40 303.13 302.68
(CE) Carlisle
D/UGL Howe & Co's Sdg 302.77
Syke Foot 301.18 Horrocks 300.75
Cotehill/ High Stand Viaduct 301.02
Low House Crossing (LH) 299.55
Drybeck Viaduct 299.12-06
ARMATHWAITE 298.09
Armathwaite Tunnel (325 yds) 296.66-51
Armathwaite Viaduct 297.30-23
Baron Wood Tunnels No.2 No.1 (252yds)(207yds)
295.67-55 295.51-42
UP DOWN
SAC LMS : Mid
LAZONBY AND KIRKOSWALD 292.50
Lazonby Tnl (99 yards) 292.30-25
Long Meg (or Eden Lacy) Viaduct 291.12-06
LITTLE SALKELD 289.56
Little Salkeld Viaduct 289.41-35
LANGWATHBY 288.23
Waste Bank Tunnel (164 yds) 285.55-48
Culgaith 284.55
Culgaith Tunnel (661 yds) 285.28-284.78
45C
E
Miles from Northallerton Station
22.34
22.13 RR
22.30 22.01
REDMIRE (620 ft)
REB 2 LNE : NE
Wensley (TMO) 19.65
Leyburn 17.28
DN REDMIRE UP
WENSLEYDALE BRANCH
Finghall Lane (TMO) 13.17
Crakehall (TMO) 9.55
Bedale (TMO) 7.42
LNE : NE (Bedale & Leyburn) LNE : NE (Newcastle & Darlington (Bedale)
Aiskew (AOCL) 6.34
A1 6.17
Leeming Bar (TMO) 5.64
Scruton (TMO) 4.26
Ham Hall (AOCL) 4.61
Ainderby Stn (TMO) 2.68
R. Swale Viaduct 3.31-3.27
Ainderby Gates (19) 2.44 (TMO)
Yafforth (10)(AOCL) 1.49
R. Wiske Viaduct 1.24-1.21
(Castle Hills Inner Jn) 0.00
2 REB 4
COM 0.48 0.28
COM
REDMIRE LINE REV. 30.63 DM 30.59 UP MN 30.59 31.09
20B: to Darlington
ECM 5
Castle Hills Jns (145 ft)
LNE : NE
20B: to Northallerton
45

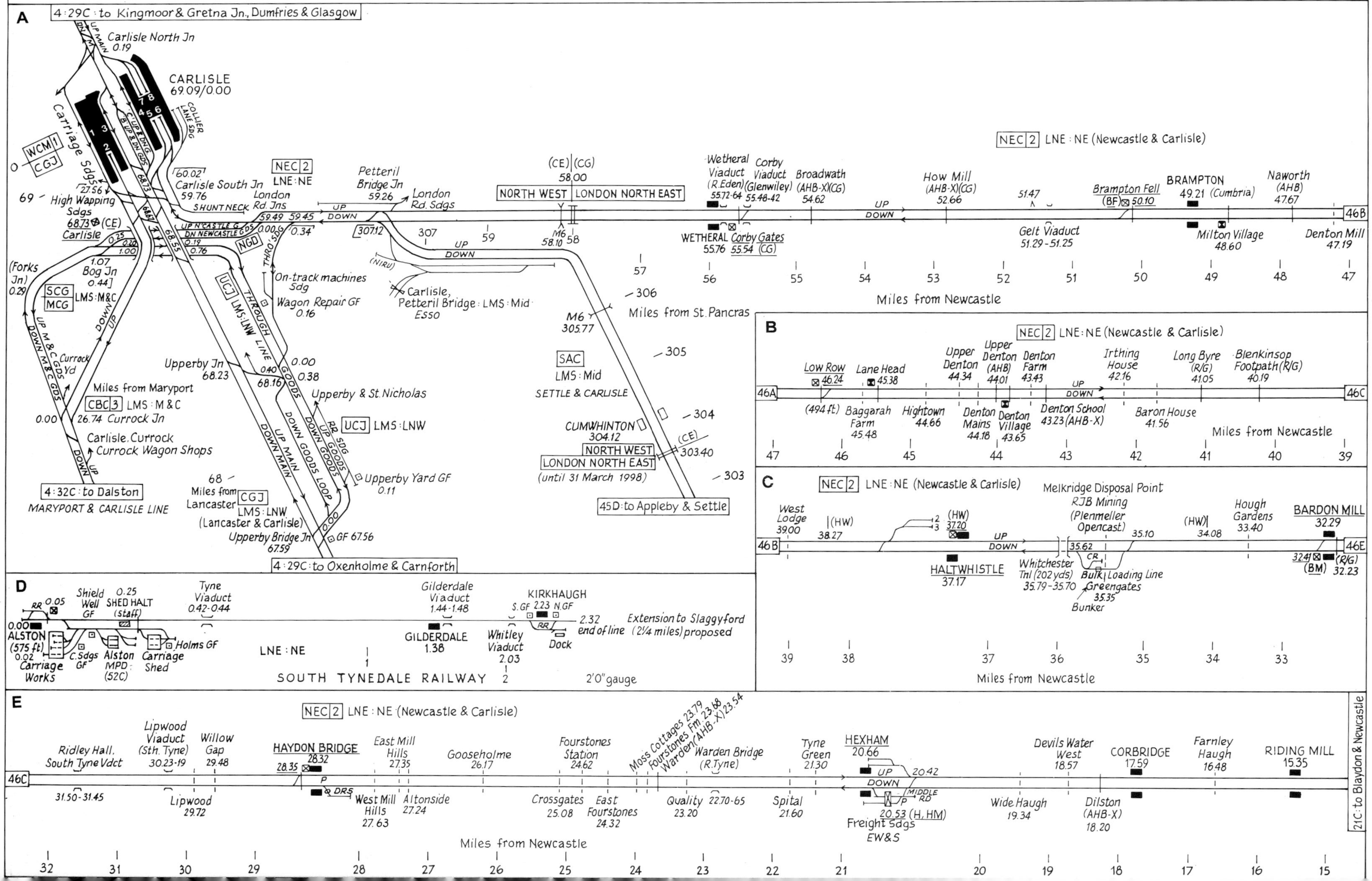
A
4:29C: to Kingmoor & Gretna Jn., Dumfries & Glasgow
Carlisle North Jn 0.19
CARLISLE 69.09/0.00
COLLIER LANE SDG
Carriage Sdgs
WCM1
CGJ
69 – High Wapping Sdgs 27.56
68.73 (CE)
Carlisle
60.02
Carlisle South Jn 59.76
NEC2 LNE:NE
London Rd. Jns
SHUNT NECK
Petteril Bridge Jn 59.26
London Rd. Sdgs
UP NCASTLE GDS
DN NEWCASTLE GDS
NGD
THRO SDG
On-track machines Sdg
Wagon Repair GF 0.16
Carlisle, Petteril Bridge: LMS:Mid Esso
(NIRU)
307.12
307
(CE) (CG) 58.00
NORTH WEST | LONDON NORTH EAST
M6 58.10 58
59
57
– 306
Miles from St. Pancras
M6 305.77
– 305
SAC LMS:Mid
SETTLE & CARLISLE
– 304
CUMWHINTON 304.12
NORTH WEST
LONDON NORTH EAST
(until 31 March 1998)
(CE) 303.40
– 303
45D: to Appleby & Settle
(Forks Jn) 0.29
SCG MCG LMS:M&C
Bog Jn 0.44
UP M&C GDS
DOWN M&C GDS
Currock Yd
Miles from Maryport
CBC3 LMS:M&C
0.00
26.74 Currock Jn
Carlisle, Currock
Currock Wagon Shops
4:32C: to Dalston
MARYPORT & CARLISLE LINE
Upperby Jn 68.23
UCJ LMS:LNW
THROUGH LINE
GOODS
Upperby & St. Nicholas
UCJ LMS:LNW
RR SDG
UP GOODS
DOWN GOODS
DOWN GOODS LOOP
UP MAIN
DOWN MAIN
Upperby Yard GF 0.11
68 – Miles from Lancaster
CGJ LMS:LNW (Lancaster & Carlisle)
Upperby Bridge Jn 67.59
GF 67.56
4:29C: to Oxenholme & Carnforth
Wetheral Viaduct (R.Eden) 55.72-64
Corby Viaduct (Glenwiley) 55.48-42
Broadwath (AHB-X)(CG) 54.62
WETHERAL 55.76
Corby Gates 55.54 (CG)
How Mill (AHB-X)(CG) 52.66
51.47
Gelt Viaduct 51.29-51.25
Brampton Fell (BF) 50.10
BRAMPTON 49.21 (Cumbria)
Milton Village 48.60
Naworth (AHB) 47.67
Denton Mill 47.19
NEC2 LNE:NE (Newcastle & Carlisle)
Miles from Newcastle
46B
B
NEC2 LNE:NE (Newcastle & Carlisle)
46A
Low Row 46.24
(494 ft)
Lane Head 45.38
Baggarah Farm 45.48
Hightown 44.66
Upper Denton 44.34
Upper Denton (AHB) 44.01
Denton Farm 43.43
Denton Mains 44.18
Denton Village 43.65
Denton School 43.23 (AHB-X)
Irthing House 42.16
Baron House 41.56
Long Byre (R/G) 41.05
Blenkinsop Footpath (R/G) 40.19
Miles from Newcastle
46C
C
NEC2 LNE:NE (Newcastle & Carlisle)
West Lodge 39.00
(HW) 38.27
(HW) 37.20
HALTWHISTLE 37.17
Whitchester Tnl (202 yds) 35.79-35.70
35.62
CR
Bulk Loading Line
Greengates 35.35
Bunker
Melkridge Disposal Point
RJB Mining (Plenmeller Opencast) 35.10
(HW) 34.08
Hough Gardens 33.40
BARDON MILL 32.29
32.41 (BM)
(R/G) 32.23
Miles from Newcastle
46E
D
ALSTON (575 ft) 0.00
0.02 Carriage Works
RR 0.05
C.Sdgs GF
Shield Well GF
0.25 SHED HALT (staff)
Alston MPD (52C)
Carriage Shed
Holms GF
Tyne Viaduct 0.42-0.44
LNE:NE
SOUTH TYNEDALE RAILWAY
Gilderdale Viaduct 1.44-1.48
GILDERDALE 1.38
Whitley Viaduct 2.03
KIRKHAUGH
S.GF 2.23 N.GF
RR
Dock
2.32 end of line
Extension to Slaggyford (2¼ miles) proposed
2'0" gauge
E
NEC2 LNE:NE (Newcastle & Carlisle)
46C
Ridley Hall, South Tyne Vdct
31.50-31.45
Lipwood Viaduct (Sth. Tyne) 30.23-19
Lipwood 29.72
Willow Gap 29.48
HAYDON BRIDGE 28.32
28.35
DRS
West Mill Hills 27.63
East Mill Hills 27.35
Altonside 27.24
Gooseholme 26.17
Crossgates 25.08
Fourstones Station 24.62
East Fourstones 24.32
Moss Cottages 23.79
Fourstones Fm 23.68
Warden (AHB-X) 23.54
Quality 23.20
Warden Bridge (R.Tyne) 22.70-65
Tyne Green 21.30
Spital 21.60
HEXHAM 20.66
20.42
MIDDLE RD
20.53 (H, HM)
Freight Sdgs EW&S
Wide Haugh 19.34
Devils Water West 18.57
Dilston (AHB-X) 18.20
CORBRIDGE 17.59
Farnley Haugh 16.48
RIDING MILL 15.35
Miles from Newcastle
21C: to Blaydon & Newcastle

# WEARDALE RAILWAY ● (DARLINGTON) – NORTON-ON-TEES ● TANFIELD RAILWAY



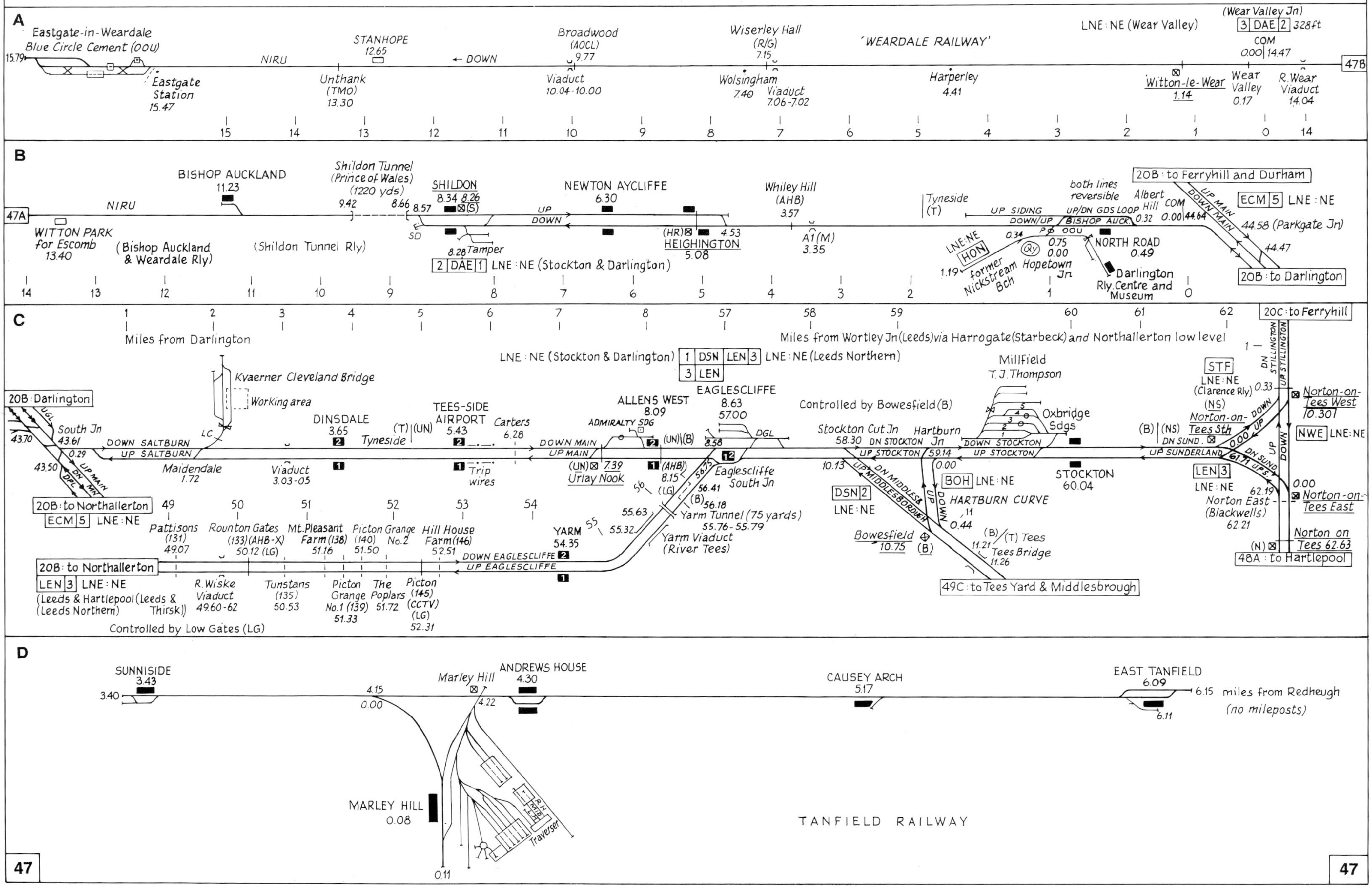

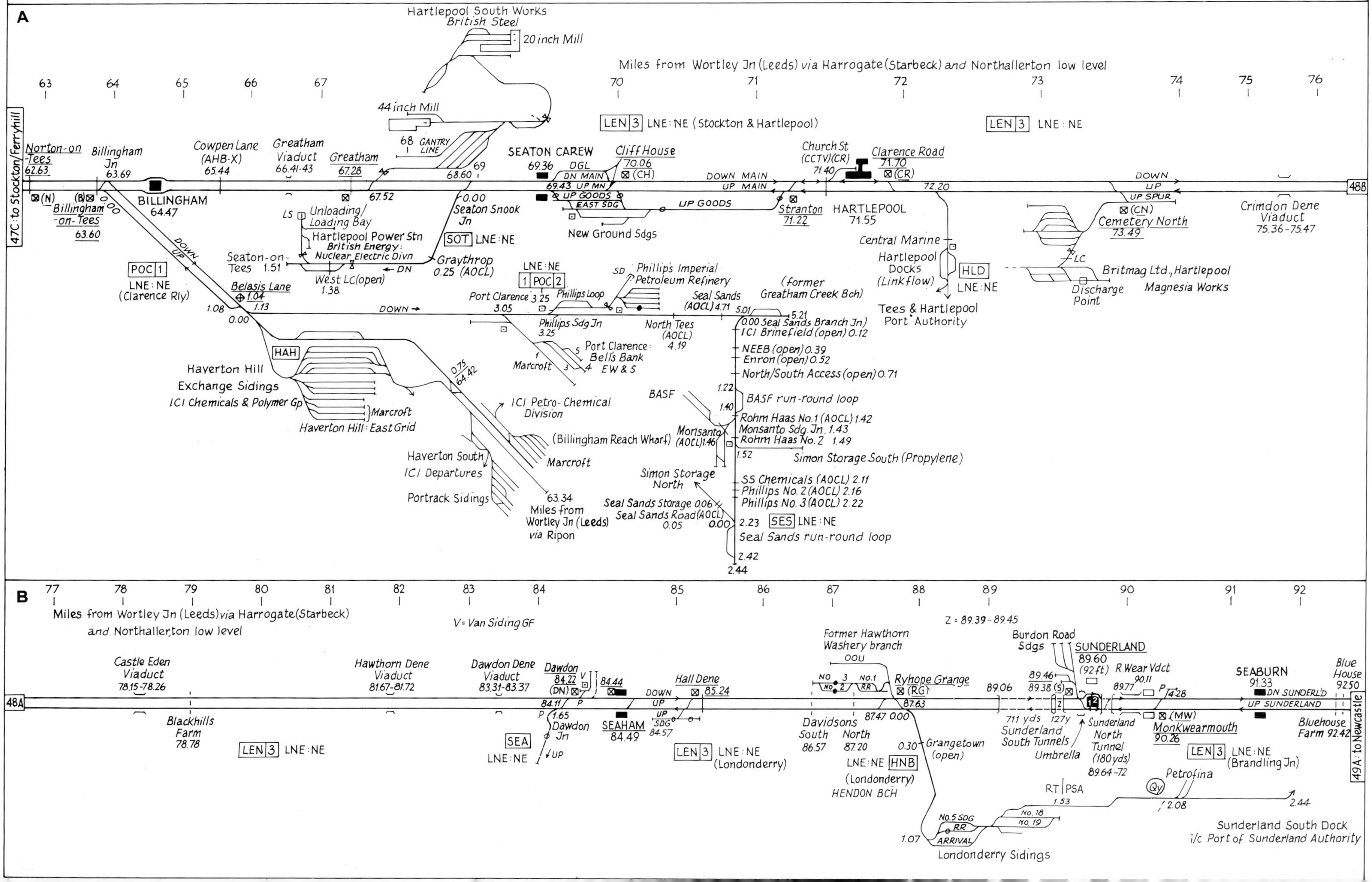
A
Hartlepool South Works
British Steel
20 inch Mill
Miles from Wortley Jn (Leeds) via Harrogate (Starbeck) and Northallerton low level
63
64
65
66
67
70
71
72
73
74
75
76
44 inch Mill
LEN 3 LNE: NE (Stockton & Hartlepool)
LEN 3 LNE: NE
47C: to Stockton/Ferryhill
Norton-on-Tees 62.63
Billingham Jn 63.69
Cowpen Lane (AHB-X) 65.44
Greatham Viaduct 66.41-43
Greatham 67.28
68 GANTRY LINE
SEATON CAREW 69.36
DGL
Cliff House 70.06
(CH)
Church St (CCTV)(CR) 71.40
Clarence Road 71.70
(CR)
DOWN MAIN
UP MAIN
72.20
DOWN
UP
UP SPUR
48B
(N)
(B)
Billingham-on-Tees 63.60
BILLINGHAM 64.47
0.00
67.52
69
68.60
DN MAIN
69.43 UP MN
UP GOODS
EAST SDG
UP GOODS
Stranton 71.22
HARTLEPOOL 71.55
(CN)
Cemetery North 73.49
Crimdon Dene Viaduct 75.36-75.47
LS
Unloading/Loading Bay
0.00
Seaton Snook Jn
SOT LNE: NE
New Ground Sdgs
Hartlepool Power Stn
British Energy: Nuclear Electric Divn
Central Marine
Hartlepool Docks (Linkflow)
HLD
LNE: NE
LC
Britmag Ltd., Hartlepool Magnesia Works
Discharge Point
DOWN
UP
POC 1
LNE: NE (Clarence Rly)
Seaton-on-Tees 1.51
DN
Graythrop 0.25 (AOCL)
LNE: NE
1 POC 2
SD
Phillips Imperial Petroleum Refinery
Belasis Lane 1.04
West LC (open) 1.38
1.08
1.13
0.00
DOWN
Port Clarence 3.25
Phillips Loop
Port Clarence 3.05
Seal Sands (AOCL) 4.71
5.01
5.21
(Former Greatham Creek Bch)
Tees & Hartlepool Port Authority
Phillips Sdg Jn 3.25
North Tees (AOCL) 4.19
0.00 Seal Sands Branch Jn)
ICI Brinefield (open) 0.12
HAH
Port Clarence: Bell's Bank EW & S
1
5
3
4
Marcroft
NEEB (open) 0.39
Enron (open) 0.52
North/South Access (open) 0.71
Haverton Hill Exchange Sidings
ICI Chemicals & Polymer Gp
0.75
64.42
ICI Petro-Chemical Division
BASF
1.22
BASF run-round loop
1.40
Marcroft
Haverton Hill: East Grid
Rohm Haas No.1 (AOCL) 1.42
Monsanto Sdg. Jn. 1.43
Rohm Haas No.2 1.49
Monsanto (AOCL) 1.46
(Billingham Reach Wharf)
Haverton South
ICI Departures
1.52
Simon Storage South (Propylene)
Marcroft
Simon Storage North
SS Chemicals (AOCL) 2.11
Phillips No. 2 (AOCL) 2.16
Phillips No. 3 (AOCL) 2.22
Portrack Sidings
63.34
Miles from Wortley Jn (Leeds) via Ripon
Seal Sands Storage 0.06
Seal Sands Road (AOCL) 0.05
0.00
2.23
SES LNE: NE
Seal Sands run-round loop
2.42
2.44
B
77
78
79
80
81
82
83
84
85
86
87
88
89
90
91
92
Miles from Wortley Jn (Leeds) via Harrogate (Starbeck) and Northallerton low level
V = Van Siding GF
Z = 89.39-89.45
Former Hawthorn Washery branch
OOU
Burdon Road Sdgs
SUNDERLAND 89.60 (92ft)
R. Wear Vdct 90.11
SEABURN 91.33
Blue House 92.50
Castle Eden Viaduct 78.15-78.26
Hawthorn Dene Viaduct 81.67-81.72
Dawdon Dene Viaduct 83.31-83.37
Dawdon 84.22 (DN)
V
84.44
DOWN
UP
Hall Dene 85.24
NO 3
NO 2
NO.1 RR
Ryhope Grange (RG)
87.63
89.06
89.46
89.38 (S)
Z
89.77
P
4.28
DN SUNDERL'D
UP SUNDERLAND
48A
84.11
P
1.65
Dawdon Jn
UP
SEAHAM 84.49
UP SDG 84.57
87.47 0.00
711 yds
127y
Sunderland North Tunnel (180 yds) 89.64-72
(MW)
Monkwearmouth 90.26
Bluehouse Farm 92.42
49A: to Newcastle
Blackhills Farm 78.78
LEN 3 LNE: NE
SEA
LNE: NE
LEN 3 LNE: NE (Londonderry)
Davidsons South 86.57
North 87.20
0.30
Grangetown (open)
LNE: NE HNB (Londonderry)
HENDON BCH
Sunderland South Tunnels
Umbrella
LEN 3 LNE: NE (Brandling Jn)
Petrofina
Qy
RT PSA
1.53
2.08
2.44
No.5 SDG
RR
ARRIVAL
1.07
No.18
No.19
Londonderry Sidings
Sunderland South Dock i/c Port of Sunderland Authority

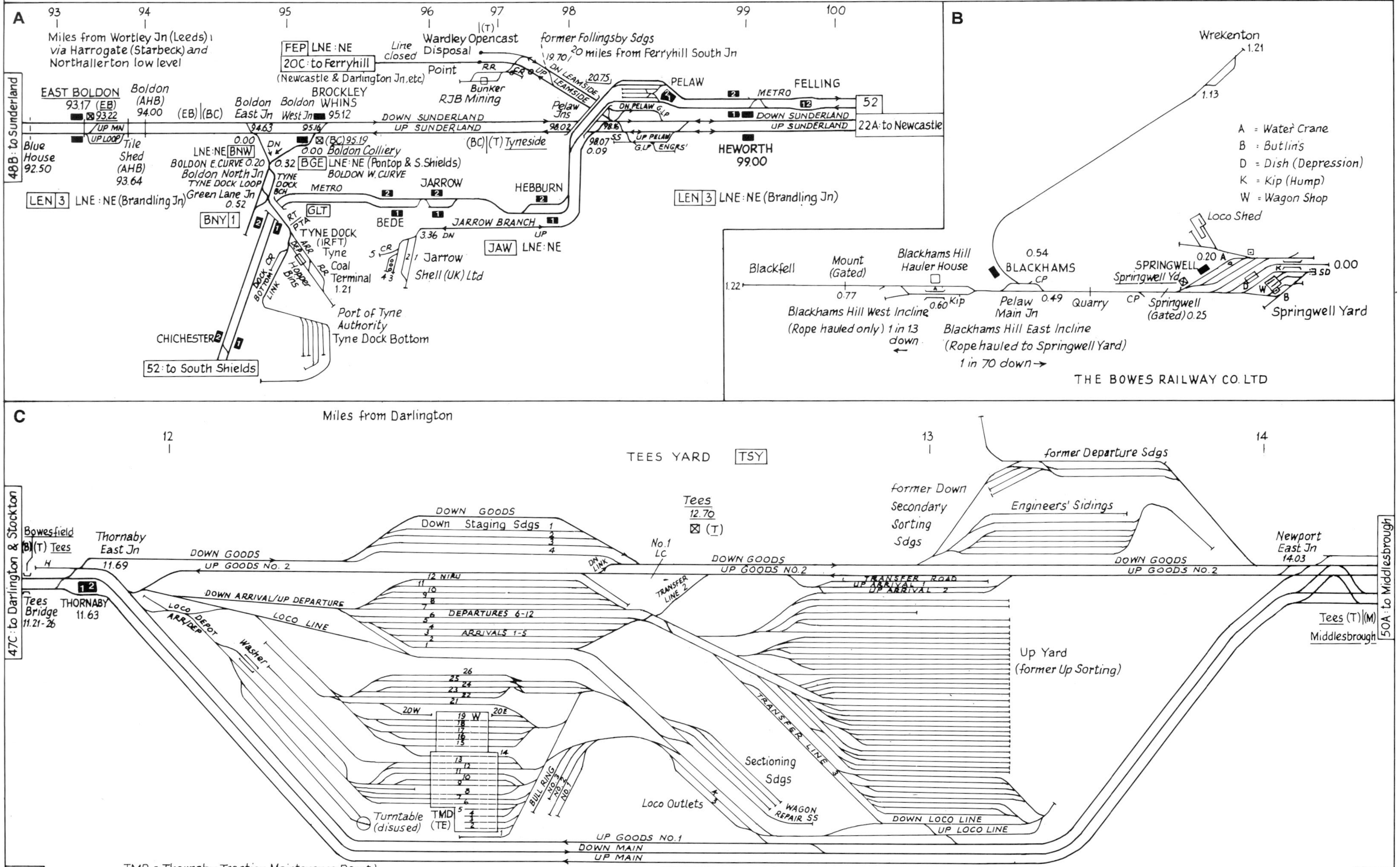


TMD = Thornaby Traction Maintenance Depot } EW&S
W = Thornaby Wagon Repair Depot

DSN 2 LNE: NE (Stockton & Darlington)

# MIDDLESBROUGH – REDCAR/NUNTHORPE



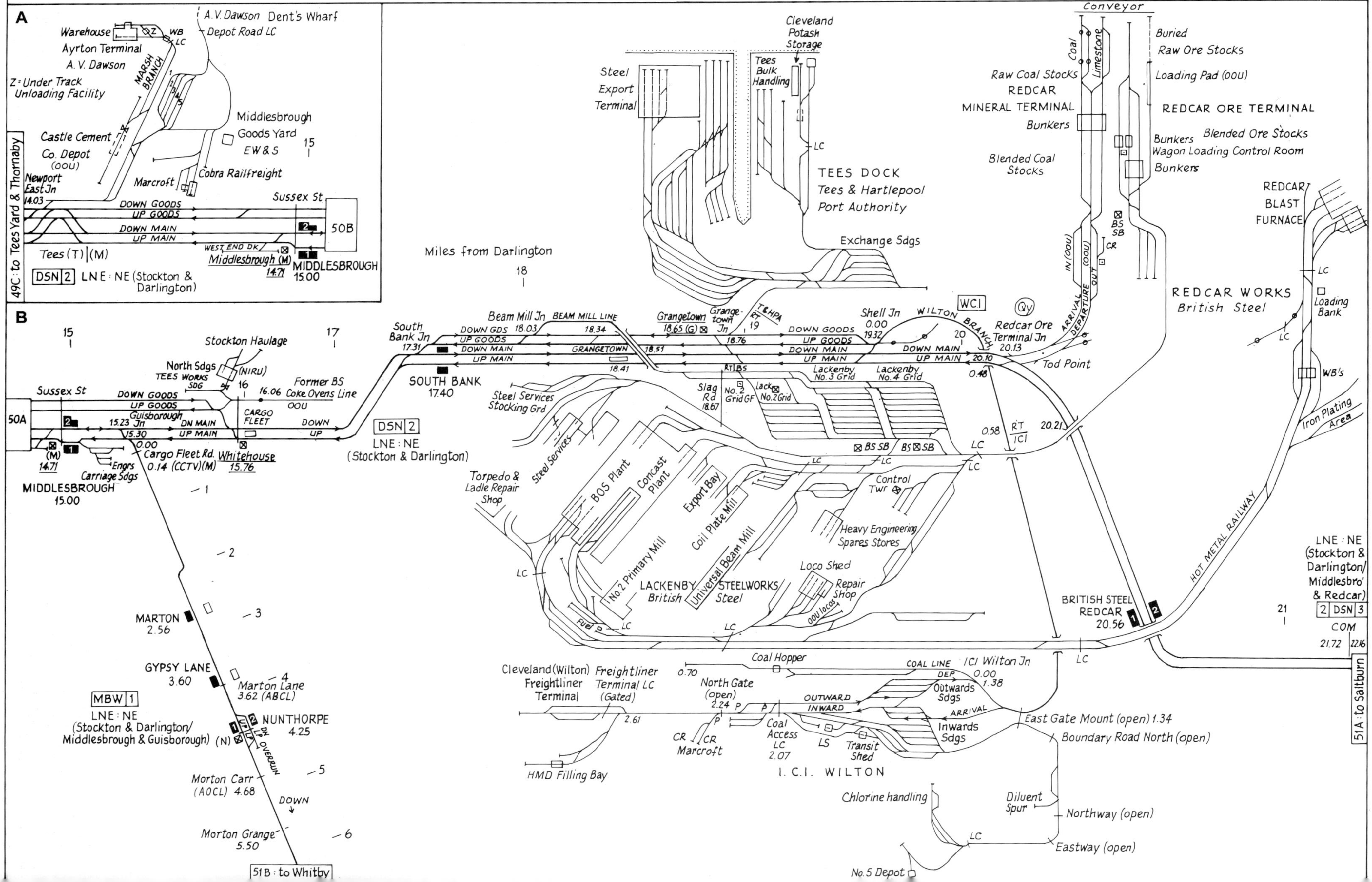

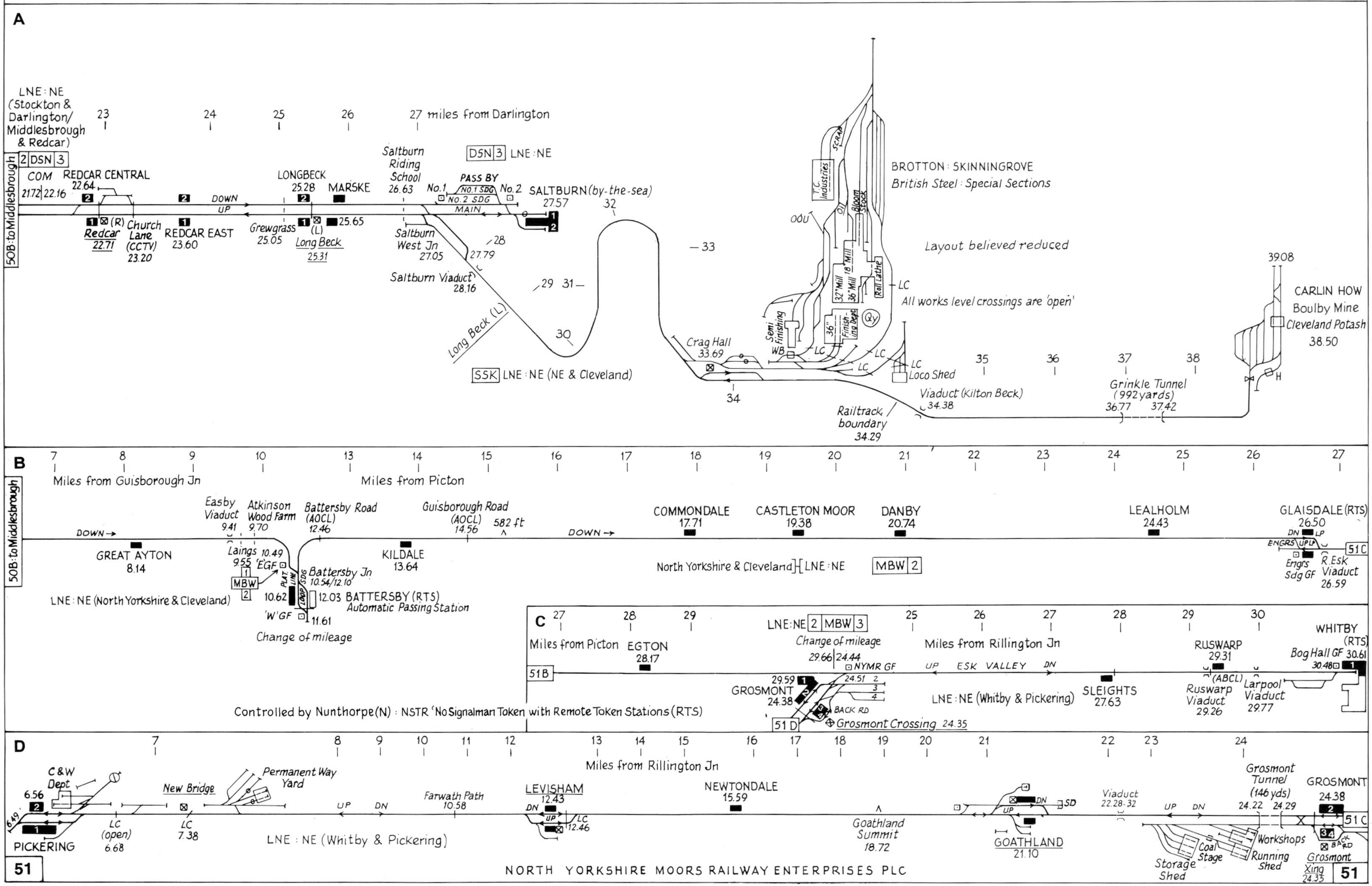
A
LNE : NE
(Stockton & Darlington/ Middlesbrough & Redcar)
23
24
25
26
27 miles from Darlington
50B: to Middlesbrough
2 DSN 3
COM
21.72 22.16
REDCAR CENTRAL
22.64
DOWN
UP
Redcar
22.71
(R) Church Lane (CCTV)
23.20
REDCAR EAST
23.60
Grewgrass
25.05
LONGBECK
25.28
MARSKE
(L)
Long Beck
25.31
25.65
Saltburn Riding School
26.63
No.1
PASS BY
NO.1 SDG
NO.2 SDG
MAIN
No.2
D5N 3 LNE : NE
SALTBURN (by-the-sea)
27.57
Saltburn West Jn
27.05
28
27.79
Saltburn Viaduct
28.16
29
31
32
30
33
Long Beck (L)
SSK LNE : NE (NE & Cleveland)
Crag Hall
33.69
34
ODU
T.C. Industries
SCRAP
Oil
Bloom Stock
18" Mill
32" Mill
36" Mill
Roll Lathe
Semi Finishing
WB
36"
Finishing Dept
Qy
LC
Loco Shed
BROTTON : SKINNINGROVE
British Steel : Special Sections
Layout believed reduced
All works level crossings are 'open'
Viaduct (Kilton Beck)
34.38
Railtrack boundary
34.29
35
36
37
38
Grinkle Tunnel
(992 yards)
36.77
37.42
39.08
CARLIN HOW
Boulby Mine
Cleveland Potash
38.50
H
B
7
8
9
10
13
14
15
16
17
18
19
20
21
22
23
24
25
26
27
Miles from Guisborough Jn
Miles from Picton
50B: to Middlesbrough
DOWN →
GREAT AYTON
8.14
Easby Viaduct
9.41
Atkinson Wood Farm
9.70
Laings 10.49
9.55 'EGF'
MBW 1 2
LNE : NE (North Yorkshire & Cleveland)
10.62
PLAT LINE
LOOP
SDG
'W'GF
11.61
Change of mileage
Battersby Road (AOCL)
12.46
Battersby Jn
10.54/12.10
12.03 BATTERSBY (RTS)
Automatic Passing Station
KILDALE
13.64
Guisborough Road (AOCL)
14.56
582 ft
DOWN →
COMMONDALE
17.71
CASTLETON MOOR
19.38
DANBY
20.74
North Yorkshire & Cleveland LNE : NE
MBW 2
LEALHOLM
24.43
GLAISDALE (RTS)
26.50
DN LP
ENGRS UPLP
Engrs Sdg GF
R. Esk Viaduct
26.59
51 C
C
27
28
29
Miles from Picton
EGTON
28.17
51 B
LNE: NE 2 MBW 3
Change of mileage
29.66 24.44
NYMR GF
29.59
GROSMONT
24.38
24.51
2
3
4
BACK RD
51 D
Grosmont Crossing 24.35
Controlled by Nunthorpe (N) : NSTR 'No Signalman Token with Remote Token Stations (RTS)
25
26
27
28
29
30
Miles from Rillington Jn
UP ESK VALLEY DN
LNE : NE (Whitby & Pickering)
SLEIGHTS
27.63
RUSWARP
29.31
(ABCL)
Ruswarp Viaduct
29.26
Larpool Viaduct
29.77
WHITBY (RTS)
Bog Hall GF 30.61
30.48
D
7
8
9
10
11
12
13
14
15
16
17
18
19
20
21
22
23
24
Miles from Rillington Jn
C & W Dept
6.56
6.49
PICKERING
LC (open)
6.68
New Bridge
LC
7.38
Permanent Way Yard
UP DN
LNE : NE (Whitby & Pickering)
Farwath Path
10.58
LEVISHAM
12.43
DN
UP
LC
12.46
NEWTONDALE
15.59
Goathland Summit
18.72
UP
DN
SD
GOATHLAND
21.10
Viaduct
22.28-32
UP DN
Grosmont Tunnel
(146 yds)
24.22 24.29
GROSMONT
24.38
51 C
Workshops
Coal Stage
Running Shed
Storage Shed
BACK RD
Grosmont Xing
24.35
NORTH YORKSHIRE MOORS RAILWAY ENTERPRISES PLC

All distances on this page are metric; station distances are from point of origin 28 metres north of Gosforth South Junction

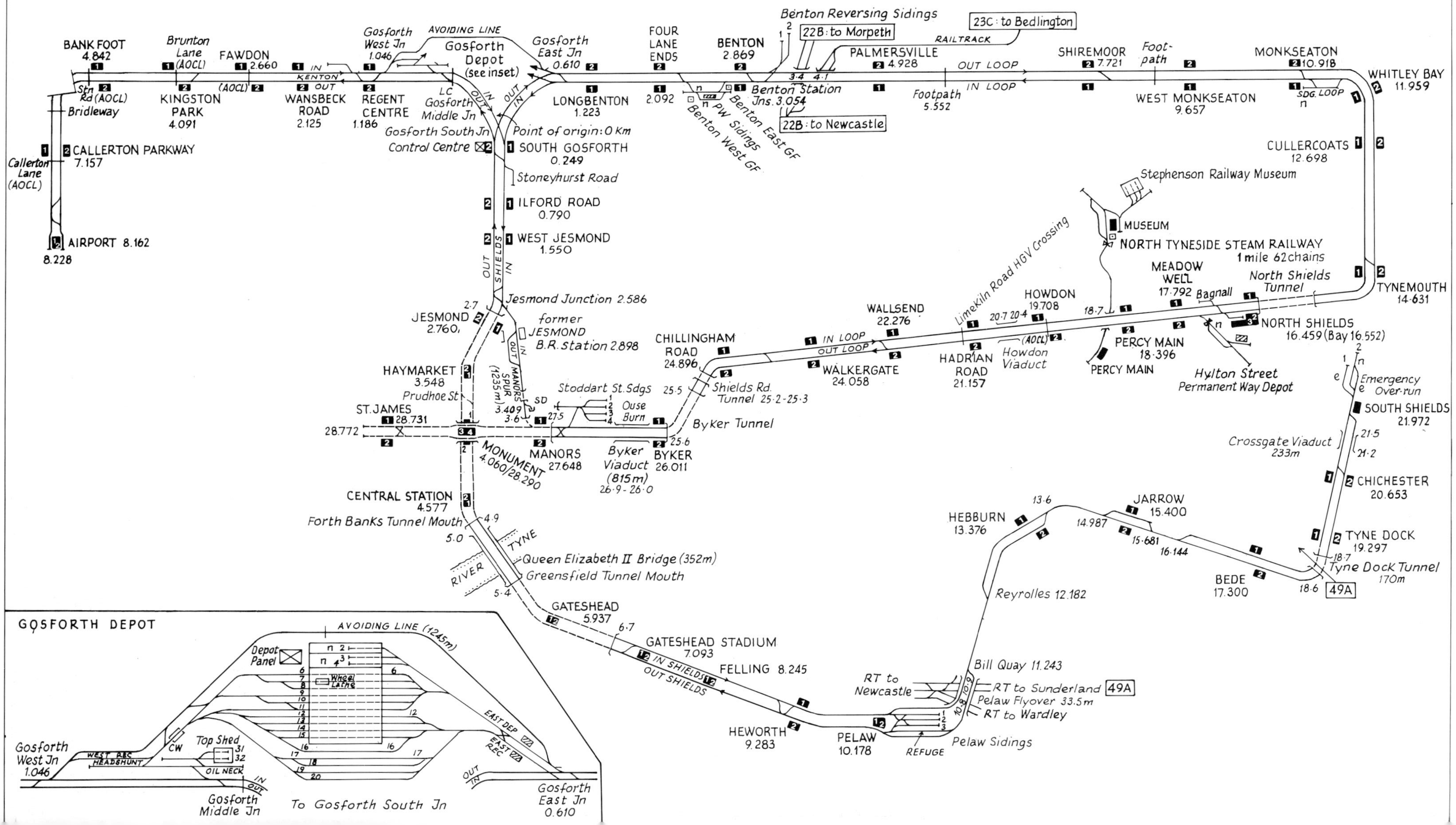

# SOUTH YORKSHIRE SUPERTRAM LTD.



Figures are distances in metres between stops (*subject to error*)

Operation franchised to Stagecoach East Midlands

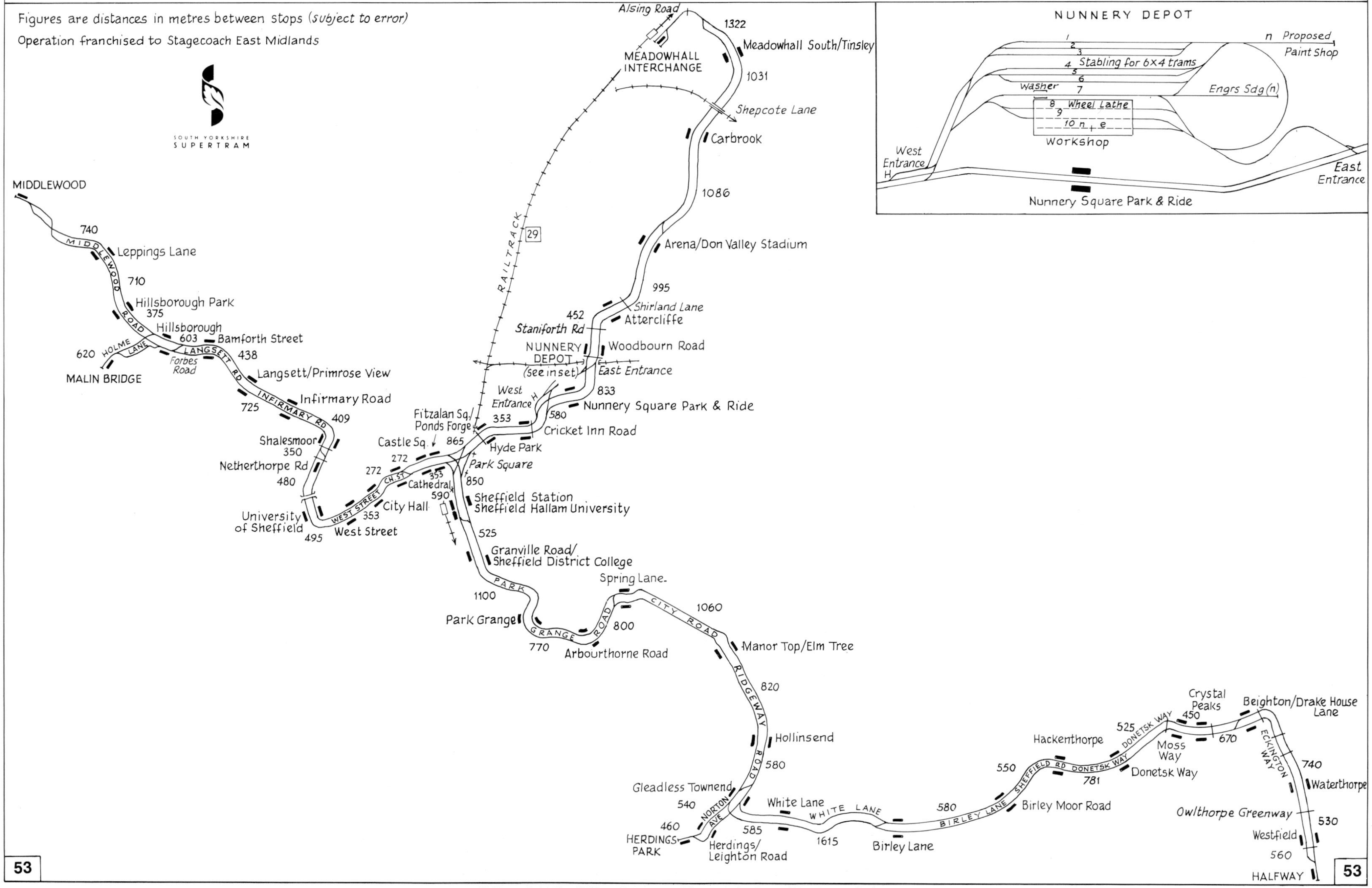

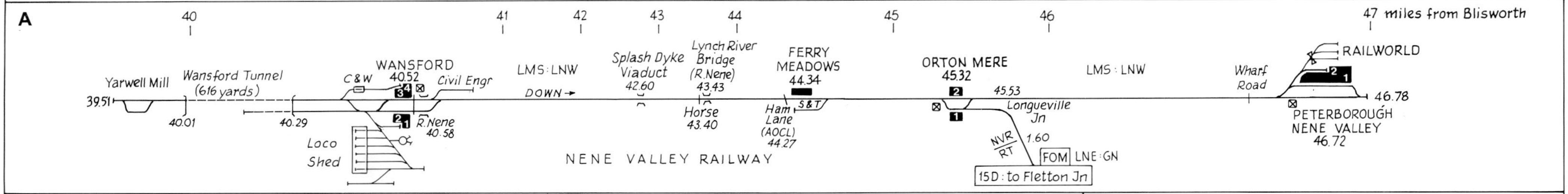
A
40
41
42
43
44
45
46
47 miles from Blisworth
Yarwell Mill
39.51
Wansford Tunnel
(616 yards)
40.01
40.29
C&W
WANSFORD
40.52
Civil Engr
R.Nene
40.58
Loco
Shed
LMS : LNW
DOWN →
Splash Dyke
Viaduct
42.60
Lynch River
Bridge
(R.Nene)
43.43
Horse
43.40
FERRY
MEADOWS
44.34
S&T
Ham
Lane
(AOCL)
44.27
NENE VALLEY RAILWAY
ORTON MERE
45.32
45.53
Longueville
Jn
NVR
RT
1.60
FOM
LNE : GN
15D : to Fletton Jn
LMS : LNW
Wharf
Road
RAILWORLD
46.78
PETERBOROUGH
NENE VALLEY
46.72

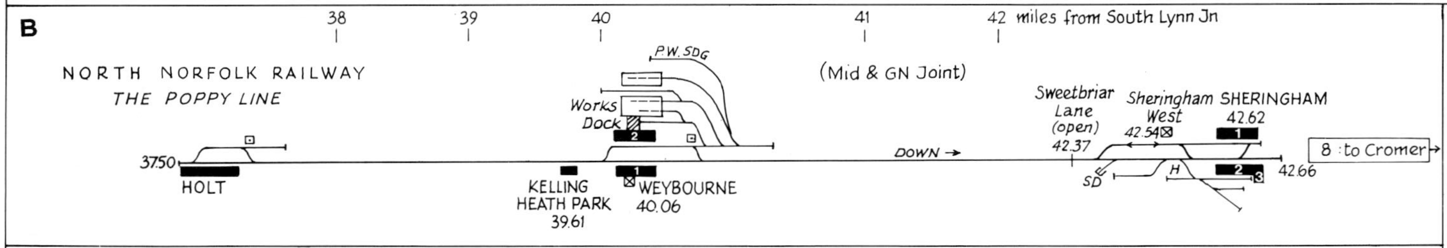
B
38
39
40
41
42 miles from South Lynn Jn
NORTH NORFOLK RAILWAY
THE POPPY LINE
3750
HOLT
P.W. SDG
Works
Dock
KELLING
HEATH PARK
39.61
WEYBOURNE
40.06
(Mid & GN Joint)
DOWN →
Sweetbriar
Lane
(open)
42.37
SD
Sheringham
West
42.54
SHERINGHAM
42.62
H
42.66
8 : to Cromer

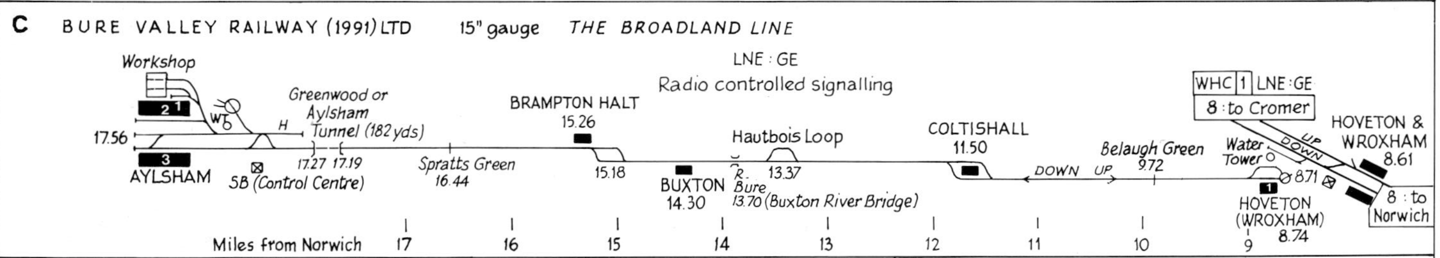
C
BURE VALLEY RAILWAY (1991) LTD
15" gauge
THE BROADLAND LINE
LNE : GE
Radio controlled signalling
Workshop
17.56
WT
AYLSHAM
SB (Control Centre)
H
Greenwood or
Aylsham
Tunnel (182 yds)
17.27 17.19
Spratts Green
16.44
BRAMPTON HALT
15.26
15.18
BUXTON
14.30
Hautbois Loop
R.
Bure
13.37
13.70 (Buxton River Bridge)
COLTISHALL
11.50
DOWN
UP
Belaugh Green
9.72
WHC
LNE : GE
8 : to Cromer
Water
Tower
8.71
UP
DOWN
HOVETON &
WROXHAM
8.61
HOVETON
(WROXHAM)
8.74
8 : to
Norwich
Miles from Norwich
17
16
15
14
13
12
11
10
9

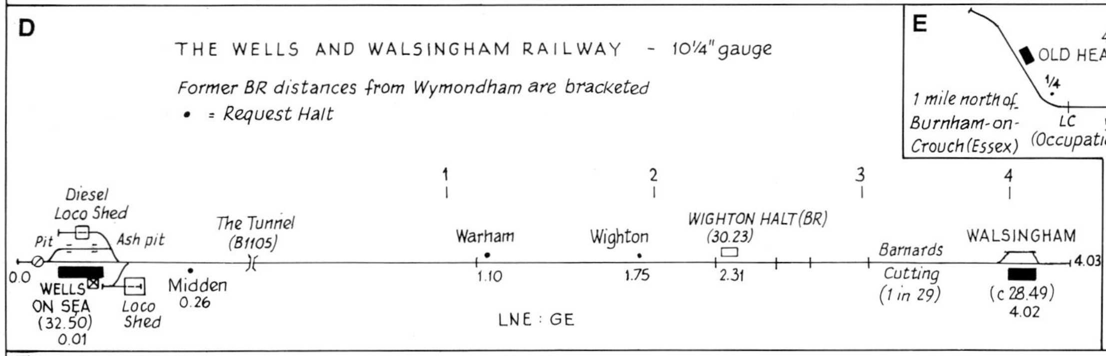
D
THE WELLS AND WALSINGHAM RAILWAY - 10¼" gauge
Former BR distances from Wymondham are bracketed
• = Request Halt
1
2
3
4
Diesel
Loco Shed
Pit
Ash pit
0.0
WELLS
ON SEA
(32.50)
0.01
Loco
Shed
Midden
0.26
The Tunnel
(B1105)
Warham
1.10
Wighton
1.75
WIGHTON HALT (BR)
(30.23)
2.31
Barnards
Cutting
(1 in 29)
WALSINGHAM
(c 28.49)
4.02
4.03
LNE : GE

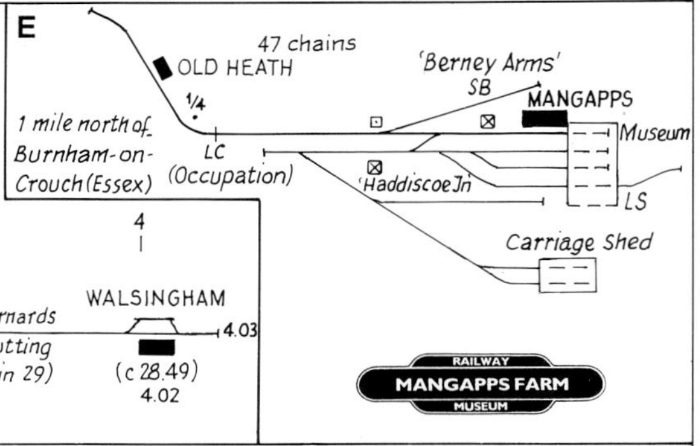
E
47 chains
OLD HEATH
¼
1 mile north of
Burnham-on-
Crouch (Essex)
LC
(Occupation)
'Berney Arms'
SB
MANGAPPS
Museum
'Haddiscoe Jn
LS
Carriage Shed
RAILWAY
MANGAPPS FARM
MUSEUM

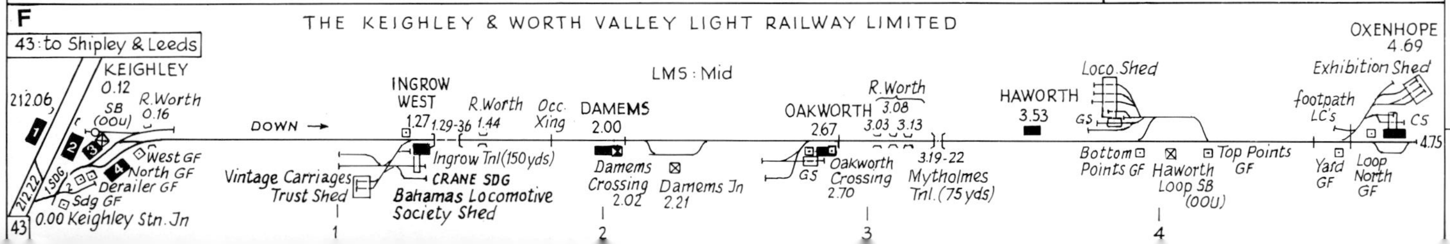
F
THE KEIGHLEY & WORTH VALLEY LIGHT RAILWAY LIMITED
43 : to Shipley & Leeds
212.06
KEIGHLEY
0.12
SB
(OOU)
R.Worth
0.16
West GF
North GF
Derailer GF
Sdg GF
1 SDG
212.22
43
0.00 Keighley Stn. Jn
DOWN →
Vintage Carriages
Trust Shed
INGROW
WEST
1.27
1.29-36
R.Worth
1.44
Occ.
Xing
Ingrow Tnl (150 yds)
CRANE SDG
Bahamas Locomotive
Society Shed
LMS : Mid
DAMEMS
2.00
Damems
Crossing
2.02
Damems Jn
2.21
OAKWORTH
2.67
R.Worth
3.08
3.03 3.13
GS
Oakworth
Crossing
2.70
3.19-22
Mytholmes
Tnl. (75 yds)
HAWORTH
3.53
Loco Shed
GS
Bottom
Points GF
Haworth
Loop SB
(OOU)
Top Points
GF
OXENHOPE
4.69
Exhibition Shed
footpath
LC's
CS
4.75
Yard
GF
Loop
North
GF
1
2
3
4

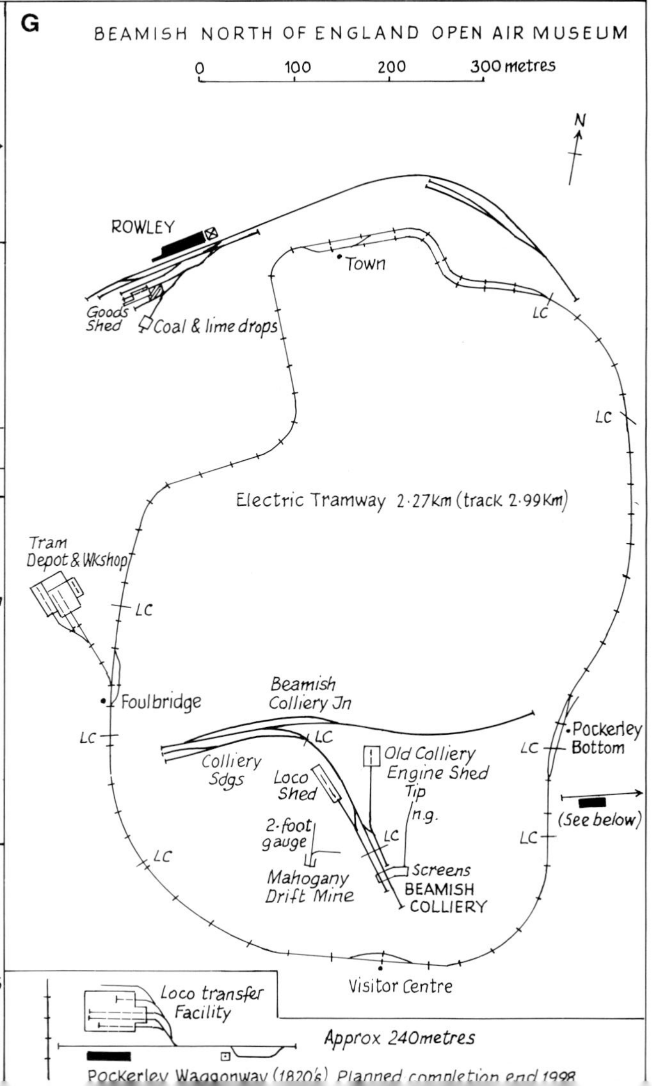
G
BEAMISH NORTH OF ENGLAND OPEN AIR MUSEUM
0
100
200
300 metres
N
ROWLEY
Goods
Shed
Coal & lime drops
Town
LC
LC
Electric Tramway 2·27km (track 2·99Km)
Tram
Depot & Wkshop
LC
Foulbridge
LC
Beamish
Colliery Jn
LC
Colliery
Sdgs
Loco
Shed
Old Colliery
Engine Shed
Tip
n.g.
LC
2-foot
gauge
Mahogany
Drift Mine
Screens
BEAMISH
COLLIERY
LC
LC
Pockerley
Bottom
LC
(See below)
Visitor Centre
Loco transfer
Facility
Approx 240 metres
Pockerley Waggonway (1820's) Planned completion end 1998